ARKHAM KNIGHT
SIGNATURE SERIES STRATEGY GUIDE

TABLE OF CONTENTS

THE DARK KNIGHT RETURNS
GAME PLAY

In the explosive finale to the *Arkham* series, Batman faces the ultimate threat against the city he is sworn to protect. The Scarecrow returns to unite an impressive roster of super villains, including Penguin, Two-Face and Harley Quinn, to destroy The Dark Knight forever. Developed exclusively for New-Gen platforms, *Batman: Arkham Knight* introduces Rocksteady's uniquely designed version of the Batmobile, which is drivable for the first time in the franchise. The addition of this legendary vehicle, combined with the acclaimed gameplay of the *Arkham* series, offers gamers the ultimate and complete Batman experience as they tear through the streets and soar across the skyline of the entirety of Gotham City.

Batman: Arkham Knight is a huge game full of surprises. Our aim is to point you in the right direction without spoiling those surprises. You can't expect to read ahead or, say, skim the Unlocks chapter prematuraly and learn absolutely nothing, but you won't spoil anything crucial. This guide offers full coverage for everything in *Batman: Arkham Knight*: the main missions to take down Scarecrow and Arkham Knight, the side missions featuring other opportunistic villains preying on Gotham City this Halloween, the AR Challenges that replicate all sorts of scenarios, and all collectibles and unlockable content.

DIFFICULTY SETTINGS AND GAME COMPLETION

You select setting when starting a new game. After that, it can be altered at any time in the options menu.

Easy: This difficulty is suitable for players inexperienced with action games or the *Arkham* game series. Enemy health, damage output, reaction time, hit accuracy, and movement speed are all at their lowest settings.

Normal: *Arkham Knight*'s standard difficulty. Enemy parameters escalate chapter by chapter. As the story progresses, foes become slightly quicker, smarter, and more powerful. On normal difficulty only, this adjustment is dynamic. If you perform gracefully, dispatching combat scenarios with freeflow ease and stalking predator scenarios unseen, difficulty increases slightly. However, if you take many hits in combat or get seen often when sneaking around then the game becomes slightly easier.

Hard: This is the setting for experienced Dark Knights. If you've cleaned out the other Arkham games and chewed up and spat out their challenge rooms, this is probably the setting for you. On Hard difficulty, enemies in a given level behave as they would five chapters later on Normal. For example, in Hard difficulty's chapter 3, enemies act like they do in Normal difficulty's chapter 8. The difficulty won't subtly adjust based on your performance, either. You're stuck at five chapters harder no matter what, though if this ends up being tougher than you'd like, you can change it back to Normal or Easy. *Arkham Knight* doesn't have Achivements or Trophies based on difficulty, and WayneTech Upgrade Points earned are the same too, so you're free to pick the difficulty setting that is most fun and rewarding for you.

GAME COMPLETION

Standard completion of *Arkham Knight* is accomplished by playing through the game's story missions. This completes the tale of this ugly Halloween in Gotham, but that isn't all the story available. To unlock the full ending, complete at least seven side missions in addition to the game's story missions. You can accomplish this without focusing on Riddler collectibles: the trophies, riddles, and puzzles Edward Nigma has rigged up all over Gotham. But that's still not quite all.

To unlock a slightly longer version of the full ending, complete *all* Most Wanted side missions in addition to the story. Since this includes the "Riddler's Revenge" side mission, this inherently includes gathering all trophies and collectibles. Completing side missions and tracking down Riddler trophies you've missed can be accomplished after completing the main story, so you don't have to worry about a point of no return for the "full" ending.

Completing missions and snagging collectibles also unlocks Showcase models, Concept Art, Bios, Gotham City Stories, AR Challenges, and (depending on your gaming platform) Achievements or Trophies.

NEW GAME PLUS AND KNIGHTMARE DIFFICULTY

Beat *Arkham Knight* on any difficulty setting and you unlock the ability to start a New Game Plus playthrough. During New Game Plus, you retain WayneTech upgrades and points you earned before, and the game is locked to a new difficulty setting called Knightmare. Knightmare is the exact opposite of Easy. Instead of enemy sturdiness, damage dealing, reactions, accuracy, and speed begin set as low as possible, these parameters are all set as high as possible, all the time. Knightmare difficulty also eliminates the danger sense that shows up on the HUD when Batman is about to be attacked. These are the signals that indicate when to Counter or Evade incoming enemy strikes. You have to really pay attention to enemy animations and positions to succeed in combat at this difficulty. Knightmare difficulty is the only setting available during New Game Plus, and cannot be selected outside of New Game Plus. Your reward for braving the dark night a second time through on the highest difficulty is the game's capstone system reward, a Platinum Trophy on PlayStation 4 and the biggest Gamerscore Achievement on Xbox One.

GAMEPLAY

At any given time as Batman, you have the run of the roofs, rafters, and other vantage points of the islands of Gotham City. Thugs affiliated with several of Batman's greatest foes have overrun the city, and are found rioting and looting and joyriding through the streets below anywhere you care to look. You can descend and thin their ranks for combat practice, WayneTech Upgrade Points, and to find Riddler Informants, but you'll never beat back the tide of goons without engaging in missions to track down their leaders.

DISPLAY

The heads-up display shows several useful pieces of information at a glance. Aspects of it fade away to clear your view when the info isn't needed.

Health is displayed at the top of the screen, left of the compass. When piloting the Batmobile, vehicle armor is shown here.

The compass helps you find your way, and is a boon for navigation among the three island cities. For example, you can always find Bleake due north, Miagani due south, and Founders' due west.

When nearby criminal comms are intercepted, this icon points you in their direction.

The Combo counter helps you track how long you've kept up a Freeflow Combo, and when Special Combat Takedowns are available. In Battle Mode Batmobile fights, the Combo counter helps you track progress toward charging up secondary weapons.

The compass atop the screen helps orient you and can point the way to current targets and waypoints. Target Details can show up onscreen when you're near an objective and facing it. Batman's health is visible on the top-left corner. Other indicators display the currently equipped Gadget and any currently available contextual controls. When you're prowling above Gotham's streets, a Local Surveillance indicator on the right points the way toward a looter or militia member below who's up to no good. When you're actively brawling with baddies or engaging in a tank skirmish, the Combo indicator appears on the left.

CHOOSING OBJECTIVES

From the Most Wanted screen (Right on the D-Pad), you can choose between the main path or a side mission as your current focus. Waypoints for the current objective appear on the map screen and the HUD. These waypoints guide you to the vicinity of your objective. The map screen, provided remotely by the Batcomputer, can also be used to set waypoints of your own and to view any collectible locations you've shaken down from Informants. The locations of any AR Challenges available are also displayed. You can filter between types of targets to help prioritize your effort. Initially, you're restricted to exploration on Bleake Island, but quickly enough the other two islands are accessible as well.

DETECTIVE MODE

When confronted with a puzzle or surrounded by foes, Detective Mode can be vital. This enhanced vision mode, activated by tapping Up on the D-Pad, uses Batman's sophisticated suit to detect many more parts of the light spectrum, revealing much information that's hidden from unassisted human eyes. Nearby people can be viewed through solid walls, electric lines and circuit pathways can be traced, and mission-critical devices are highlighted. Eventually, some foes deploy their own anti-Detective Mode countermeasures, but for most of the adventure this vision mode is one of the most powerful tools Batman has over his opposition. If you're ever in doubt where to go or what to do, be sure to scour suspect terrain with Detective Mode.

THE BATMOBILE

Having a Batmobile at your beck and call is as awesome as it sounds. You can summon the vehicle remotely, and board it smoothly from the ground or by swooping in from the air.

On top of its obvious uses in car and tank forms, the Batmobile is also crucial to solving many missions and puzzles.

You can traverse from point to point in Gotham City as in *Arkham* titles before. Batman can mount rooftops and perches instantly grappling upward with the Grapnel, and fly by gliding and diving through the air using the Batsuit's rigid, adaptive, aerodynamic cape. But, new to *Arkham Knight*, Batman can also shred the mean streets of Gotham in the rumbling Batmobile! The Batmobile is of course a powerful addition to Batman's selection of gadgets, offering both speed and ground superiority in a rapidly escalating crisis. And since it can be driven remotely within a small radius around Batman, the Batmobile is crucial for puzzling out certain situations. A parked Batmobile can even provide Environment Takedowns in hand-to-hand combat with baddies nearby.

PURSUIT MODE

The defining trait of Pursuit Mode is speed, which comes here thanks to a Lucius Fox-designed rocket boost. The Batmobile speeds up airborne Batman too, since it can eject him directly into a high-speed glide.

When pursuing runaway vehicles, drift through turns to build up Afterburner power to keep speed up. Gain an Immobilizer Signal Lock and fire away (usually several times) to kill the engines of fleeing cars, or sideswipe them until they're disabled.

Batman must be in some ways scarier than the villains he pursues if he is to inspire fear in them, and this approach is certainly true for the Batmobile. This almost (but not quite) indestructible vehicle can be outfitted with a rocket Afterburner for flight-worthy landspeeds and has the handling to drift through turns like a rally car. One actually fuels the other; you generate extra Afterburner energy by drifting aggressively through turns.

The Pursuit Mode Batmobile is durable enough to disable many enemy vehicles just by crashing into them. An onboard Immobilizer Gadget can also be used to non-lethally halt a fleeing vehicle. Pursuit Mode is capable of dispatching suspect cars and APCs, but does not hold up against military-grade assault vehicles. Thankfully, designer Lucius Fox built in the solution. When targeted in Pursuit Mode by something like a tank or gunship (or similarly stout attacker), an unmistakeable alarm warning sounds. This is your signal to either hightail it away using Pursuit Mode's speed, or to transform into Battle Mode.

BATTLE MODE

Enemy forces may have tons of drone tanks, but there's nothing in their armory like the Battle Mode Batmobile.

The HUD populates useful ballistic information in Battle Mode, like missile lock-ons in progress and projected enemy fire vectors.

Simply through holding the left trigger, the Pursuit Mode Batmobile can be almost instantly reconfigured into a formidable and agile light tank. Think of holding the left trigger for tank mode like zooming in to aim in a typical first-person shooter. While Pursuit Mode is ideal for quickly crossing Gotham City and for chasing enemy vehicles, Battle Mode is perfect for exerting dominance over immediate surroundings.

The Batmobile in tank form comes equipped with non-lethal riot-suppression rounds for use against humans, and fully live ammunition for use against military-grade unmanned drones. The army of the Arkham Knight is largely mechanized, which means the gloves come off. Battle Mode is equipped with a 60MM Heavy Cannon for engagement with enemy armor, and a rapid-fire Vulcan Gun primarily intended to shoot down incoming missiles. The Bat-tank can also quickly jet across short distances in any direction thanks to Dodge Thrusters, ideal for dodging incoming enemy rounds at the last moment. Battle Mode's advanced intelligence systems project the expected path of incoming tank rounds, giving you a chance to see exactly what space you need to immediately vacate. Battle Mode also features several vital Gadgets (not all initially available), from the Power Winch to the EMP to the Forensic Scanner Pulse, so it's as useful to puzzles as to combat.

GADGETS

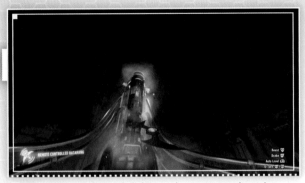

Gadgets supplement Batman's fighting and movement, and certain Gadgets are required for puzzle solutions.

It's the expert use of a wide array of specialized Gadgets that allows Batman to appear prepared for any contingency.

The Batman of *Arkham Knight* is established as a polished and well-equipped vigilante. You add more Gadgets and techniques to Batman's Utility Belt as you progress, but the Dark Knight is incredibly powerful and riding in style with the Batmobile very early on. At the start, Batman is carrying Batarangs, Remote Controlled Batarangs, the Batclaw, Explosive Gel, Line Launcher, Smoke Pellets, and (very shortly into the adventure) the Batmobile Remote.

You discover new Gadgets at certain parts of the main story, while Gadget upgrades, new combat techniques, and Batmobile customizations can be purchased using WayneTech Upgrade Points. WayneTech points are essentially XP, and you earn them by completing story missions, side missions, and by collecting Riddler trophies.

COMBAT SCENARIOS

You can't "mash" your way through combat and succeed. You must be patient and take what comes to you, countering incoming strikes, dodging any strikes that can't be countered, and getting in hits of your own when you have open shots.

Be patient and don't over-commit to attacks and Takedowns so you're always ready to Counter incoming enemy strikes. You can even Counter two or three incoming strikes at once; press Counter once for each incoming attack.

Some mission areas and AR Challenges are entirely about fighting, and it's rare for the enemy to be few in number. Batman routinely squares off against a dozen or more henchmen at once. These battles are tests of your Freeflow Combo mastery. String three moves together without being interrupted to start a Combo. During a Combo, Batman's moves reach farther and strike harder, and a Combo counter appears onscreen. At an 8-hit Combo, Special Combat Takedowns become available. Use one and keep the Combo going, and you earn another Special Takedown every five additional Combo hits. Weaving Special Takedowns into your Combos is an extremely potent way to subdue attackers more quickly, so getting a Freeflow Combo going can build momentum like a snowball rolling down a hill. For excellent Combo scenario scores (and thus lots of WayneTech XP), you must avoid getting hit, keep your Combo going continuously, and vary the combat techniques and Quickfire Gadgets you incorporate.

PREDATOR SCENARIOS

Detective Mode grants enough situational awareness to help overcome a dozen or more rifle-toting foes.

Catch patrolling sentries unawares and you can use Silent Takedowns to dispatch them without making a lot of attention-attracting noise. Thanks to the new Fear Multi-Takedown, you can get the drop on entire groups of henchmen and knock them all out before they can react.

The situation often dictates or demands a stealthy approach, rather than beating everyone into submission. This is especially true when adversaries are all packing firearms, and in critical, hostage-type situations. In Predator environments, you want to dispatch enemies as silently and efficiently as possible. Played perfectly, the enemy simply doesn't see Batman coming. Batman has the movement advantage over almost any adversary, being able to Grapple up to vantage points overhead or move quickly and silently under floor grates and through air circulation vents.

To the end of dispatching heavily-armed threats, Batman can accomplish stealth Takedowns from many different positions. Takedowns quickly remove threats from the field, non-lethally subduing them. You can sneak up behind an unaware foe for a Silent Takedown, or wait for them to approach Batman in cover before a Corner Takedown. Takedowns are possible hanging from below a ledge, or perched just above, and even from just under a grate in the ground, or just above one in the ceiling. There are a lot of ways to take out these terrorists that don't involve them getting a chance to fire their guns or alert their accomplices. Predator room scores are improved by faster completion, by not being seen or triggering alarms, and by varying Takedown methods.

ENEMIES OF THE BAT

FOOT SOLDIERS

Scarecrow's Halloween plot has attracted many villainous elements into Gotham, ranging from petty thieves and vandals, to the henchmen of classic Batman archenemies, and scaling all the way up to the military-grade forces of the mysterious Arkham Knight. As Batman, you'll stalk most of these criminals on foot. When circumstances permit, it's best to take them out silently, using unseen Takedowns from all sorts of vantage points to dwindle their ranks, while springing Fear Multi-Takedowns to incapacitate several unaware enemies at once with startling speed. But often the situation won't permit stealth, and you'll have to wade into the fray and take the enemies all on in hand to hand combat. Masterminds and supervillains are covered where appropriate for story missions and side missions elsewhere in this guide, while common foes are featured here.

STANDARD ENEMIES

They have their various motivations and allegiances, but the standard-issue thug fighter is a ubiquitous feature of the landscape in evacuated Gotham City. They're tough, but not against Batman, who can dispatch them dozens at a time with his FreeFlow Combos. Standard unarmed thugs can be easily beaten into submission with Strikes, repelled with Counters, and dispatched when floored with Ground Takedowns. Unarmed toughs can be Countered up to three at a time, in fact, so even in large numbers they can barely make Batman break a sweat.

These guys sometimes bring something along to help them, which complicates things for Batman. Note that when you K.O. a tool-using enemy, he drops his weapon and another foe can pick it up. You have to plan for other foes retrieving their fallen allies' weapons unless you destroy enemy weapons with the Special Combo, Disarm and Destroy (which is not initially unlocked).

Melee Weapons: Foes lug bats and pipes into battle, which helps them hit harder but still allows their bludgeoning swings to be easily Countered. You can even pick up their dropped melee weapons and use them to enhance Batman's strikes!

Projectiles: When hefty objects litter the combat area, enemies may pick some of them up and hurl them at Batman. You can Counter these just as against melee attacks. Press the Counter button right before an incoming projectile hits Batman. Batman catches the object and returns it to sender. The projectile can also be directed at an enemy other than the one who threw it. Otherwise, if you're not going to intercept the enemy's tossed objects, at least Evade to get out of the way.

Shields: Other foes sport riot shields, which guard against Strikes from the front. Inadvertently attacking a shield user head-on breaks your Combo and often gets Batman hit in return. Shield users are vulnerable to Cape Stun into Aerial Attack, which floors them and knocks the shield from their hands. Up close, these fighters bash with their shields, an uncounterable assault. Evade away or Redirect over them before they hit Batman. Like with other weapons, if you disarm or K.O. a shielded foe, their shield may be recovered by another foe.

Blades: Thugs who show up carrying knives are much more threatening than standard combatants. Knives can't be Countered directly by tapping the button; instead, you must hold away from the incoming attack while also holding down the Counter button for the duration of the attack. This merely evades the sharp swipes, and doesn't injure or stun the knife-wielder. It just resets the situation without Batman taking damage, and without breaking your FreeFlow Combo. (Attack again immediately after recovering from a blade dodge to keep the Combo going.) In order to punish blade users for engaging Batman, unlock the Blade Dodge Takedown, which allows you to K.O. them outright when they attack. To pull this off, you need to hold away from the incoming attack as during a normal blade dodge, but only tap and briefly hold the Counter button when the enemy is actively swiping. During gaps in the blade user's three-hit knife combo, you must *release* the Counter button.

Stun Rods: Some well financed fighters enter the fray with electrified stun rods, shock sticks that are a great deterrent against frontal assault. If you attempt to Strike a stun rod user from the front, Batman gets shocked and your Combo is broken. Their electrified pokes are also uncounterable. As against Brutes and shielded enemies, Batman's cape provides the solution, since it allows you to open a head-on assault without getting punished for it. Try Cape Stun into Aerial Attack for a quick flooring hit, or Cape Stun into Beat Down when you have time to land a series of knockout blows on one stun rod user without getting interrupted. Also like Brutes, since you have to be so specific attacking these adversaries, you can just save your Special Combo Takedowns for them and spare yourself the effort.

Guns: Gun-toting criminals are a significant threat, of course. You'll want to take them out silently whenever possible, but that's not an option when they show up during a melee brawl. It's important to keep scanning the fringes of a fistfight for all sorts of threats, like thugs starting an uncounterable tackle rush or tossing an object at Batman, but this is probably the most important. Melee fighters may rush off to a nearby weapon crate to arm themselves, or occasionally an armed patrol may happen upon your melee in progress. Once you acquire the Disruptor and the appropriate WayneTech Upgrade for it, you can sabotage weapon crates, so a foe trying to cowboy up will be in for a shocking surprise.

When a gunfighter is present, they become the top priority by default. While Evading helps a little bit against their gunfire, this is not a sustainable approach. Either Evade/Redirect toward a gunfighter so you can initiate Strikes on him immediately, or plan to keep him busy somehow. Nailing a gunfighter with a Quickfire Gadget like the Batarang or REC can knock him off balance for a few seconds and briefly prevent his fire. This is useful when you face more than one armed opponent at once; unbalance one while you work on knocking out the other. You can also Quickfire the Batclaw to disarm gunfighters. When you do K.O. or disarm these guys, keep in mind that other thugs might pick up their guns. To avoid this, permanently break their guns by targeting armed enemies with Special Combo Disarm and Destroy if you have a Combo going.

Optic deflection: The Arkham Knight's militia is absurdly well equipped, with advanced body armor and camouflage technology. Some of the Knight's guard don a sparking blue-white suit capable of rendering them invisible to Detective Mode scans. This should quickly grab your attention when stalking assault rifle toting patrols. Single out optic deflection units to reduce your surprises later, or use the Disruptor Gadget (once acquired) to sabotage their deflection suits.

Arkham Knight's Personal Guard

Combat bodysuit renders the wearer invisible to Detective Mode

Rioters

Petty criminals out to see Gotham burn

Two-Face Thugs

Bank heist crew

Penguin Thugs

Recruited from Gotham's criminal underworld

Harley Thugs

Harley Quinn's henchmen

ENEMY LIEUTENANTS

In the cutthroat criminal ranks, power largely determines hierarchy. Hulking, experienced enemy officers sometimes join the fracas themselves, bringing onto the field extra defense, more vigilante-busting strength, bigger guns, and better tools. Like enemies carrying blades, guns, or stun rods, the presence of a Brute onscreen immediately commands your attention. Thanks to their raw defense, regular Strikes don't make much headway on Brutes, and normal Counters don't deal damage at all. Against unarmed Brutes, you have to first daze them with a Cape

Stun attack, then follow up with a full Beat Down for the K.O. A Beat Down is a high-commitment attack, so you won't be able to pull this off if the Brute's allies are swarming nearby. You may have to avoid a Brute and put off taking him out until you've cleared out some of his underlings first. Otherwise, if you have a Combo going and a Super Combo Takedown ready, you can spend it to instantly subdue a Brute, greatly simplifying your plan of attack.

Brutes wielding miniguns are, it should go without saying, the center of attention whenever they're around. Should they notice Batman sneaking, they'll cut loose with a horrific torrent of bullets that Batman won't survive unless you immediately find cover or escape their field of view. In the unlikely event that you run into a minigun wielder in close quarters combat, wear them down with Beat Down after Beat Down up close. While pummeling a minigunner, be ready to Counter repeatedly, since they retaliate even in the midst of Batman's punches. Go back and forth swinging at a minigunner for several rounds to actually knock them out, so you won't be able to pull this off with any of their friends around. When stalking minigunners, look for chances to K.O. them more easily with an Environment Takedown, or with a trap set with the Disruptor or Explosive Gel.

RIDDLER ROBOTS

These robot henchmen give Riddler a large supply of foot soldiers. You run into them around some of Riddler's trophies, and during some events in story and side missions. When you find a robot around a trophy puzzle, they're usually integral to its solution. Interacting with robots to solve these puzzles usually requires that you've earned the right Gadget, like the Voice Synthesizer or Remote Hacking Device. While Riddler robots are definitely hostile, and attack if they see Batman, you can often find ways to trick them into helping you. During these puzzles, if you accidentally destroy a robot helper, you find a Batarang-activated switch in the area that restores the Riddler robot to working order for another try. If you can't seem to figure out a robot puzzle, make note of where it is and come back later when you've expanded Batman's options through story progress.

Riddler Robots
Riddler's mechanized army

Brutes
The biggest and toughest of Harley's men

Mini-Gunners
Highly dangerous foes

Mini-Gun Brutes
Harley's frontline firepower

Penguin Brutes
The biggest and toughest of Penguin's men

VEHICLES AND DRONES

The introduction of the Batmobile comes at an ideal time, as imminent threats to Gotham City's peace include a veritable army of lethal unmanned drones. Against conventional vehicles like stolen cars and jeeps, the Batmobile's sheer thrust and bulk in Pursuit Mode can be enough to easily win a vehicle encounter—just ram them off the road, basically. That armor isn't just for looks. But against unconventional vehicles, specifically the Arkham Knight's unmanned vehicle horde, you need serious firepower, which is where Battle Mode comes in hand. Ingeniously, WayneTech head Lucius Fox engineered the Batmobile to transform from Pursuit Mode to Battle Mode almost instantly with just the pull of a trigger. The Batmobile is uniquely equipped to pacify Gotham City's streets (and sometimes tunnels) no matter the adversary.

JOYRIDING RIOTERS

Stolen and used by rioters during the occupation

With Gotham City's sudden evacuation, its formidable taxicab force has been abandoned or left otherwise unattended, ripe for looter theft. Periodically, you'll see stolen cars swerving back and forth over city streets. Come upon them in the Batmobile and they'll naturally try to get away, a retreat you can easily interrupt with the Immobilizer or with brute force. If they come upon Batman on foot, they'll try to run him down, then get out of the car to finish him off. When a car bears down, either dive out of the way at the last moment by Evading, or hit the Counter button just before impact. Similarly, if you're gliding above a stolen car in the streets, you can also initiate a car Takedown with the Strike button from this position. Keep a particularly watchful eye out for cars when you're engaging with thugs at street level. Engaging rioters doesn't prevent other thugs from showing up in cars. They may attempt to run down Batman, and then pull over and get out to join the melee.

ARMORED VEHICLE

Militia personnel transport

The Arkham Knight's militia is considerably better equipped and funded than the street-level toughs who are just taking advantage of the chaos. They use armored trucks as their standard transport. Sometimes, a passenger aboard may even hang out the window with a rocket tube trying to dissuade any vigilante who may be in hot pursuit using a high-tech armored rocket car. When pursuing these trucks, you can't let a little rocket launcher be a deterrent. Slalom back and forth in the road to cause their shells to miss, and either attempt to slam or side-swipe the truck, or take locked-on shots at it using the Immobilizer. Beware more than one of these trucks at a time; they may attempt to ram *you*, and it's never good to have more people shooting rockets at you. You won't get a ballistic projection of the shells here like you will in Battle Mode, so drive unpredictably, battering one truck target while firing the Immobilizer at another.

MILITIA APC

Transport for the militia's senior command

The militia's slouching armored personnel carriers are heavily plated and can withstand much more abuse than the militia's armored trucks. Your method for dispatching them is the same, however: smack into the APCs using Afterburners, side swipe them up close, and lock on and fire with the Immobilizer when tailing them. When trying to waylay an APC, you may also come under fire from an escort of armored vehicles, so watch out and counter accordingly.

RATTLER DRONE

Militia assault tank

The really surprising thing about the Arkham Knight's force is the sheer hardware, which almost matches Batman's sophistication, and certainly wins the battle of numbers. The foundation of this force is the Rattler drone, a light unmanned tank equipped with a single heavy turret. For taking over an urban center en masse, these are unstoppable. The Batmobile isn't just another police car for a tank to overpower, though. No single Rattler stands a chance against the Batmobile in Battle Mode, but they aren't going to attack with just one. Rattlers may trundle up into the fray from all directions at once. This forces you to be agile dodging their crossfire, while also drawing a bead on their turrets. Land a heavy turret shell square on a Rattler turret to obliterate it in one shot.

COBRA DRONE

Militia heavy armor tank

This is not just another variant of the Rattler. This is a bonafide heavy tank, a vehicle capable of outgunning the Batmobile head-on. These behemoths move slowly down Gotham's streets, scanning the road ahead for threats to militia dominance. Their blue tracking scanners turn red when a target is discovered, and their high-powered turrets lock on for several seconds before launching a high-energy explosive shell. These shots are devastating even to the Batmobile, so taking these drones on from the front is terribly ill-advised. Instead, play hide and seek with these units, crawling up behind them unseen. If cover big enough to hide you from their scanners is available, you can park the Batmobile, allow the Cobra to pass, then crawl after it. If you're detected and the scanner goes red, get out of there immediately, even dropping back into Pursuit Mode and Afterburning around the nearest street corner to break line of sight. When you manage to approach a Cobra from behind, you'll begin to lock Battle Mode's heavy turret on the exposed core of the Cobra. After several seconds of lock-on time, a single 60mm round fired from the Batmobile shatters the Cobra drone. The trick is getting into position to take them out in the first place.

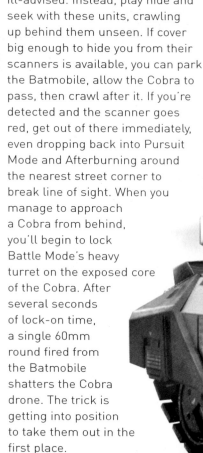

MAMBA DRONE

The missile platform variant of the Rattler. This tank's launcher works differently, lazing the Batmobile with a target lock-on for several seconds before launching guided missiles. During the initial lock-on period, the Batcomputer sounds an alarm and projects the lock-on's direction onscreen, allowing you to track down the Mamba attacker. If you can't destroy the tank before it fires, shoot the missiles out of the air using the Vulcan Gun. This is easier than it sounds—the Batcomputer highlights the incoming missiles—as long as you know which direction the missiles are coming from, so keep an eye out for Mamba targeting when they're around.

Mobile missile platform

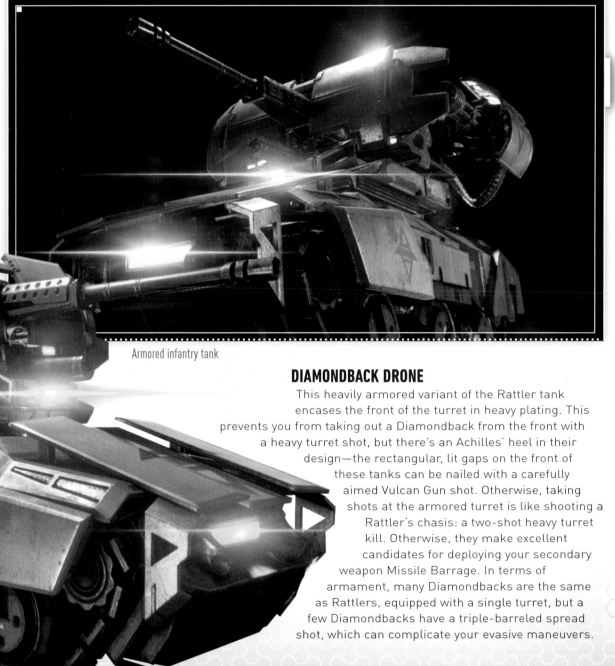

Armored infantry tank

DIAMONDBACK DRONE

This heavily armored variant of the Rattler tank encases the front of the turret in heavy plating. This prevents you from taking out a Diamondback from the front with a heavy turret shot, but there's an Achilles' heel in their design—the rectangular, lit gaps on the front of these tanks can be nailed with a carefully aimed Vulcan Gun shot. Otherwise, taking shots at the armored turret is like shooting a Rattler's chasis: a two-shot heavy turret kill. Otherwise, they make excellent candidates for deploying your secondary weapon Missile Barrage. In terms of armament, many Diamondbacks are the same as Rattlers, equipped with a single turret, but a few Diamondbacks have a triple-barreled spread shot, which can complicate your evasive maneuvers.

DRAGON DRONE

Rapid assault aircraft

This heavy flying drone is basically a small unmanned attack helicopter. They supplement the land forces of Rattlers and Rattler variants, launching air-to-ground rockets at the Batmobile. Like against Rattler shells, the Batcomputer displays a projection of the incoming attack, giving you a little bit of advance notice and a chance to dash away with dodge thrusters. Predators aren't as heavily armored as ground units, so once you sight them they can be shot down quickly with the Vulcan Gun.

PYTHON DRONE

Static missile platform

Naturally, this rapidly deploying occupying force doesn't neglect stationary weapons platforms. Setting up Python drones increases militia firepower at chosen chokepoints and intersections, forcing you to stay on your toes in their presence. As with Mambas, their projectiles can be shot down using the Vulcan Gun. Pythons are usually deployed in areas with nearby cover, giving you a place to play peek-a-boo, strafing out to fire a 60mm shell then strafing back behind cover when the Pythons fire.

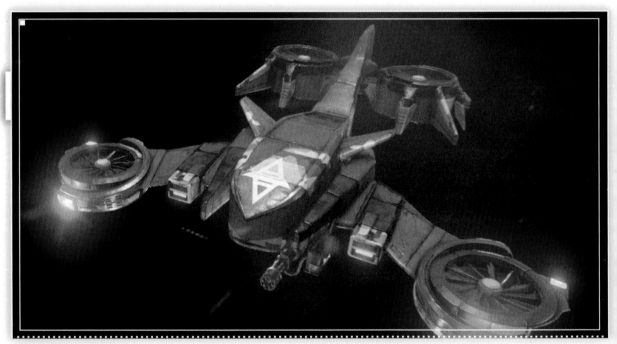

Militia surveillance aircraft

SERPENT DRONE

These more rugged, durable versions of the Boa sentry drone are piloted by militia command, and can't be disabled by taking out some drone controller. They function as eyes in the sky for the militia forces patrolling Gotham City. They can be blinded for a bit by the Remote Hacking Device, but otherwise can't be engaged head-on by Batman on foot. Instead, target these drones from above during their patrols along Gotham's skyline. Glide in carefully from above, land on them, deploy Explosive Gel, then dismount and glide away. Land upon a perch somewhere and get the rigged Serpent drone in your sights to remotely detonate the gel, destroying the drone.

Heavy fire support tank

TWIN RATTLER DRONE

Twin Rattlers offer the militia an offensive upgrade over the standard Rattler. The dual heavy barrels increase the gauntlet of tank shells through which you must dodge. When Rattlers, Twin Rattlers, and tri-barreled Diamondbacks are roaming the battlefield, there will be projected shell headings criss-crossing your HUD and forcing you to put the Batmobile's dodge thrusters to the test. Prioritize Twin Rattlers over Rattlers to reduce enemy firepower more quickly.

BOA SENTRY DRONE

These hovering anti-infantry drones scan urban areas for Batman. These scaled-down versions of Serpent drones are piloted by a drone operator. The Boa drone itself can be blinded temporarily by the Remote Hacking Device, or you can take out the drone operator troop piloting the drone. The drone operator's control module can also be sabotaged several different ways by the Disruptor Gadget, destroying the drone or shocking the operator. You can also just avoid the drone. Detective Mode shows the link between drone and operator, making it easy to keep tabs on the drone's location, while you keep your ears perked for the drone's telltale engine hum.

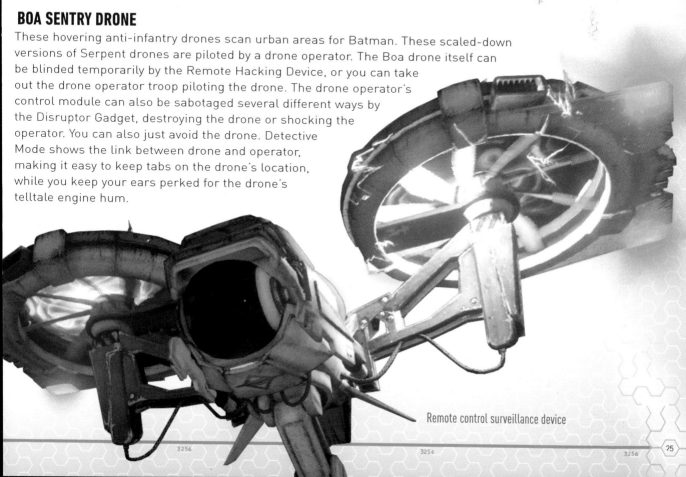

Remote control surveillance device

WAYNETECH ARSENAL

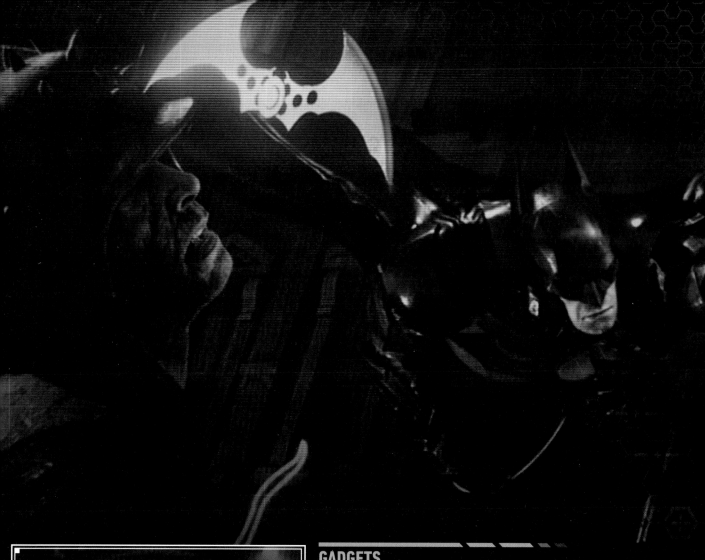

GADGETS

Batman succeeds, in part, due to his preparation and his resourcefulness. You almost always have the right tool for the job right there on Batman's belt, unless you just haven't acquired a particular Gadget yet. For example, you'll probably start to see terminals begging to be hacked before you actually acquire the Remote Hacking Device. Make note of puzzles and places to which you need to return with a new gadget or solution.

When hidden from foes, or at least not directly engaged with them, you can use Batman's Gadgets through careful aim. When facing off with several foes in a fistfight, there usually isn't time. Here, Quickfire functions are very useful. These commands allow you to snap-fire a particular Gadget, without having to specifically equip and aim that Gadget first. Using them successfully affords a big advantage in combat scenarios, widening your options against varied gangs of thugs. You'll also benefit from increased combat scores—thus more WayneTech XP—thanks to increased variety. A Quickfired Gadget that hits keeps your FreeFlow Combo going as long as you attack quickly afterward.

SMOKE PELLET

Floods an area with disorientating smoke and allows for a quick escape. During combat, target a group of enemies and take them down silently during the confusion.

GADGET QUICKFIRE COMMANDS

Smoke Pellet	When under fire, tap △ / Ⓨ
Batarang	Tap L2 / LT
Explosive Gel	L2 + □ / LT + Ⓧ
Batclaw	L2 + △ / LT + Ⓨ
Remote Electrical Charge (not initially available)	L2 + ◯ / LT + Ⓑ
Freeze Grenade (not initially available)	R2, R2 / RT, RT

UPGRADES

Veteran crimefighter Batman comes thoroughly trained and well equipped at the outset. And yet Lucius Fox continues iterating at WayneTech, providing Batman with a new Batsuit and Batmobile very near the beginning of his adventure. These provide his first few upgrades, built-in. From there, other gadgets and Batmobile components are earned and upgrades become available for purchase. You can do this from the WayneTech pane in the menu, using WayneTech Upgrade Points. You earn XP toward WayneTech Upgrade Points through most normal gameplay actions, like completing story and side missions, clearing combat and predator scenarios, and completing Riddler puzzles.

On top of Batman's huge starting moveset, there are upgrade categories for Combat Abilities, the Batsuit, the Batmobile in Pursuit Mode and in Battle Mode, Tech Gadgets, and Skill Gadgets. Many upgrades have prerequisites, where you must unlock other upgrades along the way. Upgrades can have a huge effect on combat efficacy, opening up new knockout approaches and increasing survivability. The most expensive (and usually meaningful) upgrades cost eight WayneTech points and are often gated behind other upgrades, so carefully consider where you invest points.

Some upgrades are just incremental (like extra Batsuit or Batmobile armor) or very situational (like a specific new function for a particular Gadget), whereas some upgrades grant big boosts for situations that come up all the time. For example, Special Combo Boost enhances all future FreeFlow Combos by lowering the number of hits needed for your first Special Takedown from eight to five. Special Combo Multi Ground Takedown gives you the chance to K.O. lots of downed foes at once for the cost of one Special Combo Takedown in combat. For the same thing in predator scenarios, Fear Multi-Takedown x4/x5 lets you clear four or five unaware sentries at once, clearly a significant upgrade. And a Batmobile upgrade like Dodge Thruster Boost allows two bursts in a row from the Battle Mode Batmobile's dodge thrusters, permanently doubling drone dodging ability.

BETTER XP THROUGH COMBOS

Combat in the *Arkham* series is about finesse. Above all else, your primary goals in combat should be to avoid getting hit, and to avoid dropping your FreeFlow Combo. In FreeFlow, Batman (and any other fighter who becomes playable) hits harder and moves faster and farther, using agile melee attacks not available outside of FreeFlow. This makes it quite easy to keep a combo going just by pinballing back and forth between enemies with aimed Strikes and Countering as needed when foes attack. At a Combo counter of x8, a Special Combo move is available. These are special finishers in several variations—you can instantly K.O. a single enemy, K.O. all floored foes at once, or break the weapon of an armed enemy, among others. Keep the Combo going and use the Special Combo move in the flow, to earn another with five more Combo hits. You won't start building to the next Special Combo move without using one you've already earned, so don't hold back. If you get hit, miss an attack, or there's a gap of longer than a second between consecutive actions, the FreeFlow Combo ends and you must build up three Combo hits again to enter FreeFlow—eight to gain another Special Combo move.

Apart from Special Combo Takedowns, which you must build up via the Combo counter, you can also use Ground Takedowns during predator stalking. If you knock a foe down with a Strike or Counter, you can transition right into a Ground Takedown. This even keeps the Combo going, and is actually one of the highest point value actions you can weave into a Combo.

Be careful, though, since you can easily be hit during a Takedown attempt. Only go for Ground Takedowns mid-Combo when you've knocked down a thug on the edge of the group, one who isn't right near other enemies.

There are layers on top of this when tougher enemies show up, but that's the basic combat refrain. To avoid hits, keep the camera oriented toward the most foes as you leap among them with attacks. Keep an eye out for any incoming attacks so you can Counter or Evade them. If you've already started up a Strike and you realize an attack is incoming, you can make a judgment call. If Batman will literally beat the opponent to the punch, you can just let the Strike hit; if it looks like the enemy will hit Batman first, you can interrupt Batman's swing by Countering, up to a point. For many actions, you're totally committed, and can't "take it back" by canceling into a Counter, but while ping-ponging between enemies with normal Strikes, you can weave in Counters as needed. Once more challenging enemies show up, like foes with shields or weapons, or huge Brutes, then you can think of the normal thugs as the medium you move through as you deal with these higher-ranking threats.

Counterable Attacks

Uncounterable Attacks

Requires specific Counter

When you're comfortable dodging and Countering standard attacks, start watching out for attacks that cannot be Countered, which are indicated with red intuitive flashes above enemy heads instead of blue flashes. You must Evade or interrupt these. For example, when a thug charges with a tackle attempt from afar—definitely one of the prime threats from the fringe of a melee—a Quickfired Batarang in his direction is an assured K.O. Otherwise, Evade or Redirect out of his way immediately. There are always two or three toughs coming in close to try close range attacks, but keep the guys on the edges in mind. These are the ones who charge from afar, start throwing objects, or even produce a gun and start shooting. You don't want it to come from an angle you neglected to check. Be ready to reprioritize quickly when this happens.

If you feel swarmed or unsure of action on the fringes, you can Redirect or Evade out of the enemy gang's midst to the edges without dropping your FreeFlow Combo. You just have to make sure you hit with some action just after dodging to the edge of the group. A common way to escape a crowd and grab a mental breather is to Evade out of the way, then immediately Quickfire a Batarang back at the group. This gets you some space, keeps the Combo alive, and buys you a couple of beats to plan your next move and reposition the camera.

Avoiding hits and building up Combos have some positive natural consequences. Obviously, avoiding hits is good for Batman's longevity and your progress in the game. Keeping your Combo going is not only fun, but vital for good combat XP scoring. By beating up enemies of Gotham City gracefully, in unbroken Combos with varied moves, you gain more XP and accrue WayneTech Upgrade Points more quickly. Combos work as a raw multiplier to your combat actions, so it's easy to see how it quickly increases—a Strike only gets 10 XP outside of a Combo, but is worth 200 points as hit 20. Combat encounters are scored based on avoiding hits, building up Combos, and injecting those Combos with variety.

Stealthy predator scenarios are scored based on going unseen and for varying your Takedown methods. Invisible predator scenarios can devolve into combat, but that's usually a bad idea, as the villains are all usually armed in these encounters. Attracting a lot of attention is likely to end poorly. Patience and planning are paramount. Use Detective Mode to get full situational awareness, seeing all patrols, drones, and items of interest in the area. Stay hidden and moving, pick off enemies with a variety of grate, vent, perch, and ledge Takedowns, and plan for one or two dramatic Fear Multi-Takedowns against clusters of foes you can't split up. Depending on the environment and your Gadget selection, you can bend things in your favor. The Remote Hacking Device allows you to manipulate gates and alarms, confusing foes. The Disruptor lets you set all sorts of traps, depending on upgrades. You can prime a weak wall or patrol spot with Explosive Gel. And the Batarang itself can be used to misdirect or stun foes. In fact, the first time you're spotted in a predator scenario, you have a split-second just to Quickfire a Batarang, giving you a chance to subdue the onlooker before he makes too much noise and warns others. If you are discovered and an onlooker calls for backup, it's usually best to just run. Vacate the area and find a new vantage point where you can monitor the enemies. They'll be on high alert in the area where you were seen, but you'll have new chances to pick them off once they separate and start patrolling again.

STANDARD MOVEMENT

ABILITIES MOVEMENT

Left Stick	Move
Left Stick + ⊗ / Ⓐ	Run/Climb/Glide
R2 / RT	Crouch

Traverse the streets and rooftops of Gotham City with ease. While running, you automatically climb over obstacles, jump between structures, and launch into a Glide. When crouched, movement is quick and silent, making this a very useful tactic for a stealthy approach.

GLIDE

Hold ⊗ / Ⓐ while airborne	Glide
Left Stick	Steer glide

When gliding, your cape takes on a rigid form, allowing you full control of pitch and yaw. Mastering this move, in combination with the Dive Bomb, is key to moving quickly and effectively around Gotham City's streets. If you glide directly into a wall, you can kick off into another glide. From a glide you can also grapple to a perch, Grapnel Boost right past the perch into another glide, initiate a Glide Kick or Car Takedown on foes below, or create a perch in place with Line Launcher Tightrope. Certain upgrades allow particular Gadgets to be fired while gliding.

LINE LAUNCHER TIGHTROPE

Press in and hold Left Stick while gliding or tap R1 while zipping with the Line Launcher	Create Line Launcher Perch

This upgrade to the Line Launcher enables you to use the zip line as a tightrope. This can be used to create new positions to observe and attack enemies, or to collect Riddler trophies. While on the cable, you can move above an enemy to perform a Drop Attack, Glide Kick, or Takedown.

EVADE

Left Stick + ⊗ ⊗ / Ⓐ Ⓐ	Evade

Use Evade to quickly dodge attacks and gunfire, reducing damage sustained while in combat. You can also evade through glass or over railings. When Batman's combat intuition shows red indicators above a charging thug's head, their grapple attempt cannot be Countered. You need to get out of the way by Evading, or K.O. the approaching thug with a Quickfired Batarang to the noggin. Evading can also be useful when enemies bring guns to a fistfight, though you won't be able to dodge gunfire forever, so you'll still need to stun, disarm, or K.O. gunfighters as soon as possible. You can Evade during a FreeFlow Combo and keep the Combo going as long as you do some other action when the Evasion move recovers. If you happen to Evade right into an enemy, you flip over their heads with a Redirect instead.

DETECTIVE MODE

Tap Up on D-Pad	Toggle Detective Mode

Gain an immediate tactical analysis of the current location, identifying potential threats, even through solid walls. Enemies carrying firearms are highlighted in orange. All other personnel in the vicinity are highlighted in blue. This scan mode also highlights items of interest in the environment, providing information via a direct connection to the Batcomputer.

ENVIRONMENTAL ANALYSIS

Hold Up on D-Pad	Environmental Analysis

The Environmental Analysis can be used to scan the solutions to riddles, as well as Riddler trophies. If these are currently unobtainable, adding their locations to the map screen allows you to return and collect them later.

GRAPNEL

R1 / RB	Grapple

The Grapnel is an essential part of your navigation equipment. To use it, simply look at any ledge and fire the Grapnel to move there almost instantly. While running or gliding, the Grapnel continuously targets the nearest valid ledge, meaning this move can be used at almost any time. The Grapnel also enables Grapnel Boosts, which contribute greatly to Batman's ability to travel quickly throughout Gotham City.

GRAPNEL TARGETING

Hold L2 / LT while gliding	Aim

Quickly locate your nearest available Grapnel point while running or gliding. Keep the Grapnel engaged and chain multiple points together to traverse fluidly and reach high Vantage Points.

GRAPNEL BOOST

and hold while grappling	Boost

When grappling over medium to long distances, this gadget boosts the speed of the grapple, launching you high into the air above the target point. Combine this move with the Dive and Glide maneuvers to cover long distances without ever touching the ground. Ejecting from the Batmobile can provide a similar function.

GRAPNEL BOOST MK II

and hold while grappling	Boost

The gadget upgrade boosts the speed of the grapple, launching you higher and further into the air above the target point. When combined with the Dive and Glide maneuvers vast distances can be covered swiftly, greatly reducing travel times.

STANDARD COMBAT

STRIKE

	Strike

The Strike is your primary close range attack. Once you have delivered three sequential blows in a fight, you enter FreeFlow. In this state, you cover a much greater distance with your attacks and your strikes increase in power, knocking most enemies to the ground. Grounded enemies are susceptible to Ground Takedowns and upgrades like the Special Combo Multi Ground Takedown. To maintain the FreeFlow, you must continue to successfully Strike and Counter enemies without being hit and without leaving a gap of more than a moment between actions.

CAPE STUN

⊙ / Ⓑ	Cape Stun

Use the weighted tips of your cape to disorientate attacking enemies and temporarily stun them. The move affects all enemies standing immediately in front of you, making it useful for crowd control. Certain enemies are adept at soaking up normal Strikes, but are staggered easily by Cape Stuns. The Cape Stun is also the first stage of several advanced techniques.

SUPER STUN

⊙⊙⊙ / ⒷⒷⒷ	Super Stun

Use three Cape Stuns in quick succession on one target to perform the Super Stun. This move knocks down most enemies for an extended period of time, leaving them vulnerable to attack. It's particularly effective against Brutes, causing them to lower their guard and leaving them open to a Beat Down attack.

BEAT DOWN

⊙ > □ / Ⓑ > Ⓧ	Beat Down

Unleash a flurry of rapid, focused blows on a single enemy, these finish them off in one attack. The Beat Down is effective against armored opponents, but leaves you vulnerable to attack from other enemies while it is performed. You can interrupt a Beat Down and Evade/Counter against an incoming attack, but the Beat Down victim won't be knocked out if you don't complete the move. Beat Downs are also noteworthy since they add so many hits to the current Combo, likely readying another Special Combo move for you.

WEAPON STEAL

Ⓧ + □ / Ⓐ + Ⓧ	Grab Weapon

Steal weapons from stunned opponents or retrieve dropped weapons from the floor during combat. Using weapons increases the damage inflicted by your strikes and allows you to directly strike armored or electrified enemies, as well as foes wielding Stun Batons or shields.

AERIAL ATTACK

⊙ > ⓍⓍ / Ⓑ > ⒶⒶ	Aerial Attack

Stun an enemy, then attack from above to come crushing down on them. This is especially useful against enemies using shields as they cannot block an Aerial Attack. This move can also be redirected to attack another enemy by selecting an alternate target while airborne.

BATCLAW SLAM

L2 + △ > □ / LT + Ⓨ > Ⓧ	Batclaw Slam

Fire the Batclaw at enemies during combat and follow up immediately with a Strike attack to knock assailants down, rendering them unconscious if it's the final blow. This inflicts double the damage of a normal Strike, but takes longer to perform, leaving you vulnerable to attack. Against an incoming attack, simply change plans after the Quickfired Batclaw rather than pressing □ / Ⓧ to complete the attack.

REDIRECT

Left Stick + ⓍⓍ / Left Stick + ⒶⒶ toward an enemy	Redirect

This move flips you over the head of an attacking enemy. Effective when surrounded, giving you time and space to launch your next attack, it can also be used on charging enemies to send them sprawling. Your FreeFlow Combo won't be interrupted by a Redirect as long as you get back to a Strike, Counter, or Quickfired Gadget quickly after recovering.

SLIDE

Tap R2 / RT while running	Slide

Use the Slide to navigate through very small gaps, allowing access to new areas. It can also be used to kick straight through vent covers, eliminating the need to remove them by hand, but at the cost of making more noise and potentially alerting nearby threats. Finally, the slide can be used to initiate combat as the first strike of a combo attack.

COUNTER

	Counter
	Multi-Counter

The Counter is one of the most important moves in your arsenal and mastery of this is critical to success in combat. This move instantly turns an enemy's attack back against them and keeps you on the offensive. When multiple enemies strike simultaneously, tap once for each attacker to fend them off. Batman can counter up to three concurrent attacks.

Batman doesn't have to be completely at rest for you to Counter. You can attempt a Counter from many other actions, especially if you attempt to Counter on the tail end of a move. Always keep an eye out for the way enemies telegraph their attacks, and for Batman's intuition to reveal their imminent attacks with blue flashes over their heads. Don't go into battles jamming on the Strike button. Instead, get into a dance-like rhythm with the shifting gang around Batman, Striking where you can and deftly Countering enemies that dare swing at the Bat.

BLADE DODGE

Left Stick + hold ▲ / Ⓨ away from attacker	Blade Dodge

Enemies armed with knives and other sharp objects attack with multiple swipes in quick succession. To avoid these repeated attacks, you must perform a number of dodges in a row by moving away from the assailant while holding the Counter button. The excellent Blade Dodge Takedown upgrade allows, given precise timing on your part, for this dodge sequence to end with the blade-wielder unconscious.

INTERROGATION

▲ / Ⓨ on Riddler Informants	Interrogate

Interrogate Riddler's Informants to learn the location of his trophies and riddles. Informants are visible in Detective Mode as green-hued criminals. To extract information from an informant, you must first knock out every other enemy in the vicinity. Use the Evade or Redirect move to vault over the informant should he attack and keep him conscious for questioning.

PROJECTILE COUNTER

▲ / Ⓨ	Projectile Counter

Use the Counter move to catch projectiles and throw them back at the attacker. A thrown object can be redirected toward a different enemy by pushing in their direction as it is caught.

THROW COUNTER

Left Stick + ▲ / Ⓨ toward enemy	Throw Counter

Time your Counter strike to perfection and incapacitate opponents with a critical throw. This move allows you to counter and throw multiple enemies simultaneously and double the damage against your attackers. Throw Counters can also be useful since you'll knock back attacking enemies into their comrades, staggering the next incoming wave.

COMBAT PICK UP

R2 + Ⓞ / RT + Ⓑ near downed enemy	Pick Up

Pick up a downed opponent and initiate a critical Beat Down while they're stunned. An extremely effective maneuver, but one that may leave you vulnerable to enemy attacks.

SPECIAL COMBO TAKEDOWN

⊙ + △ / Ⓑ + Ⓨ with full Combo meter	Special Combo Takedown

Immediately incapacitate most enemies in a single move, regardless of their health or current weapon. The Combo meter flashes when Special Combo Moves are available. Special Takedowns can be a huge help in difficult combat scenarios; build your FreeFlow Combo up on run-of-the-mill combatants, then unleash the Special Combo Takedown on the toughest enemy on the field.

BATMOBILE ASSISTED TAKEDOWN

⊗ + ▢ / Ⓐ + Ⓧ	Batmobile Assisted Takedown

The Batmobile Assisted Takedown lets you knock an enemy into the path of an auto-targeted Batmobile Slam Round, rendering them unconscious. This is basically an Environment Takedown, courtesy of the Batmobile.

GROUND TAKEDOWN

R2 + △ / RT + Ⓨ on a downed enemy	Ground Takedown

This powerful move knocks out a downed enemy in one attack and is very effective in both combat and predator situations. While performing the Ground Takedown you are vulnerable to attack, so ensure that there's enough time for the move to complete successfully before committing to it. Unlike certain other attacks, like Beat Downs in progress or winding up a Strike, you can't Counter or Evade out of the middle of a Ground Takedown attempt.

ENVIRONMENT TAKEDOWN

⊗ + ▢ / Ⓐ + Ⓧ	Environment Takedown

Use environmental objects to instantly incapacitate enemies in creative ways. Environmental objects that can be used during a Takedown are highlighted in blue. Enemies are highlighted in blue once they're in range.

SILENT TAKEDOWN

△ / Ⓨ while undetected	Silent Takedown

This signature move allows you to sneak up on an unaware enemy and take them down silently. There are many variations on the basic Silent Takedown. In predator scenarios, try to take out as many foes as possible with unnoticed Silent Takedowns. Keep an eye on enemy groups and patrol routes, wait for them to split up, catch them unaware, or lure them into your clutches, then knock them out silently.

CORNER COVER TAKEDOWN

△ / Ⓨ while in corner cover	Corner Cover Takedown

While hidden in Corner Cover, you can take out any approaching, unaware enemies when they move into close proximity. This move quickly grabs your target and silently chokes them into unconsciousness while leaving you undetected.

KNOCKOUT SMASH

▢ / Ⓧ during Silent Takedown	Knockout Smash

While performing a Silent Takedown, use the Knockout Smash to instantly render the thug unconscious. The noise alerts nearby enemies. This is usually employed during a Silent Takedown gone wrong, in which Batman is spotted by other enemies anyway. Stealth is blown at that point, so smashing your prey is the fastest way to begin dealing with others.

DROP ATTACK

▢ / Ⓧ directly above target	Drop Attack

When overlooking an enemy, launch a surprise attack directly down onto your target. Combo directly from this attack if there are other enemies nearby, or launch immediately into a Ground Takedown.

GLIDE KICK

 / ⊗ while gliding	Glide Kick

When gliding through the streets or perched up high, you can target any enemy within range for a Glide Kick, indicated where possible with a Bat symbol over the enemy's head. This move knocks most enemies to the ground, making it an effective way to initiate combat with a group. Hold the Dive Bomb button after locking on for more damage. Upgrades allow some Gadgets to be fired while diving in with a Glide Kick.

SMOKE PELLET

L2 + R2 / LT + RT	Throw
While under fire ⃤ / Ⓨ	Quickfire Drop
While in smoke ⃤ / Ⓨ	Silent Takedown

Target a group of enemies with the Smoke Pellet and take them down silently during the confusion. When used in combat, enemies panic and attack wildly, often hitting each other. Requires a recharge time after use.

VENT TAKEDOWN

 ⃤ / Ⓨ when behind a vent cover	Wall Grate Takedown

When behind a vent cover, smash through and knock your chosen target unconscious. Be careful, this move is not silent and attracts other enemies to your location.

WINDOW TAKEDOWN

⃤ / Ⓨ when behind a window	Window Takedown

Smash through a window and take out the target on the other side. The noise attracts nearby enemies, so evaluate the position of other combatants before initiating this move.

DROP DOWN TAKEDOWN

⃤ / Ⓨ when above target	Drop Down Takedown

When positioned above an enemy, drop seamlessly into a Silent Takedown.

LEDGE TAKEDOWN

⃤ / Ⓨ when hanging from ledge	Ledge Takedown

While hanging from a ledge, reach up and grab an enemy on the walkway to silently knock them unconscious before dropping back down.

SWING DOWN TAKEDOWN

⃤ / Ⓨ when perched above an enemy	Swing Down Takedown

While perched on a ledge, target an enemy directly below you and swing down to perform a long range Silent Takedown.

GRATE TAKEDOWN

⃤ / Ⓨ while in a floor grate	Grate Takedown

When under a floor grate, use the Takedown move to leap out and knock a nearby enemy unconscious. Be careful, this move is not silent and attracts other enemies, who search nearby floor grates on discovering the victim.

WOODEN WALL TAKEDOWN

⃤ / Ⓨ when behind a weak wall	Weak Wall Takedown

Smash through a weak wall, grab the unsuspecting enemy and choke them into unconsciousness. Be careful, this move attracts nearby enemies, so plan your escape route.

CEILING TAKEDOWN

△ / Y when above target	Ceiling Takedown

Target your enemy from above and smash down through a weak ceiling directly into a Takedown. The noise attracts nearby enemies, so evaluate the position of other combatants before initiating this move.

INVERTED TAKEDOWN

△ / Y when hanging from Vantage Point	Inverted Takedown

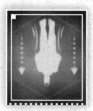

While hanging from a Vantage Point, drop down and grab an enemy directly below you, leaving them suspended from your perch. Plan your escape as the screaming victim attracts nearby enemies to your location.

FEAR MULTI-TAKEDOWN

Right Stick	Select Target
□ / X	Fear Takedown

The new Batsuit allows you to approach enemies undetected and neutralize multiple unaware targets in quick succession. Upgrades allow you to chain ever higher numbers of targets together and wipe them out in a single attack. The power to unleash a Fear Multi-Takedown comes from intimidation, which you build up by using Silent Takedowns on criminals and not being spotted. When a Fear Multi-Takedown is ready to be deployed in predator scenarios, "Fear" is displayed on the HUD. After using a Fear Multi-Takedown, you must silently take out more enemies in order to earn another Fear Takedown. With enemies coming after Batman in larger, more aggressive groups in *Batman: Arkham Knight*, the Multi-Takedown becomes one of the most potent sneaking tools in Batman's arsenal.

LINE LAUNCHER TAKEDOWN

△ / Y while on zip line	Line Launcher Takedown

While using the Line Launcher, target unaware combatants and drop down to perform a powerful takedown. Nearby enemies are alerted, so plan your attack carefully.

STANDARD BATMOBILE COMPONENTS

SUMMON AND EJECT

L1 / LB	Call Batmobile
X X / A A while in Pursuit Mode	Slingshot Eject
L1 / LB while in Pursuit Mode	Parachute Eject

Utilize your suit and car's synchronized subsystems to signal and enter the Batmobile at will. Eject while driving to be shot high into the air and transition seamlessly into a glide, or use your cape as a chute to slow your motion and bring you safely to the ground. Slingshot Eject can be used somewhat like a Grapnel Boost in order to achieve top gliding speed quickly.

BATMOBILE HANDLING

Hold R2 / RT	Accelerate
Hold □ / X	Brake/Reverse
△ / Y	Afterburner
Hold R2 + □ / RT + X	Wheel Spin
Hold R2 + □ + Left Stick / RT + X + Left Stick	Donut

Whether in transit or during enemy pursuit, engage and utilize any number of the Batmobile's high performance capabilities to your advantage. The Afterburner isn't initially available, but is unlocked very shortly into the adventure. Afterburner energy depletes quickly when boosting, but replenishes slowly over time, or quickly if you slide into turns with □ / X .

PURSUIT IMMOBILIZER

◎ / Ⓑ while in Pursuit Mode	Track Vehicle / Fire Immobilizer

After tagging an enemy vehicle with the Vehicle Tracker, you can track its movements and immobilize the target with a small infrared homing missile. Heavily armored transports require multiple strikes. You can also immobilize some vehicles simply by using the Batmobile to batter their vehicles until they're disabled.

BATTLE MODE

Hold L2 / LT	Battle Mode
Left Stick	Move
Left Stick + ⊗ / Ⓐ	Dodge Thrusters

Effortlessly transform the Batmobile from Pursuit Mode to Battle Mode to engage drones or enemies on foot. Also ideal for traversing difficult terrain. To revert to Pursuit Mode, simply release the trigger.

RIOT SUPPRESSOR

While targeting enemies on foot L2 + R2 / LT + RT	Fire

Heat signature recognition automatically disengages live rounds and engages the Riot Suppressor during combat. The weapon fires non-lethal Slam Rounds that immobilize combatants with minimal long-term trauma.

VULCAN GUN

Hold L2 + R1 / LT + RB	Fire

This rapid rate of fire chaingun delivers armor-piercing incendiary shells, ideal for precision-targeting drone weak spots, neutralizing incoming missiles, and engaging aerial drones.

MISSILE BARRAGE

▢ / ⊗ when charged	Missile Barrage Level 1
▢ ▢ ▢ ▢ / ⊗ ⊗ ⊗ ⊗ when fully charged	Missile Barrage Level 2

With simultaneous targeting capabilities, you can mark multiple enemy drones and deliver GPS guided missiles that neutralize the target on impact. A choice weapon for reducing enemy numbers during intense battles. Activate the Missile Barrage by destroying multiple drones to charge up weapon energy. Think of this like a Special Combo Takedown in a tank.

60MM CANNON

Hold L2 + R2 / LT + RT	Fire

This high powered weapon delivers Kinetic Energy Penetrator shells specifically designed to combat armored vehicles. Make every shot count as turret strikes can destroy an enemy with a single hit. Use dodge thrusters to stay out of the paths of incoming enemy shells while lining up turret shots. There are valuable upgrades that hasten the reload rate of the Batmobile's Heavy Turret.

POWER WINCH

Hold L2 + R1 / LT while targeting Winch Point + RB	Fire Power Winch
Left Stick	Move

This multipurpose grapple claw is an essential component of the Batmobile's armory. Attach to winch points to move heavy objects, pull down walls or deliver high powered electrical charges. The winch is even strong enough to anchor and lower the Batmobile down sheer vertical surfaces.

BATMOBILE COMPONENTS INITIALLY UNAVAILABLE

FORENSIC SCANNER

Hold Up on D-Pad while in Battle Mode	Fire Forensic Scanner

This device emits a sonar pulse that can scan the immediate topography of an environment and detect forensic anomalies. Drone targets are also identified, providing a tactical advantage in combat.

EMP

Tap ◎ / Ⓑ	EMP Blast

This powerful weapon emits an Electro-Magnetic Pulse designed to temporarily immobilize drones and scramble incoming missiles. A must-have addition to the armory when fighting large numbers.

DRONE VIRUS

Hold △ / Ⓨ	Hack Drone

This virus infiltrates drone systems and overrides targeting protocols, causing an infected drone to target other militia vehicles instead of the Batmobile. During battles, multiple targets can be infected, causing disarray among enemy forces and giving you the tactical advantage.

CLOSE COMBAT UPGRADES

SPECIAL COMBO BATARANG

WayneTech Points required	4
Hold L2 / LT with full Combo meter	Special Combo Batarang

The Special Combo Batarang lets you unleash up to three explosive Batarangs, which detonate upon impact with target.

SPECIAL COMBO BOOST

WayneTech Points required	4
Prerequisite	Special Combo Batarang

All Special Combo Moves are available after achieving a combo of x5 instead of the normal requirement of x8. This upgrade is applied to all playable characters. A very high return on investment for your WayneTech Points, this lets you roll Special Combo Takedowns into your FreeFlow Combos much faster (or, if you unlock the FreeFlow Focus Mk II upgrade, this gives you an overall damage boost earlier).

SPECIAL COMBO EXPLOSIVE GEL

WayneTech Points required	4
Prerequisite	Special Combo Batarang
Hold L2 + ☐ / LT + Ⓧ with full Combo meter	Special Combo Explosive Gel

The Special Combo Explosive Gel has an increased area of effect, allowing you to stun multiple enemies in a single blast.

SPECIAL COMBO BATCLAW

WayneTech Points required	8
Prerequisite	Special Combo Batarang
Hold L2 + △ / LT + Ⓨ with full Combo meter	Special Combo Batclaw

The Special Combo Batclaw technique allows Batman to render Armored Brutes unconscious in one shot, which is why it is so valuable and expensive.

CRITICAL STRIKES

WayneTech Points required	1
Prerequisite	Acquire new Batsuit

Time your next strike perfectly to double the damage of your attacks. To perform this technique, initiate your next strike the moment your current attack lands.

BLADE DODGE TAKEDOWN

WayneTech Points required	3
Prerequisite	Critical Strikes
Hold Left Stick away + (△) / (Y), release Counter button between each swipe	Blade Dodge Takedown

Instantly take out an enemy that attacks with a blade or sharp object. To successfully complete this move, the Counter button must be held as an enemy attacks, then released and held again in between each of the attacker's swipes. This upgrade is applied to all playable characters. Usually, a Counter just evades an incoming attack and briefly discombobulates a foe (or two or three), but with this technique, an assaulting blade-wielder is doing you a favor.

SPECIAL COMBO MULTI GROUND TAKEDOWN

WayneTech Points required	4
Prerequisite	Critical Strikes
(X) + (O) / (A) + (B) with full Combo meter	Multi Ground Takedown

Instantly incapacitates all enemies that are currently knocked down by flipping up into the air and throwing out a number of Batarangs simultaneously. This move can be very effective if timed correctly, but fails if there are no targets currently on the ground. If you can time this when several enemies are briefly downed, it's just about the most efficient possible use of your Combo meter, and a boon in combat scenarios and AR Challenges.

SPECIAL COMBO DISARM AND DESTROY

WayneTech Points required	6
Prerequisite	Critical Strikes, Multi Ground Takedown
(□) + (△) / (X) + (Y) with full Combo meter	Disarm and Destroy

Disarm an enemy and permanently destroy their weapon to prevent it from being reused by other enemies. Use this move tactically to eliminate dangerous weapons from the fight early on. For obvious reasons, this is particularly useful to spring on enemies packing firearms.

FREEFLOW FOCUS MK II

WayneTech Points required	8
Prerequisite	Critical Strikes

Fill up your Special Combo meter to enable increased damage when striking enemies. Using a Special Combo Move during FreeFlow Focus Mk II depletes the Combo meter and returns damage levels to normal. If there are no particularly dangerous enemies encouraging you to use Special Combo Takedowns, and if there's no good chance to use a Special Combo Multi Takedown on several floored foes, it may be best to just keep the FreeFlow Combo going with the bonus from this upgrade active.

AERIAL JUGGLE

Prerequisite	Acquire new Batsuit
(◎) (◎) (◎) (□) / (B) (B) (B) (X)	Super Stun to Aerial Juggle
Hold (◎) > (□) / (B) > (X)	Charged Super Stun to Aerial Juggle

Perform a Super Stun, then initiate this powerful strike to deliver extra damage to your opponent. This move is ineffective against Brutes and instead triggers a normal Beat Down attack.

BATCLAW SUPER STUN

WayneTech Points required	2
Prerequisite	Aerial Juggle
L2 + △ > ◎ / LT + Ⓨ > Ⓑ	Quickfire Batclaw to Super Stun

Fire the Batclaw at an enemy and pull them toward you into a Stun, instantly hitting them with the same force as a Super Stun.

CHARGED SUPER STUN

WayneTech Points required	3
Prerequisite	Aerial Juggle, Batclaw Super Stun
Hold ◎	Charged Super Stun

Perform a Super Stun without having to perform three Stun attacks first. Hold down the Stun button to execute this move. Can lead into Aerial Juggle follow-up.

WEAPON STEAL MK II

WayneTech Points required	2
▢ + ✕ / Ⓧ + Ⓐ	Steal Weapon

Increase the length of time you can wield a weapon grabbed from an enemy before it breaks, letting you do increased damage for longer.

BATMOBILE ASSISTED TAKEDOWN BOOST

WayneTech Points required	3
Prerequisite	Weapon Steal Mk II

The Batmobile Assisted Takedown is available after achieving a combo of x6 instead of the normal requirement of x9. Somewhat like the Special Combo Boost upgrade, this boosts your Takedown potential for all FreeFlow Combos that take place near the Batmobile.

SPECIAL COMBO REC

WayneTech Points required	4
Prerequisite	Special Combo Batarang, acquire REC Gadget
Hold L2 + ◎ / LT + Ⓑ with full Combo meter	Special Combo REC

The Special Combo REC damages multiple enemies at once with chained arcs of electricity, leaving them shuddering in place and helpless for a few seconds.

SPECIAL COMBO FREEZE BLAST

WayneTech Points required	6
Prerequisite	Special Combo Batarang, acquire Freeze Blast Gadget
R2, R2 / RT, RT and hold with full Combo meter	Special Combo Freeze Blast

The Special Combo Freeze Blast has an expanded radius from the target, encasing nearby enemies in ice. Be advised that Freeze Blasts do not prevent armed enemies from firing their weapons.

BATSUIT UPGRADES

GRAPNEL BOOST MK III

WayneTech Points required	6
R1 / RB	Grapple
✕✕✕✕ / ⒶⒶⒶⒶ and hold	Boost

Launch yourself higher and faster with the upgraded Grapnel Boost.

GRAPNEL BOOST MK IV

WayneTech Points required	8
Prerequisite	Grapnel Boost Mk III
R1 / RB	Grapple
⊗⊗⊗⊗⊗ / ⒶⒶⒶⒶⒶ and hold	Boost

The fully upgraded Grapnel Boost allows you to launch yourself skyward at maximum height and speed. Traversing Gotham City, and unlocking certain Achievements, Trophies, and AR Challenges, is made easier through Grapnel Boost upgrades.

GRAPPLE TAKEDOWN

WayneTech Points required	1
Prerequisite	Acquire new Batsuit
R1 > △ / ▢ or RB > Ⓨ / ⊗	Grapple into Takedown or Fear Takedown

Grapple to a ledge below an enemy and perform a Takedown or Fear Takedown to vault the ledge and smash them into the ground, knocking them out instantly. When using the Fear Takedown variant of a Grapple Takedown, you can naturally transition into taking out two to four of your initial target's accomplices, if they're nearby (and if you've upgraded Fear Multi-Takedown to x4 or x5).

BALLISTIC ARMOR LEVEL 1

WayneTech Points required	1
Prerequisite	Acquire new Batsuit

Provides a 25% increase to the Batsuit's ability to withstand firearm damage. Whether you invest WayneTech Upgrade Points in Ballistic Armor probably centers on your combat prowess. If you can go through fights without getting hit, then your armor is irrelevant and you're free to spend points on other upgrades. But if you're having trouble surviving combat encounters, these upgrades are a big help. The same tradeoff applies to Batmobile armor upgrades, which you can prioritize or bypass.

BALLISTIC ARMOR LEVEL 2

WayneTech Points required	2
Prerequisite	Ballistic Armor Level 1

Provides a 50% increase to the Batsuit's ability to withstand firearm damage.

BALLISTIC ARMOR LEVEL 3

WayneTech Points required	3
Prerequisite	Ballistic Armor Level 2

Provides a 75% increase to the Batsuit's ability to withstand firearm damage.

BALLISTIC ARMOR LEVEL 4

WayneTech Points required	4
Prerequisite	Ballistic Armor Level 3

Provides a 100% increase to the Batsuit's ability to withstand firearm damage.

SHOCKWAVE ATTACK

WayneTech Points required	3
Hold ⊗ + R2 / Ⓐ + RT while gliding	Dive Bomb
◎ / Ⓑ on impact	Shockwave

Land after Dive Bombing and detonate the Shockwave Attack to unleash a wave of kinetic energy that knocks down any standard-sized enemies in the immediate vicinity. Great for getting the drop from above on an unaware group of loitering looters.

GLIDE BOOST ATTACK

WayneTech Points required	3
Prerequisite	Shockwave Attack
Hold ⬜ + R2 / ✕ + RT	Boost

This incredibly powerful attack can be used to take down multiple enemies in a single move. Glide Kick to lock onto your target and then initiate a Dive Bomb. If you can fill the Bat-symbol icon before impact, then you instantly knock out your target and any enemies standing directly behind them.

FEAR MULTI-TAKEDOWN X4

WayneTech Points required	6
Right Stick	Select Target
⬜ / ✕	Fear Takedown

Lock an extra enemy in your sights and vanquish up to four opponents in a seamless, chained attack. This move is highly effective for neutralizing large groups quickly and efficiently. Between Fear Multi-Takedown moves, you'll have to build intimidation back up among remaining enemies by performing other Takedowns before another Fear Takedown is available.

FEAR MULTI-TAKEDOWN X5

WayneTech Points required	8
Prerequisite	Fear Multi-Takedown x4
Right Stick	Select Target
⬜ / ✕	Fear Takedown

The ultimate Fear Multi-Takedown. Incapacitate up to five enemies in a seamless, chained attack that quickly depletes enemy numbers and neutralizes the threat with devastating force. One of the predator-themed AR Challenges actually requires this upgrade for completion.

MELEE ARMOR LEVEL 1

WayneTech Points required	1
Prerequisite	Acquire new Batsuit

Provides a 25% increase to the Batsuit's level of defense against melee attacks.

MELEE ARMOR LEVEL 2

WayneTech Points required	2
Prerequisite	Melee Armor Level 1

Provides a 50% increase to the Batsuit's level of defense against melee attacks.

MELEE ARMOR LEVEL 3

WayneTech Points required	3
Prerequisite	Melee Armor Level 2

Provides a 75% increase to the Batsuit's level of defense against melee attacks.

MELEE ARMOR LEVEL 4

WayneTech Points required	4
Prerequisite	Melee Armor Level 3

Provides a 100% increase to the Batsuit's level of defense against melee attacks.

SMOKE PELLET - DURATION

WayneTech Points required	2
L2 + R1 / LT + RB	Drop
L2 + R2 / LT + RT	Throw
△ / Ⓨ under fire	Quickfire Drop

A lingering cloud of smoke keeps enemies disorientated for longer and grants more time for you to escape or to dispatch foes unseen. Requires recharge time before reuse.

SMOKE PELLET – AREA OF EFFECT

WayneTech Points required	2
Prerequisite	Smoke Pellet - Duration

Increase the size of the cloud created by a Smoke Pellet, providing more cover and enveloping more enemies at once.

EXPLOSIVE GEL 1 – INSTANT TAKEDOWN

WayneTech Points required	1
Prerequisite	Acquire new Batsuit
L2 + R2 / LT + RT	Spray Explosive Gel
Push in Left Stick while facing Gel	Detonate

Instantly incapacitates the nearest enemy when placed Explosive Gel is detonated. Other nearby enemies are still stunned. Particularly effective through a weak wooden wall. Does not apply to Quickfired Explosive Gel.

EXPLOSIVE GEL 2 – STUN DURATION

WayneTech Points required	2
Prerequisite	Explosive Gel 1 – Instant Takedown

Increase the length of time an enemy is stunned by an Explosive Gel detonation. This upgrade applies only to placed Explosive Gel, not to Quickfired Explosive Gel.

EXPLOSIVE GEL 3 - RANGE

WayneTech Points required	2
Prerequisite	Explosive Gel 1 – Instant Takedown

Increase the range at which enemies are affected by an Explosive Gel detonation. This upgrade applies only to placed Explosive Gel.

FREEZE BLAST – PROXIMITY MINE

WayneTech Points required	2
Prerequisite	Acquire Freeze Grenade
L2 + R2 / LT + RT	Throw

The Proximity mine automatically detonates and encases an enemy in ice on approach. Can be useful to delay patrols in predator scenarios, or to waylay a Medic who is attempting to revive incapacitated accomplices.

FREEZE CLUSTER

WayneTech Points required	4
Prerequisite	Freeze Blast – Proximity Mine
L2 + R1 / LT + RB	Throw

The Freeze Cluster produces an ice blast that can lock multiple enemies in place simultaneously. The freezing effect applies only to the lower body of your targets, which doesn't prevent firearm-packing foes from using them.

FREEZE CLUSTER – PROXIMITY MINE

WayneTech Points required	4
Prerequisite	Freeze Grenade – Freeze Cluster
L2 + R1 / LT + RB	Throw

An enhanced Freeze Blast Proximity Mine, the Freeze Cluster Mine detonates when an enemy draws near, locking multiple targets in place. The freezing effect only applies to the lower body of your targets.

FREEZE BLAST – FREEZE DURATION

WayneTech Points required	4
Prerequisite	Freeze Cluster – Proximity Mine

Hold enemies encased in ice for longer periods. This upgrade applies to all ice-based weapons.

DISRUPTOR – SABOTAGE DETECTIVE MODE SCANNER

WayneTech Points required	3
Prerequisite	Acquire Disruptor
L2 + R2 / LT + RT	Fire Disruptor

Sabotage the Detective Mode Scanner to target its user. When the scanner has locked onto your signal while in Detective Mode, it shocks and incapacitates the operator. An effective counter-measure against enemies who can track down Batman using Detective Mode.

DISRUPTOR – SABOTAGE DETECTIVE MODE JAMMER

WayneTech Points required	3
Prerequisite	Disruptor – Sabotage Detective Mode Scanner

Sabotage the Detective Mode Jammer to instantly disable it and cause it to emit a high-frequency signal, deafening any nearby militia.

DISRUPTOR – SABOTAGE SENTRY GUN DISPENSER

WayneTech Points required	2
Prerequisite	Disruptor – Sabotage Detective Mode Scanner

Sabotage a Sentry Gun Dispenser to explode, incapacitating the enemy attempting to use it. Situationally quite useful, depending on the enemy's configuration and equipment.

DISRUPTOR – OPTIC DEFLECTION ARMOR

WayneTech Points required	3
Prerequisite	Disruptor – Sabotage Sentry Gun Dispenser

Disrupt an enemy's Optic Deflection Armor to render them visible again in Detective Mode. Neutralizes the advantage held by some of the enemy's elite forces.

DISRUPTOR – SABOTAGE MEDIC

WayneTech Points required	4
Prerequisite	Acquire Disruptor

Instantly incapacitates Medics when they try and resuscitate downed enemies. Medics can greatly complicate a combat scenario, undoing your Takedowns and prolonging encounters if you don't prioritize them as targets or sabotage them.

DISRUPTOR – SABOTAGE MINE

WayneTech Points required	3
Prerequisite	Disruptor – Sabotage Medic

Detonate mines and incapacitate nearby enemies. Mines placed upon Vantage Points can also be targeted and disabled.

DISRUPTOR – SABOTAGE STUN STICKS

WayneTech Points required	4
Prerequisite	Disruptor – Sabotage Medic

Sabotage an enemy's Stun Stick to electrocute and incapacitate the user when they attempt to attack. Stun Stick combatants can't be assaulted directly with Strikes, so this can be a streamlined way to take them down.

DISRUPTOR – SABOTAGE AMMO

WayneTech Points required	8
Prerequisite	Disruptor – Sabotage Medic

Equip the Disruptor with a fourth charge, allowing you to disrupt the weapons of up to four enemies, or to overload two enemy weapons at once.

SABOTAGE BOA DRONE CONTROLLER

WayneTech Points required	2
Prerequisite	Acquire Disruptor

Sabotage the Boa Sentry Drone Controller to create an explosive feedback loop. When the operator's drone attempts to attack you, the control device shocks and incapacitates the operator instead.

REMOTE HACKING DEVICE – DRONE HACKER MK II

WayneTech Points required	1
Prerequisite	Sabotage Boa Drone Controller

Increase the duration of the Remote Hacking Device's jamming effect, leaving drones blind to your presence for longer.

DISRUPTOR – SABOTAGE DRONE

WayneTech Points required	8
Prerequisite	Sabotage Boa Drone Controller

Sabotage a drone's weapon systems, causing it to self-destruct when it next attempts to fire. Only one drone can be sabotaged at any time.

SKILL GADGET UPGRADES

TWIN AIMED BATARANGS

WayneTech Points required	2
L2 + R1 / LT + RB	Toggle Multi-Batarangs
L2 + R2 / LT + RT	Throw

Take aim from any position and select up to two targets before unleashing simultaneous Batarangs. A highly effective method of attack when engaging small groups of enemies.

TRIPLE AIMED BATARANGS

WayneTech Points required	3
Prerequisite	Twin Aimed Batarangs

Take aim from any position and select up to three targets before unleashing simultaneous Batarangs.

BATARANG STUN DURATION

WayneTech Points required	1
Prerequisite	Acquire new Batsuit

Increase the amount of time an enemy remains stunned after being hit by an Aimed Batarang. Highly effective during combat situations and when attacking enemies unawares.

REMOTE CONTROLLED REVERSE BATARANG

WayneTech Points required	2
Prerequisite	Batarang Stun Duration
Hold L2 / LT	Aim
Hold R1 / RB	Lock On
Release R1 / RB	Throw

This programmed Remote Batarang loops back on itself to hit an enemy from behind. Disorientated enemies then search for their attacker in the wrong direction, creating the perfect opportunity to sneak up on them.

BATARANG COMBAT DAMAGE

WayneTech Points required	4
Prerequisite	Batarang Stun Duration

Increase the power of one of your most trusted gadgets, causing Batarang strikes to do greater damage to enemies during combat.

BATCLAW – DISARM FIREARM

WayneTech Points required	1
Prerequisite	Acquire new Batsuit
L2 + R2 / LT + RT	Fire Batclaw
L2 + △ / LT + Ⓨ	Quickfire Batclaw

Surprise an armed attacker by firing the Batclaw at range to snatch the weapon from their hands. This can be used effectively in combat situations by using the Quickfire Batclaw.

GADGETS WHILE GLIDING – BATARANG

WayneTech Points required	2
Tap L2 / LT while gliding	Batarang

Throw Batarangs in mid-air, stunning your targets before you even reach the ground. Aiming during a glide slows down time and allows you to select your targets.

GADGETS WHILE GLIDING – FOUR GADGETS

WayneTech Points required	3
Prerequisite	Gadgets While Gliding – Batarang
▢ / Ⓧ while gliding	Glide Kick
Tap L2 / LT	Batarang
L2 + △ / LT + Ⓨ in range of target	Batclaw
L2 + ▢ / LT + Ⓧ while gliding	Explosive Gel
L2 + ◎ / LT + Ⓑ	Remote Electrical Charge
R2, R2/ RT, RT	Freeze Grenade

Use up to four gadgets while gliding toward an enemy group. You still need to unlock the individual Gadgets While Gliding upgrades for each Gadget.

GADGETS WHILE GLIDING – BATCLAW

WayneTech Points required	2
Prerequisite	Gadgets While Gliding – Batarang
L2 + △ / LT + Ⓨ in range of target while gliding	Batclaw

Fire the Batclaw while gliding toward an enemy, disarming or knocking them off balance before you even reach the ground.

GADGETS WHILE GLIDING – EXPLOSIVE GEL

WayneTech Points required	2
Prerequisite	Gadgets While Gliding – Batarang
L2 + ▢ / LT + Ⓧ while gliding	Explosive Gel

Throw Explosive Gel charges while gliding toward an enemy, preparing the battleground before you even touch down.

GADGETS WHILE GLIDING – REMOTE ELECTRICAL CHARGE

WayneTech Points required	2
Prerequisite	Gadgets While Gliding - Batarang
L2 + ◎ / LT + Ⓑ while gliding	Remote Electrical Charge

Fire the Remote Electrical Charge while gliding toward an enemy, stunning combatants before you even reach the ground.

GADGETS WHILE GLIDING – FREEZE BLAST

WayneTech Points required	2
Prerequisite	Gadgets While Gliding - Batarang
R2, R2 / RT, RT	Freeze Blast

Throw a Freeze Blast projectile while gliding toward an enemy and trap them in ice before you attack.

GADGETS WHILE GLIDING – FIVE GADGETS

WayneTech Points required	2
Prerequisite	Gadgets While Gliding - Four Gadgets
▢ / Ⓧ while gliding	Glide Kick
Tap L2 / LT	Batarang
L2 + △ / LT + Ⓨ in range of target	Batclaw
L2 + ▢ / LT + Ⓧ while gliding	Explosive Gel
L2 + ◎ / LT + Ⓑ	Remote Electrical Charge
R2, R2 / RT, RT	Freeze Grenade

Use up to five gadgets while gliding toward an enemy group. You still need to unlock the individual Gadgets While Gliding upgrades for each Gadget.

BATMOBILE PURSUIT MODE UPGRADES

SUPER EJECT LEVEL 1

WayneTech Points required	4
✖ ✖ / Ⓐ Ⓐ and hold	Super Eject

Eject further and faster from the Batmobile.

SUPER EJECT LEVEL 2

WayneTech Points required	8
Prerequisite	Super Eject Level 1

Eject from the Batmobile at maximum speed and soar to incredible heights. Can be used much like Grapnel Boosting past rooftops, instantly putting Batman into a fast, altitude-gaining glide.

AFTERBURNER RECHARGE LEVEL 1

WayneTech Points required	2

Increase the automatic recharge rate of the Batmobile's Afterburner, when not in a powerslide.

AFTERBURNER RECHARGE LEVEL 2

WayneTech Points required	4
Prerequisite	Afterburner Recharge Level 1

Further increase the automatic recharge rate of the Batmobile's Afterburner, when not in a powerslide.

DODGE THRUSTER BOOST

WayneTech Points required	8
Prerequisite	Afterburner Recharge Level 1
Left Stick + ⊗ > Left Stick + ⊗ / Left Stick + Ⓐ > Left Stick + Ⓐ	Double Dodge

Trigger two successive bursts of the Dodge Thrusters while in Battle Mode to cover greater distances with ease. Highly effective in combat for evading drone missile fire, and well worth the WayneTech Upgrade Points spent. Tank-on-drone combat isn't too different from hand-to-hand; the most important thing is to avoid getting hit.

RAM CHARGE

WayneTech Points required	4
R2 + △ / RT + Ⓨ in Pursuit Mode	Ram Charge

Increase the damage delivered to enemy vehicles when rammed by the Batmobile.

ARMOR LEVEL 1

WayneTech Points required	1
Prerequisite	Acquire Batmobile

Increase the Batmobile's armor defenses by 25%.

ARMOR LEVEL 2

WayneTech Points required	2
Prerequisite	Armor Level 1

Increase the Batmobile's armor defenses by 50%.

ARMOR LEVEL 3

WayneTech Points required	3
Prerequisite	Armor Level 2

Increase the Batmobile's armor defenses by 75%.

ARMOR LEVEL 4

WayneTech Points required	4
Prerequisite	Armor Level 3

Increase the Batmobile's armor defenses by 100%.

BATMOBILE BATTLE MODE UPGRADES

60MM CANNON – RELOAD SPEED

WayneTech Points required	2

Reduce reload time on the 60mm cannon by 16%, allowing for increased rate of fire during battle.

60MM CANNON – RELOAD SPEED 2

WayneTech Points required	4
Prerequisite	60mm Cannon-Reload Speed

Reduce reload time on the 60mm cannon by 33%, allowing for maximum possible rate of fire during battle. A big help in clearing opposing drone armies quickly and giving you an edge in Battle Mode AR Challenges.

ENERGY STORAGE PROTECTION

WayneTech Points required	8
Prerequisite	Emergency Weapon Energy

Prevent the loss of the Batmobile's Weapons Generator energy levels when taking damage.

60MM CANNON – CHASSIS SHOT DAMAGE

WayneTech Points required	4
Prerequisite	60mm Cannon-Reload Speed
R2 / RT during Battle Mode	Fire

Increase the amount of damage caused to a drone by a direct shot to the chassis.

VULCAN GUN ACCURACY

R1 / RB in Battle Mode	Fire

Increase the Vulcan Gun's accuracy, allowing you to fire with precision targeting for longer periods.

60MM CANNON – TURRET SHOT DAMAGE

WayneTech Points required	4
Prerequisite	60mm Cannon-Reload Speed
R2 / RT during Battle Mode	Fire

Increase the amount of damage caused to a drone by a direct shot to the turret.

ENERGY ABSORPTION EFFICIENT

WayneTech Points required	4

Increase the amount of Weapons Generator energy gained for each enemy destroyed.

EMERGENCY WEAPON ENERGY

WayneTech Points required	2

Instantly charge up the Weapons Generator meter to level 2 when the Batmobile's armor level drops to critical.

60MM CANNON COBRA LURE

WayneTech Points required	3
Prerequisite	Acquire Batmobile
R2 / RT while in Battle Mode	Fire

Shots from the 60mm cannon attract the militia's Cobra drones to the location of the blast. A highly effective means of creating diversions and setting up ambush opportunities. Can be a lifesaver during late-game missions, and during the "Big Game Hunter" AR Challenge.

STORY MODE

The ending of **Batman: Arkham City** saw the death of Gotham's most fearsome villain, Joker—taken down by the Dark Knight himself. Bracing for a power struggle within Gotham, the GCPD prepared for the worst, but over the next nine months they saw a drop in crime. In Gotham City, though, that can't last forever...

Batman: Arkham Knight is the conclusive third game in Rocksteady's **Batman: Arkham** series. The blockbuster games have revolutionized the action-adventure genre with expansive exploration, fluid FreeFlow Combat, and mind-boggling puzzles. The finale steps it up once again with an even bigger world, improved methods for disposing of thugs, more side missions, and the Batmobile. This mode of transportation is brand new to the series, allowing Batman to quickly move around the islands and providing a way to launch even higher into the air. It also becomes a necessity as tanks are sent in to take down the Dark Knight.

BATMAN

PROFILE

REAL NAME	**Bruce Wayne**
OCCUPATION	**World's Greatest Detective**
BASED IN	**Gotham City**
EYE COLOR	**Blue**
HAIR COLOR	**Black**
HEIGHT	**6 Ft. 2 Inches**
WEIGHT	**210 Lbs**
FIRST APPEARANCE	*Detective Comics* **#27 [May 1939]**

ATTRIBUTES

-Trained to physical and mental peak
-Arsenal of gadgets, vehicles, and advanced technology
-Inventor, detective, genius-level intellect
-Expert in most known forms of martial arts
-Trained in all aspects of criminology

When his parents were gunned down in front of him, young Bruce Wayne resolved to rid Gotham City of the criminal element that took their lives.

He trained extensively to achieve mental and physical perfection, in addition to mastering martial arts, detective techniques, and criminal psychology.

Dressing as a bat to prey on criminals' fears, Batman fights crimes with the aid of specialized gadgets and vehicles, operating out of his secret Batcave below Wayne Manor.

Following the events of Arkham City, many of Gotham's citizens are convinced that Batman broke his defining rule by killing his arch-nemesis, The Joker.

BRUCE WAYNE

PROFILE

REAL NAME	**Bruce Wayne**
OCCUPATION	**CEO/Philanthropist**
BASED IN	**Gotham City**
EYE COLOR	**Blue**
HAIR COLOR	**Black**
HEIGHT	**6 Ft. 2 Inches**
WEIGHT	**210 Lbs**
FIRST APPEARANCE	*Detective Comics* **#27 [May 1939]**

ATTRIBUTES

-Billionaire playboy by day, Batman by night
-Gotham's most eligible bachelor

Born into the wealthy Wayne family, Bruce Wayne had an idyllic childhood. But after witnessing his parents' violent murder in Crime Alley, Bruce dedicated his life to battling criminals.

He circled the globe for years, training his mental and physical abilities to their peak. Gotham City welcomed him home, not knowing that high society's favorite billionaire playboy is also the Batman.

Following the Arkham City debacle and the prison's subsequent closure, Bruce Wayne once again came to Gotham's rescue, footing the bill for its extensive redevelopment.

ALFRED

PROFILE

REAL NAME	**Alfred Pennyworth**
OCCUPATION	**Butler**
BASED IN	**Gotham City**
EYE COLOR	**Blue**
HAIR COLOR	**Gray (formerly black)**
HEIGHT	**6 Ft.**
WEIGHT	**160 Lbs**
FIRST APPEARANCE	***Batman* #16 [April–May 1943]**

ATTRIBUTES

-Skilled actor
-Trained in emergency medical techniques
-Proficiency with mechanical and computer systems
-Expert in domestic sciences
-Unflappable manner

After a varied career, Alfred Pennyworth was employed as the Wayne family's butler. When Bruce Wayne's parents were killed, Alfred raised the young orphan and reluctantly aided him in his quest to become the Batman.

Alfred's many skills, ranging from cooking to combat medicine, make him Batman's staunchest ally, and his formal demeanor helps ground the Dark Knight and deflect those who might otherwise suspect Bruce Wayne's true identity.

The Story Mode chapter covers everything you need to defeat Batman's new nemesis, the Arkham Knight, and complete the campaign. Full details on the collectibles and side missions can be found in the Collectibles and Most Wanted chapters.

After Officer Owens places his order at Pauli's Diner, investigate the mysterious man in the corner to set off the evening's events. Shots can be fired once you gain control of the policeman, but it is not necessary. The only difference comes later in the game as a small amount of dialog is changed.

SCARECROW

PROFILE

REAL NAME	Jonathan Crane
OCCUPATION	Criminal mastermind psychiatrist
BASED IN	Gotham City
EYE COLOR	Blue
HAIR COLOR	Brown
HEIGHT	6 Ft.
WEIGHT	140 Lbs
FIRST APPEARANCE	*World's Finest* #3 [September, 1941]

ATTRIBUTES

-Master of Fear
-Professor of psychology
-Expert chemist

The self-proclaimed Master of Fear, Dr. Jonathan Crane is an obsessive and deranged former psychiatrist who uses a combination of experimental drugs and psychological tactics to exploit his victims' fears and phobias.

Prolonged exposure to his own toxin has rendered Scarecrow unable to experience the fear he so desperately craves. The only person who can still elicit terror from Scarecrow is Batman.

Following his attacks on the Dark Knight in Arkham Asylum, Scarecrow was mauled by Killer Croc. Rumor has it he has since reconstructed his face to resemble his iconic mask, while plotting his revenge against Batman and Gotham.

IT'S GOING TO BE A LONG NIGHT...

THE CHAPTER AT A GLANCE

OBJECTIVES

- **A** Meet Commissioner Gordon
- **B** Rescue the Missing Police Officer
- **C** Interrogate the Driver of the Military Vehicle
- **D** Investigate Scarecrow's Safe House
- **E** Run Battle Mode Weapon Energy System Diagnostics
- **F** Destroy the Squadron of Drone Tanks
- **G** Take Ivy to the GCPD Lockup
- **H** Meet Oracle at the Clock Tower
- **I** Use Panessa Studios Antenna
- **J** Collect the Power Winch for the Batmobile
- **K** Power Up the Panessa Studios Antenna
- **L** Use the Antenna at the Falcone Shipping Yard

NEW AR CHALLENGES

- **1** Weapon Energy Diagnostics
- **2** One Man Army
- **3** Combo Master
- **4** Summon, Eject & Glide
- **5** Fear Multi-Takedown
- **6** Grapnel Boost MK II
- **7** Throw Counter
- **8** Predator Fundamentals
- **9** Road Rage

AVAILABLE SIDE MISSIONS

 — The Line of Duty

 — The Perfect Crime

 — Riddler's Revenge

TO ACE CHEMICALS

N

Start

D

Panessa Studios

F

2

E 1

B

I K

3

J

C

Clock Tower

H 9

G A

6 7 8

4 5 L

GCPD

Falcone Shipping Yard

A MEET COMMISSIONER GORDON BY THE BAT-SIGNAL ON THE GCPD ROOFTOP

Fearing Scarecrow's toxin, all remaining civilians are bused off the three islands as criminals take over the area. There is one man with the ability to save Gotham City from this imminent threat. Perched on a tower in central Bleake Island, Batman spots the Bat-Signal in the distance. This indicates the location of the first objective, meet up with Commissioner Gordon.

WAYPOINTS

The current objective is marked with an exclamation point on the map, as well as on the compass at the top of the heads-up display. Open the map to find the exact location or simply line up the triangle at the center of the compass with the waypoint to face the correct direction. Target Detail is given on the right side of the HUD at this point.

A Custom Waypoint can be set anywhere when viewing the map. Simply place the cursor at the desired location and press the Set Custom Waypoint button.

Jump off the tower and glide toward the objective. Land on the platform next to Gordon as he finishes up with a phone call. After learning about a suspicious military vehicle speeding through the city and a missing patrol car, Batman disappears over the railing.

GLIDE AND DIVE

Press and hold the Run button to let Batman glide through the air. Press up on the left stick to speed up or pull it back to slow down and gain distance. The latter keeps the vigilante in the air longer.

Hold the Crouch button while gliding to perform a Dive Bomb. Batman picks up a lot of speed as he descends directly downward. This speed can be translated into distance by letting go of the Crouch button and pulling back on the stick. (If the flight control is not inverted in the Options, push up.) This gives you greater height while in flight, allowing Batman to remain in the air for a longer time and distance.

JIM GORDON

PROFILE

REAL NAME	James W. Gordon
OCCUPATION	Police Commissioner
BASED IN	Gotham City
EYE COLOR	Blue
HAIR COLOR	White (formerly brown)
HEIGHT	6 Ft.
WEIGHT	180 Lbs
FIRST APPEARANCE	*Detective Comics* #27 [May 1939]

ATTRIBUTES

-Experienced police officer
-Trained criminologist
-Proficient in hand-to-hand fighting
-Expert marksman

Police Commissioner James W. Gordon dedicated his career to cleaning up the corruption in the Gotham City Police Department, a goal he has come a long way toward accomplishing.

He has been equally tough on crime, In the pursuit of making Gotham City safe for all its citizens, Gordon has forged an uneasy alliance with Gotham's other top crime fighter, the mysterious vigilante known as Batman.

Since the closure of Arkham City and the death of The Joker, Gordon has overseen a period of relative calm in Gotham, with crime steadily declining. On the back of these successes, many see Gordon as a prime candidate to become the city's next mayor.

B RESCUE THE MISSING POLICE OFFICER

With help from ally, Oracle, the location of the missing squad car is marked with a waypoint. Jump off the pole and glide along the street to the northwest. Land or grapple onto a good vantage point as Batman nears the objective. From there, observe the thugs who surround the downed policeman at the traffic circle.

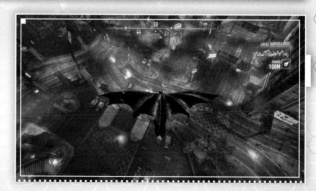

IT'S GOING TO BE A LONG NIGHT

ORACLE

PROFILE

REAL NAME	Barbara Gordon
OCCUPATION	Information Broker
BASED IN	Gotham City
EYE COLOR	Blue
HAIR COLOR	Red
HEIGHT	5 Ft. 11 In.
WEIGHT	126 Lbs
FIRST APPEARANCE	*Suicide Squad #23 [January 1989]*

ATTRIBUTES

-Eidetic memory—recall of everything she sees and reads
-Extensive headquarters in Gotham City's Clock Tower
-High-level hacking and computer skills
-Remains skilled with Escrima Sticks and Batarangs

The daughter of Gotham City's Police Commissioner James W. Gordon, Barbara Gordon fought crime alongside Batman as Batgirl until she was paralyzed from the waist down and confined to a wheelchair.

Barbara has since adopted the new identity of Oracle, and now supports Batman with her computer expertise, providing him with a constant stream of information in the field to aid his battle against crime.

Over the years, Barbara has become romantically involved with Tim Drake, aka Robin.

RIDDLER

PROFILE

REAL NAME	Eddie Nashton a.k.a. Edward Nigma
OCCUPATION	Professional Criminal
BASED IN	Gotham City
EYE COLOR	Blue
HAIR COLOR	Brown
HEIGHT	6 Ft. 1 In.
WEIGHT	183 Lbs
FIRST APPEARANCE	*Detective Comics #140 [October 1948]*

ATTRIBUTES

-Genius intellect
-Driven to test others by leaving clues to his crimes
-Compulsive need for attention and validation

With an obsessive-compulsive need for attention, Edward Nigma is determined to be the cleverest of Gotham City's criminals, plotting elaborate trails of clues and riddles around his crimes.

Batman has proven a worthy opponent, capable of unraveling the Riddler's most intricate plans, but Nigma is dedicated to creating a mystery that will confound the Dark Knight, even if he has to kill someone to do it.

Humiliated by Batman on Arkham Island, and again in Arkham City, Nigma is more determined than ever to make the Caped Crusader bow before his superior intellect. The Collectibles and Most Wanted chapters hold complete details on completing Riddler's Revenge.

EXPLORATION

The police officer is in need of help, but you are free to explore Bleake Island along the way. You can earn extra experience by taking out packs of thugs. Also,

throughout the area, Riddler and his men have placed Trophies, Destructibles, and Riddles. Refer to the Collectibles chapter for full details on locations and solutions to the puzzles. Within the groups of enemies, look out for informants, indicated by a green outline. Save this guy for last and interrogate him to reveal a few locations.

THE ELEMENT OF SURPRISE

Targeting a thug from a high vantage point or directly from a glide gives Batman an extra element of surprise. A group

approached on foot spots the vigilante before you can perform an attack. Press the Strike button when targeting an enemy from above to perform a Glide Kick. This immediately starts the combo with a knockdown. Eventually you can purchase a takedown with WayneTech Upgrade Points and immediately eliminate a foe.

Target one of the baddies and perform a Glide Kick to start the brawl. Take out the group with one fluid combo and a mix of moves and gadgets to maximize the XP earned. This experience translates to WayneTech Upgrade Points, which in turn can be spent on upgrades at the WayneTech tab in the menu.

FREEFLOW COMBAT

The FreeFlow Combat from previous *Batman: Arkham* games returns with more ways to take thugs down. Weapons can be stolen or picked up and used on opponents, items such as overhead lights and panels provide dramatic environmental takedowns, and the Batmobile can offer assistance when parked nearby. Later on in the game, an ally joins Batman with the ability to switch between the two and combine for a Dual Team Takedown. Complete details on how best to utilize these new moves are given in the Intro and Basics chapter.

TIMING IS KEY

Mastering the timing of strikes, counters, and redirects is key in clearing out big groups of henchmen. As an attack hits, push in the direction of your next victim and press the Strike button to continue the combo. Be ready to counter enemies who attack, indicated by the blue bolts above their heads. Red bolts indicate a charge attack. Instead of countering these guys, perform a redirect—evading overhead and gaining an advantageous position behind the foe. Throw in some gadgets and a variety of takedowns to earn maximum experience.

IT'S GOING TO BE A LONG NIGHT

Once you've taken care of the thugs, approach Officer Kevern, lying in the middle of the circle, and help him up. Batman uses his grapnel to narrowly escape an incoming SUV. When prompted to do so, target the street below and press the given button to call for the Batmobile. Batman automatically dives into the driver's seat.

BATMOBILE

The Batmobile is Batman's primary mode of transportation around the three islands. At first, it is used in Pursuit Mode, which allows for racing around the city, immobilizing vehicles, and launching high into the air. Battle Mode becomes relevant a little later in the chapter as tanks are deployed against the Dark Knight.

Enemies can be non-lethally run down while driving, but no XP is earned for this maneuver. It is possible to target a thug on the street and press a button to launch into an attack. Once available, you can trigger a Batmobile Assisted Takedown during a fight that fires a shot at a targeted foe.

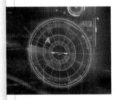

Radar appears in the lower-right corner of the HUD when inside the Batmobile. This becomes extremely valuable when fighting in Battle Mode as enemy vehicles show up as red triangular icons. Knowing where they are at all times goes a long way toward defeating them.

On the consoles, the Left Trigger is used to initiate Battle Mode, while the Square/X button brakes and reverses. This may take time to get used to, but it becomes more natural with practice. Try the Batmobile AR Challenges as they become available to improve skill with this incredibly powerful vehicle. Not only are your abilities tested during the Story, but a few side missions require proficiency in Pursuit and Battle Modes.

C INTERROGATE THE DRIVER OF THE MILITARY VEHICLE FOR INFORMATION ON SCARECROW

Immediately hold down the accelerator and take off after the military vehicle as it drives south and then southwest. A squad car is already in pursuit, though that does not last long as Gordon attempts to call it off. Once the target vehicle is within shot, a circle appears around it. This shrinks inside a diamond on the back. Quickly fire the Immobilizer. A shot fired as the car rounds a corner may end up missing. Hit it three times in all to cause the SUV to crash.

TRACKING THE VEHICLE

There are three indicators of the target vehicle's location. When not in view, a distance in meters is shown in white text. Arrows along the road indicate the automobile's path. And, a green icon appears on the Radar that displays the target's exact location and facing direction. Use these to keep track of the objective.

ARMORED VEHICLE

Militia SUVs carry soldiers of Arkham Knight's militia. They can be taken down with the Batmobile in Pursuit Mode. Fire the Immobilizer until the vehicle crashes.

IT'S GOING TO
BE A LONG NIGHT

Approach the driver as he feebly attempts to crawl away from the burning vehicle. Press the Counter button to interrogate him and obtain a sample of the toxin. Batman runs an analysis on the substance and tasks Oracle to find out more about it.

D   INVESTIGATE SCARECROW'S SAFE HOUSE

In the meantime, Scarecrow's safe house in Chinatown is marked on the HUD and map. Grapple and climb onto the rooftop of the penthouse. A glass portion of the ceiling reveals a small group of thugs who stand guard. Target one and perform a takedown to get another fight started. Take care of the rest of the enemies before moving toward the window ahead.

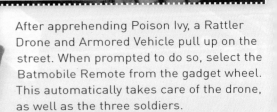

After apprehending Poison Ivy, a Rattler Drone and Armored Vehicle pull up on the street. When prompted to do so, select the Batmobile Remote from the gadget wheel. This automatically takes care of the drone, as well as the three soldiers.

GADGET SELECT

Selecting a gadget is different in *Batman: Arkham Knight* than previous games in the series. Press the Gadget Select button to bring up a circle with all available gadgets. Press in the direction of the desired device and let go to select it. Down selects the Batmobile Remote.

Switch to Battle Mode as more Rattler Drones enter Chinatown. Six drones surround the Batmobile's location. Fire the Heavy Cannon to take each one out while using the Dodge Thrusters to avoid their shots. This fight serves as a good primer to Battle Mode as the enemy does not gang up too much. Once the Rattlers have been eliminated, drive into the rectangular marker on the street, where Poison Ivy is loaded into the back of the Batmobile.

IT'S GOING TO
BE A LONG NIGHT

BATTLE MODE

The Batmobile has several weapons at its disposal. The Heavy Cannon is the weapon of choice against enemy vehicles while the Vulcan Gun is great for shooting missiles out of the air. Build up the meters surrounding the reticle to enable a Missile Barrage. As the player progresses through the Story, a Winch, Drone Virus and EMP are added. Upgrades can also be purchased to improve performance.

RATTLER DRONE

The Rattler Drone is the weakest of the militia tanks. It fires a missile with plenty of warning. A line indicates an incoming shot with arrows pointing in the direction of the shot. Follow the tracer to the start to find the drone. This line turns red when the Batmobile is targeted. Dodge to the side to avoid getting hit. A well-placed shot from the Heavy Cannon just under the Rattler's gun barrel can take the vehicle out in one shot. Use these guys to build up your combo and enable special attacks such as the missile barrage.

A variety of vehicles is added to the militia as the story continues, making for much tougher fights—especially within the AR Challenges and side missions.

Destroy the passive Rattler Drones to charge the Secondary Weapon energy, which is represented by the two meters surrounding the reticle. Once the left is full and turns green, press the Missile Barrage button to launch a single rocket at your target. Charge the Secondary Weapon energy to level 2 this time by filling up both meters. Press the button four times to launch Missile Barrage Level 2 or four guided rockets. Next, the Rattler Drones fire at the Batmobile. Taking damage depletes the weapon energy, so dodge to the side to avoid incoming shots while again charging the Missile Barrage to level 2. Release the attack to destroy 4 active targets and complete the challenge.

E RUN BATTLE MODE WEAPON ENERGY SYSTEM DIAGNOSTICS

Before delivering your prisoner to GCPD, drive southeast to the next waypoint. Drive into the hologram of a wheel, which represents the AR Challenge. This challenge demonstrates how to use the Missile Barrage in Battle Mode.

AR CHALLENGES

AR Challenges are tests of Batman's skills found throughout the city. Drive or step up to one of these holograms to display a description of the test on the right side of the HUD along with the requirements for completion. You earn WayneTech Upgrade Points when accomplishing these challenges.

A handful of introductory challenges are required to proceed through the story, but most are optional and are unlocked by completing specific requirements. Once an AR Challenge is available, it can also be selected from the Main menu by selecting AR Challenges. Our AR Challenges chapter provides full details and requirements for each.

POISON IVY

PROFILE

REAL NAME	Pamela Lillian Isley
OCCUPATION	Professional Criminal
BASED IN	Gotham City
EYE COLOR	Green
HAIR COLOR	Red
HEIGHT	5 Ft. 8 In.
WEIGHT	115 Lbs
FIRST APPEARANCE	*Batman* #181 [June 1966]

ATTRIBUTES

- Able to direct the growth of all plant life
- Plant genes mixed with her DNA
- Exudes natural pheromones that control victims
- Skin secretes a deadly toxin
- Pathological drive to protect nature from humanity

Botanist Pamela Isley was transformed by a science experiment gone wrong into a plant-human hybrid. With chlorophyll flowing through her veins instead of blood, she developed a toxic touch and a pheromone-fueled talent for seduction.

Her unique brand of eco-terrorism often puts her into conflict with Batman, whose iron will usually protects him from her seductive powers.

She was recently captured by Nightwing and imprisoned in Blüdhaven until Harley Quinn staged an audacious break-out.

IT'S GOING TO BE A LONG NIGHT

F DESTROY THE SQUADRON OF DRONE TANKS OCCUPYING PANESSA STUDIOS

On the way to GCPD, a call comes in from Gordon about a group of drones attacking Gotham. Stop by Panessa Studios to find 12 Rattler Drones. Activate Battle Mode and start picking them off from a distance. Avoid getting surrounded and dodge the enemy rockets while building up your combo. Release Missile Barrage Level 2 once available and finish off the squadron.

G IVY TO THE GCPD LOCKUP

Now Batman is free to drive to GCPD on the south side of the island and enter through the Prisoner Detention entrance on the right side. Continue down the path and park at the dead end.

GCPD

Once Poison Ivy has been placed in the isolation chamber, you're free to explore the lockup, where three riddles and a trophy  are available. Thugs and villains can be found inside the cells as the story progresses and side missions are completed. Strike up conversations if you like. The evidence room and archive hold many items from past and present criminals.

With Poison Ivy locked up, find Commissioner Gordon at the maximum-security desk. He has Aaron Cash fill Batman in on three incidents, which begin the first three Most Wanted side missions. You can investigate these anytime Batman is between objectives, earning WayneTech Upgrade Points upon completion. Select your next objective, either a side mission or main story, and exit GCPD.

MOST WANTED MISSION SELECT

Press the Mission Select button to bring up the Mission Select wheel. This allows the player to choose the next objective. For now,  three side missions are available, but more present themselves as you progress through the story. Push down to check the Most Wanted status and up to return to hunting down Scarecrow.

AARON CASH

PROFILE

REAL NAME	Aaron Cash
OCCUPATION	GCPD Officer
BASED IN	Gotham City
EYE COLOR	Brown
HAIR COLOR	Black
HEIGHT	6 Ft.
WEIGHT	200 Lbs
FIRST APPEARANCE	*Arkham Asylum: Living Hell* #1 [July 2003]

ATTRIBUTES

-Missing left hand
-Proficiency with firearms
-Great physical strength

A Gothamite through and through, Aaron Cash has spent his entire working life serving the city's law enforcement and security services.

He rose to become one of the most senior and respected guards at Arkham Asylum, which was also where he suffered a violent attack by Killer Croc, resulting in the loss of his hand and a long standing hatred of the villainous creature.

He is a trusted friend of both Batman and Commissioner Gordon, who, following the closure of Arkham City, reinstated him back to GCPD where he started his career.

THE LINE OF DUTY

Locate and rescue missing members of Station 17 fire crew.

A crew of firefighters appears to be missing and it is up to Batman to track each one down. They are scattered throughout the city and are protected by groups of thugs. Refer to the Most Wanted chapter for locations and types of enemies found at each.

THE PERFECT CRIME

Find and stop the killer displaying bodies throughout Gotham.

Investigate the body found on Merchant Bridge to begin The Perfect Crime. A series of bodies requires a thorough investigation. Hopefully the findings will lead Batman to the mastermind who must be brought to justice. Refer to the Most Wanted chapter for full details on solving the crime.

RIDDLER'S REVENGE

Riddler has been spotted milling around the Train Yard and, undoubtedly, he must be up to no good.

To start the most extensive of the side missions, investigate his last known location at the Train Yard. Riddler has set up a series of puzzles for Batman, as well as collectible trophies, destructible items, and riddles to solve. To reach 100% completion, you must complete all of these. Refer to the Most Wanted and Collectibles chapters for locations and complete solutions.

H MEET ORACLE AT THE CLOCK TOWER TO HELP LOCATE SCARECROW

Drive back outside and continue north and west to the Clock Tower. Grapple to the top of the building and find the secret entrance, given away by the waypoint. Drop inside and activate Detective Mode. This reveals a Retinal Scan Unit hidden inside a bust on the bookshelf. Use the sculpture and then the computer that appears to meet up with Oracle.

I USE PANESSA STUDIOS ANTENNA TO PINPOINT SCARECROW'S LOCATION

Glide or drive to Panessa Studios on the northeast side of the island and grapple to the rooftop. Find the panel on a back wall along the lower section. Attach a remote access device, though it appears you must bypass the damaged generator to power it up.

J COLLECT THE POWER WINCH FOR THE BATMOBILE

An attachment for the Batmobile is currently in development at Wayne Enterprises, which can provide the necessary power as well as pull the vehicle onto the rooftop—perfect for this situation. Fortunately, it is ready for deployment and Lucius Fox sends the Power Winch to the island. Glide to the dirt road next to the lighthouse, call the Batmobile, and drive into the marker. The Batwing delivers the device directly to the automobile.

IT'S GOING TO BE A LONG NIGHT

LUCIUS FOX

PROFILE

REAL NAME	Lucius Fox
OCCUPATION	CEO of Wayne Enterprises
BASED IN	Gotham City
EYE COLOR	Brown
HAIR COLOR	Black
HEIGHT	5 Ft. 9 In.
WEIGHT	195 Lbs
FIRST APPEARANCE	*Batman* #307 [January 1979]

ATTRIBUTES

-Incredible business acumen
-Inventor and entrepreneur
-Warm, friendly, intensely loyal

Current CEO and President of Wayne Enterprises, Lucius Fox is a sought after businessman all over the corporate world, and one of Bruce Wayne's closest allies.

Fox is a shrewd and experienced businessman, entrepreneur, and inventor. Aside from running Wayne Enterprises and the Wayne Foundation, Fox also takes pride in developing weapons, gadgets, vehicles, and armor for Bruce Wayne's alter-ego, Batman.

His latest contributions to the Dark Knight's arsenal include the new Batmobile, and a whole suite of new and upgraded gadgets.

BATWING

When Batman needs an upgrade delivered to his current location, the Batwing provides the service with precision and speed. It can even install an item directly onto the Batmobile.

K POWER UP THE PANESSA STUDIOS ANTENNA WITH THE BATMOBILE POWER WINCH

The objective is simple enough; use the Power Winch to power up the antenna, though getting there requires a bit more effort.

POWER WINCH

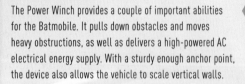

The Power Winch provides a couple of important abilities for the Batmobile. It pulls down obstacles and moves heavy obstructions, as well as delivers a high-powered AC electrical energy supply. With a sturdy enough anchor point, the device also allows the vehicle to scale vertical walls.

Facing an anchor point or electrical panel, enable Battle Mode and press the Vulcan Gun button to attach. Moving backward pulls the obstruction down or out of the way. To deliver electrical energy, lightly pull the Heavy Cannon trigger, keeping the needle in the orange until power has been provided.

BATTLE MODE FOR NAVIGATING TIGHT SPACES

When navigating tight areas with the Batmobile, enable Battle Mode. This allows for sliding in any direction with improved control. This works great for crossing the rooftops during this objective. Be careful when using this during a timed challenge, though, as it does bring the vehicle to a complete stop.

Fire the Power Winch at the anchor point ahead and pull back to bring the Urbarail Station sign down. With access to the station's roof, hold the Afterburner down and jump the gap. Pressing up and down allows for a little air control when airborne.

Turn to the right, attach to another point ahead, and pull back to provide a ramp. Jump onto the corner roof.

Turn left and carefully follow the narrow path, being careful not to drop off the roof. There is no need to avoid the ornamental globes as you can easily drive through them.

Fire the Power Winch and slowly rev the engine, keeping the needle inside the orange. This provides the necessary electricity and powers the antenna.

Follow the roof around to the left until an anchor point on the far building is within reach. Fire the Power Winch to attach and drive off the building.

While suspended, push forward to drive up the wall until safely onto Panessa Studios. Detach the winch and drive to the left until you reach the objective.

IT'S GOING TO
BE A LONG NIGHT

ROBIN

PROFILE

REAL NAME	**Tim Drake**
OCCUPATION	**Student**
BASED IN	**Gotham City**
EYE COLOR	**Blue**
HAIR COLOR	**Black**
HEIGHT	**6 Ft.**
WEIGHT	**189 Lbs**
FIRST APPEARANCE	***Batman* #436 [August 1989]**

ATTRIBUTES

- Keen detective skills
- Trained to fight crime by Batman
- Arsenal of gadgets and advanced technology
- Near-genius level intellect

Young Tim Drake was in the audience the night the Flying Graysons were murdered, where he witnessed Batman leap to the scene. Inspired by Batman's heroics, Tim closely followed the chronicles of Batman and Robin.

Eventually deducing their secret identities using his self-taught detective skills, Tim convinced Bruce Wayne and Dick Grayson—now Nightwing—that a new Robin was needed in the never-ending battle for justice.

Tested by the Dark Knight himself with a grueling training regimen, Tim earned the right to become Robin, and has since lived up to the name.

Over the years, Tim has become romantically involved with Barbara Gordon, aka Oracle.

L USE THE ANTENNA AT THE FALCONE SHIPPING YARD TO LOCATE SCARECROW

With the Batmobile busy powering the Panessa Studios antenna, grapple and glide to the Falcone Shipping Yard. Access to the antenna is housed inside a small room atop the building. Detective Mode reveals five hostiles inside, all armed. Grapple onto the vantage point above their position and then swing over to another perch to survey the environment.

Select the Batarang from the gadget select and toss a projectile at the door to lure two enemies out of the building. Let them split up, glide behind the nearest one, and drop him with a silent takedown. Crouch, quietly move behind the second guy, and eliminate him in the same manner.

That leaves three guys inside the room. Move over to the waypoint on the other side of the roof and access the Batpod to receive a new and improved Batsuit.

BATSUIT V8.03

A new and improved suit, Batsuit V8.03, gives Batman the ability to move faster and hit harder than ever before. Counter-attacks become more effective with Counter Throws. Multiple unaware targets can be neutralized quickly with the Fear Multi-Takedown. Gain increased height with access to an ejection mechanism on the Batmobile. The Grapnel Boost MK II upgrade allows for significantly higher and faster launches following a grapple.

COMPLETE AR TRAINING PROGRAMS TO EARN WAYNETECH UPGRADE POINTS

Five AR Challenges become available on the Falcone Shipping rooftop: Summon, Eject & Glide; Fear Multi-Takedown; Grapnel Boost MK II; Throw Counter; and Predator Fundamentals. These training sessions demonstrate the abilities of the new Batsuit. As far as AR Challenges go, they are relatively straightforward and each one earns a WayneTech Upgrade Point, so it is well worth the time to complete each one. Refer to the AR Challenges chapter for full details on these programs.

Now it's time to dispose of the last three thugs inside the building. Enter the floor grate and move underneath the hostiles until one is highlighted. Perform a Fear Multi-Takedown on him and continue the attack against the other two. Help the hostage onto his feet, approach the panel on the wall, and attach the uplink.

FEAR MULTI-TAKEDOWN

The new suit allows Batman to take down multiple unaware targets in quick succession. The word FEAR highlights in the upper-left corner of the HUD when the move is available. Perform Silent Takedowns to charge it back up.

Approach an oblivious enemy from behind, above, or below, then press the Strike button to take him down. Move the camera around to highlight your next target and hit the button again to chain together up to three takedowns. Upgrades become available that increase the number of targets to four and then five.

Move outside and wait for the Batarang to set up high in the air with a good view of the city. As the Microwave and Radio Receivers come online, their signals can be rotated with the movement and look controls, respectively. As microwave radiation and radio transmissions are detected, they are marked on the map. Point them both to Ace Chemicals, on the far right, to determine exactly where Scarecrow is producing the fear toxin.

IT'S GOING TO
BE A LONG NIGHT

PATIENCE IS A VIRTUE

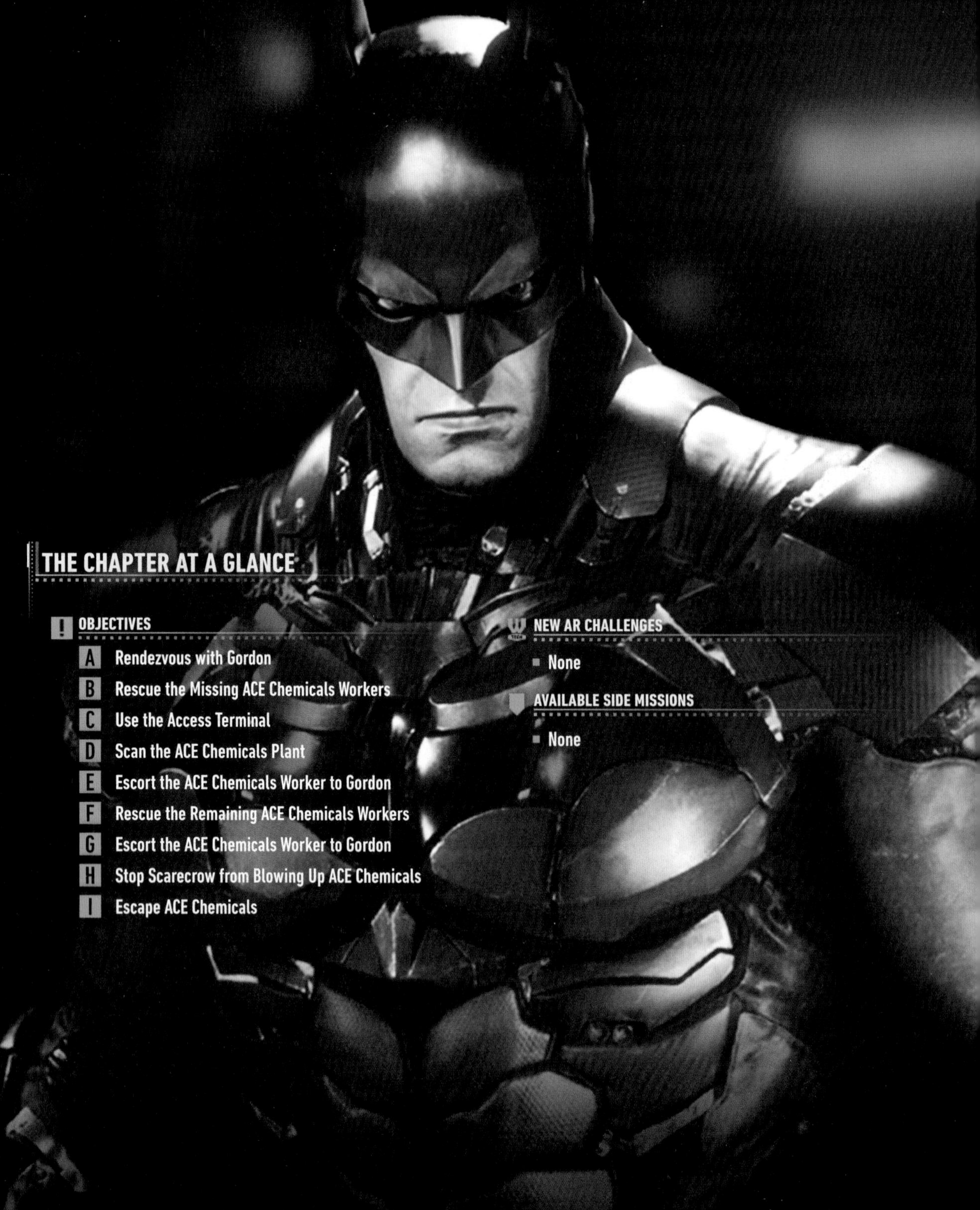

THE CHAPTER AT A GLANCE

! OBJECTIVES

A Rendezvous with Gordon

B Rescue the Missing ACE Chemicals Workers

C Use the Access Terminal

D Scan the ACE Chemicals Plant

E Escort the ACE Chemicals Worker to Gordon

F Rescue the Remaining ACE Chemicals Workers

G Escort the ACE Chemicals Worker to Gordon

H Stop Scarecrow from Blowing Up ACE Chemicals

I Escape ACE Chemicals

NEW AR CHALLENGES

- None

AVAILABLE SIDE MISSIONS

- None

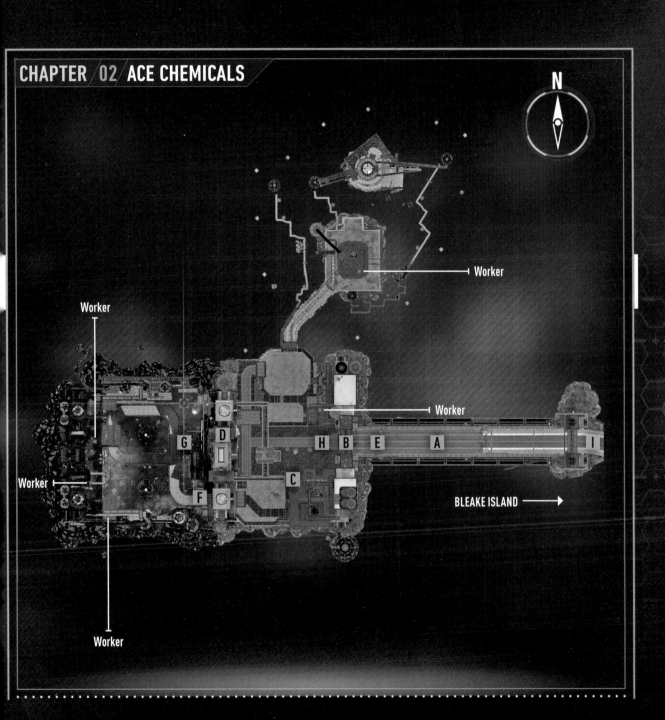

N

Worker

Worker

Worker

Worker

G D

H B E A I

C

F

Worker

Worker

BLEAKE ISLAND →

A RENDEZVOUS WITH GORDON AT THE ACE CHEMICALS PLANT

Located on the northwest corner of Bleake Island, a bridge leads out to the ACE Chemicals plant. Commissioner Gordon awaits Batman's arrival along with a group of officers. A skeleton crew of workers remains inside.

B RESCUE THE MISSING ACE CHEMICALS WORKERS TO GET INFORMATION ON SCARECROW

After a brief confrontation with the Arkham Knight, grapple to the top of the gate ahead, where Batman checks in with Oracle.

ARKHAM KNIGHT

PROFILE

REAL NAME	**Unknown**
OCCUPATION	**Military Commander**
BASED IN	**Unknown**
EYE COLOR	**Unknown**
HAIR COLOR	**Unknown**
HEIGHT	**6 Ft.**
WEIGHT	**200 Lbs**
FIRST APPEARANCE	*Batman: Arkham Knight* [June, 2015]

ATTRIBUTES

–Expert knowledge of Batman's tactics and fighting style

–Highly skilled military tactician

–Robotically synthesized voice

Besides the discovery of a militia training facility in South America, virtually nothing is known of the Arkham Knight until his arrival in Gotham where he quickly earned himself a fearless reputation amongst the city's leading criminals.

Working together with Scarecrow, he has sworn to kill Batman and will stop at nothing until he is dead.

C USE THE ACCESS TERMINAL TO RETRIEVE THE WORKERS' PERSONAL ID FREQUENCIES

A nearby terminal should allow Batman to retrieve personal ID frequencies of the workers, which would allow them to be tracked. Activate Detective Mode and survey the situation below. Five armed soldiers guard the area, so stealth is in order. The hostiles are spread out, so getting behind each one for a Silent Takedown is relatively simple. Take out the left two first, followed by the right guy who wanders. Drop into the floor grate, approach the terminal, and eliminate the final two with one takedown. Use the computer to obtain the ID codes for the five personnel.

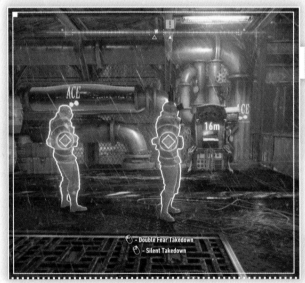

PATIENCE IS
A VIRTUE

VENT CHUTES

In predator scenarios such as this, vertical vents often give Batman quick access to floor grates. Found on walls or rooftops, you can slide down directly into the floor. From there, grapple back up to the roof or perch. Use the grapnel to access a vent on a wall.

UNCONSCIOUS VICTIMS

Unconscious bodies left behind are often discovered by hostiles, followed by a thorough investigation of the surrounding area. As the number of enemies goes up in predator situations, the likelihood of this increases. Moving away from your victims to avoid being found is often a good idea, but with the Fear Multi-Takedown you can quickly dispose of a small group of investigating thugs.

D SCAN THE ACE CHEMICALS PLANT TO PINPOINT THE LOCATION OF THE MISSING WORKERS

A high Vantage Point is required to scan the plant. Grapple and climb to the very top of the main building ahead, above the ACE Chemicals sign. Once deployed, the BatScanner slowly circles around the facility. Move the target around until a signal is displayed. Hold the Run button to analyze it and reveal a worker's location. Continue this process until you've found all five.

Glide down to the roof (or glide-kick into the roof when the diamond symbol is present) of the small building next to the front gate. Use a Fear Multi-Takedown on one of the hostiles below and continue the combo until all five guys are unconscious. Unfortunately, the hostage has been killed. Step over to the gate release that hangs between two windows and throw the switch to open the main gates.

ENVIRONMENT TAKEDOWNS

Items with a blue outline can be used in an Environment Takedown. With a highlighted hostile nearby, press Strike + Run to perform special takedowns with overhead lights, electric panels, and more.

Select the Batmobile Remote, fire the Power Winch at the anchor point ahead, and pull the road back to create a ramp. Hit the Afterburner and jump through the gate, where three Rattler Drones and a Diamondback Drone await. Take care of them with the Heavy Cannon, avoiding incoming attacks with the Dodge Thrusters.

DIAMONDBACK DRONE

These tanks are heavily armored, but still manageable with the Batmobile's 60mm Heavy Cannon. Two or three direct hits take one down. The Diamondback fires a spread of three rockets at a time, requiring Batman to be ready with the Dodge Thrusters.

Approach another anchor point next to the main building. Use the Power Winch to open the gate follow the path up a level, and spot the worker to the northeast. Drive the Batmobile through the railing, pipes, and barricades to the circular structure. Knock out the three soldiers and continue around to the backside. Take down the wall with the Power Winch and eliminate the hostiles inside. Enter a door in the far-right corner to reach a chained up hostage.

The Arkham Knight shows up with a handful of soldiers, confident that they have Batman right where they want him. Select the Batmobile Remote and knock down all of the hostiles as the boss grapples away. With the guns knocked out of their hands, take them all down with some melee attacks.

PATIENCE IS
A VIRTUE

BATMOBILE ASSISTED TAKEDOWN

When parked nearby, the Batmobile can assist in melee combat. An icon on the left side of the HUD signifies that the Batmobile Assisted Takedown is available. Press the Strike + Run buttons to knock your target in the air as the vehicle fires a shot at the foe.

E ESCORT THE ACE CHEMICALS WORKER TO GORDON ON THE BRIDGE

Free the hostage, hop into the Batmobile, and take the worker to Gordon just outside the main gate.

F RESCUE THE REMAINING ACE CHEMICALS WORKERS TO GET INFORMATION ON SCARECROW

Head back into the facility, drive up the ramp, and exit the vehicle. Grapple up to the crane platform above, where six hostiles hang out. Make the two armed-thugs a priority while taking them all down. Four combat experts take their place. Counter their acrobatic sword attacks and finish them off before accessing the crane controls.

The controls are listed in the lower-right corner of the screen. The crane can be moved, rotated, and lowered. Move the ramp toward the Batmobile and set it down on the edge of the upper level. Select the

Batmobile Remote and jump the gap with the help of the Afterburner. Turn right and drive toward the Loading Dock.

Six Rattlers and two Diamondback Drones block the path. Concentrate on the stronger two first, as their triple shot is tougher to avoid. Deploy the Missile Barrage when available and eliminate the tanks with the Heavy Cannon.

PATIENCE IS A VIRTUE

Face toward the Loading Dock at the back of the area. With a diamond target on the window above, eject from the Batmobile to perform a Glide Kick through the glass. Five soldiers and a Medic are housed inside. Defeat the group, select the Explosive Gel, and spray it onto the weak wall in the back of the room. A gas leak blocks your way. Use the Batmobile remote and winch the exposed pipe below the Loading Dock to stop the leak. Once the way is clear you find another deceased worker.

MEDICS

Medics start appearing in many of the predator and combat fights from now on. They wear white and have the ability to pick up a total of three downed enemies. Make these guys a priority or you'll have to take down some thugs multiple times. Eventually, you can purchase an upgrade that allows Batman to disable the Medic's ability to heal.

A weak section of the floor ahead can be destroyed, allowing access to the lower floor. Gas leaks block the path to the next worker. Place Explosive Gel on the wall in the back of the room and detonate it to reveal a pipe. Pull the cover off the electric panel on the front wall to raise the adjacent shutter. This gives line of sight to the Batmobile. Switch to the Batmobile, fire the Power Winch at the exposed pipe, and pull it apart to stop the leaks. Duck under the opening ahead to find a third dead worker.

Continue forward and pull the cover off the box on the left wall. This opens a gate to the outside. Select the Batmobile Remote and drive the vehicle to the opening, where bollards restrict admission. Take down the weak wall inside with the Heavy Cannon and then fire the Power Winch. Move backward until an elevator appears ahead and reaches its highest point. Leave the winch attached and climb inside the elevator. Take control of the vehicle and push forward to lower Batman.

Just ahead you can see the final hostage, along with 11 hostiles. Move around to the right and grapple into a small opening in the ceiling. Crouch and move through the short access until you reach a big fan. Pull the vent cover off the left wall and crawl inside for a better view of the enemy. Six soldiers join three combat experts and a medic. Line up for a Fear Multi-Takedown and drop in on the

thugs. Take down the entire crew and then talk to the worker.

Return to the elevator, take control of the Batmobile, and pull all the way back to free the hostage. As Batman hops in to the car, three Rattler Drones, two Diamondbacks, and a Gunship show up. Avoid the barrage of attacks while picking off the tanks. With the ground drones out of the way, release the Missile Barrage at the chopper and focus the Vulcan Gun on it. Stay on the move as it deploys numerous projectiles your way. Continue to deplete its health, indicated by the bar in the upper-right corner of the HUD.

PATIENCE IS
A VIRTUE

ARKHAM KNIGHT'S GUNSHIP

The Gunship is an unmanned chopper with three deadly attacks: guided missiles, a cluster attack, and a single rocket. The latter is a quick shot that displays a circle on the ground at the point of impact. A red indicator means that the Batmobile is within range of the blast. Dodge away to avoid taking damage. As the fight goes along, more rockets are fired in quick succession, so do not let your guard down.

Watch out for the big clusters of rockets as they are launched across the width of the area. Stay on the move, using the Dodge Thrusters to escape an imminent strike.

A beep indicates an incoming guided missile. Quickly target these projectiles as they are released from the ship and knock them out of the air with the Vulcan Gun.

G ESCORT THE ACE CHEMICALS WORKER TO GORDON ON THE BRIDGE

After downing the Gunship, look to the east to find the exit blocked and a switch on the nearby wall, which raises and lowers the adjacent platform. Drive onto this platform, exit the Batmobile, and push the button. Hop back into the vehicle and deliver the survivor to Commissioner Gordon just outside the main gate.

H STOP SCARECROW FROM BLOWING UP ACE CHEMICALS

With the survivors safe and sound, it's time to go after Scarecrow, who readies his bomb deep inside the plant. Back in the facility, valuable information from Oracle gives Batman an idea on how to get inside. Fire the Heavy Cannon at the cursor on the building ahead. Be sure the car is outside the "Keep Clear" area, eject into the air, and grapple to the crane platform. Take control of the machine and position the ramp inside the rectangle so that it faces the new hole in the wall. Use it to launch the Batmobile into the plant.

PATIENCE IS A VIRTUE

Drive around the corner and destroy the two Diamondback Drones at the bottom of the hill. Eject from the car, and grapple to the ledge above the gate. On the other side, two soldiers and a Militia Sentry Gun mean certain death if taken on directly. Instead, swing into one of the vents on the side to get into the floor. Once the turret swings away from the soldiers, perform a Fear Multi-Takedown on them, and drop back into the floor grate. With the gun pointing away, get in close and destroy it. Find the emergency gate release on the nearby wall and use it to open the gates.

Call the Batmobile and move further inside, where another gate blocks progress. Twenty unarmed hostiles, including two Medics, occupy the area on the other side. Lamps, electric boxes, and fans provide several opportunities for Environment Takedowns. Focus attention on the healers first as the group is disposed of with melee attacks, counters, and takedowns. Return to the gate, pull the cover off the gate release, and hop into the automobile once available.

Spikes above the next gate do not allow for the grapnel, so eject from the cockpit and glide over them. Inside the mixing chamber, you can see Scarecrow in the central room with eight armed soldiers spread around the outside. A few Sentry Guns also guard the area.

You must take care of the eight hostiles before going after the boss. Beams offer Vantage Points through much of the area. Just below the starting point, two Sentry Guns guard the gate. The right wing is mostly closed in with glass ceilings, allowing for takedowns from above, though the noise does make others aware of your location. Take cover at the corners for Silent Takedowns on unsuspecting foes. Move away from your victims as other soldiers discover them.

On the opposite side of the chamber, a beam runs above two stationary hostiles. Eliminate them with a silent, double takedown. A Fear-Multi Takedown can be used on them, but quickly leave the area as the noise attracts attention. The remaining wing is guarded by a single Sentry Gun, which is easily accessed from the floor gate. Use the wall vents to move between the upper and lower levels.

Once the soldiers have been taken care of, enter the central chamber through the door on the backside to confront Scarecrow. Approach the Chamber Control Terminal in the middle of the room and use it to prepare the neutralizing agent. Four canisters of the agent appear to the right. Collect one, slowly pulling back on the move controls, since it is extremely volatile. Moving too quickly causes it to explode, ending the game. On the other side of the chamber, two pairs of receptacles are ready for deployment of the agent. Carefully move over to one and insert the canister, lightly pressing forward to avoid an explosion. Do this with all four containers to reduce the blast radius.

STEADY DOES IT

Lights around the outside of the neutralizing agent canisters indicate the safeness of the chemical as Batman moves them. Green lights mean that you can speed up while red signifies it will explode if you do not slow down.

During a flashback, the player controls Commissioner Gordon as he is dropped off at the Panessa Studios landing pad. Walk into the VIP elevator ahead and press the button to ride it down to the hideout. Talk to the four prisoners to find out what's going on there.

CHRISTINA BELL

PROFILE

REAL NAME	Christina Bell
OCCUPATION	Executive Director, Queen Industries
BASED IN	Star City
EYE COLOR	Blue
HAIR COLOR	Brown
HEIGHT	5 Ft. 9 In.
WEIGHT	145 Lbs
FIRST APPEARANCE	*Batman: Arkham Knight* [June, 2015]

ATTRIBUTES

-Expert business acumen
-Violent obsession with Batman
-Highly unpredictable

After a successful career in finance, Christina recently joined the board of directors at Queen Industries in Star City.

During a blood transfusion following a miscarriage, Christina was exposed to Joker's Titan-infected blood. On returning to work, she took a knife to a board meeting and brutally murdered 11 senior executives, carving smiles on her victims' faces.

Christina has adopted several facets of Joker's personality, notably his obsession with Batman.

PATIENCE IS A VIRTUE

ALBERT KING

PROFILE

REAL NAME	Albert King
OCCUPATION	Heavyweight Boxer
BASED IN	Gotham City
EYE COLOR	Brown
HAIR COLOR	Black
HEIGHT	6 Ft. 7 In.
WEIGHT	284 Lbs
FIRST APPEARANCE	*Batman: Arkham Knight* [June, 2015]

ATTRIBUTES

-Highly proficient fighter
-Superhuman strength
-Uncontrollable rage

Albert King aka The Gotham Goliath is a legendary prizefighter with the most consecutive knockouts since records began.

Days before his testimonial fight, King checked into Gotham General for a routine procedure, only to become infected with Joker's mutated blood.

Hospitalizing his entire family in a fit of rage, King appears to have taken on the more violent and sadistic aspects of Joker's personality.

HENRY ADAMS

PROFILE

REAL NAME	Henry Adams
OCCUPATION	Principal/Teacher
BASED IN	Gotham City
EYE COLOR	Blue
HAIR COLOR	White (formerly blond)
HEIGHT	5 Ft. 9 In.
WEIGHT	160 Lbs
FIRST APPEARANCE	*Batman: Arkham Knight* [June, 2015]

ATTRIBUTES

–Principal of McCallum Academy
–Professor of biology

Highly respected principal of the esteemed McCallum Academy, Henry Adams was exposed to Joker's blood during a routine treatment at Gotham General.

Displaying none of the symptoms experienced by the other victims, Henry's immunity could be the key to developing a cure. Though initially cooperative, Henry's patience is wearing thin, and he's desperate to return home to his family.

JOHNNY CHARISMA

PROFILE

REAL NAME	Jonathan Browne
OCCUPATION	Singer
BASED IN	Gotham City
EYE COLOR	Green
HAIR COLOR	Brown
HEIGHT	5 Ft. 10 In.
WEIGHT	172 Lbs
FIRST APPEARANCE	*Batman: Arkham Knight* [June, 2015]

ATTRIBUTES

-Trained vocalist

-Narcissist

-Baritone

Jonathan Browne, aka Johnny Charisma, made a name for himself on the cabaret circuit before hitting the bigtime when he was discovered by a national talent show.

Charisma is no stranger to controversy with a string of drug offenses and a DUI, but his assault on a groupie was uncharacteristically violent.

Since his infection, Charisma has been displaying signs of megalomania, with his behavior echoing the sadistic showmanship of The Joker.

PATIENCE IS A VIRTUE

▌ ESCAPE ACE CHEMICALS

Select the Batmobile Remote, fire the Power Winch at the anchor point ahead, and pull down the side of the chamber. Enter the car and drive out of the plant onto the bridge as the facility collapses.

IT IS DANGEROUS OUT THERE

THE CHAPTER AT A GLANCE

OBJECTIVES

A	Meet Gordon Outside GCPD Prisoner Detention
B	Escort Gordon to the Clock Tower
C	Take Out the Arkham Knight Militia Forces
D	Investigate the Clock Tower
E	Track the Arkham Knight's Vehicle
F	Investigate the Militia Device
G	Defend the Virus Upload
H	Defuse the Bomb with a Controlled Explosion
I	Track the Arkham Knight's Vehicle
J	Proceed on Foot to the Grand Avenue Station
K	Head to the Abandoned Orphanage
L	Return to Mercy Bridge
M	Track the Arkham Knight's Vehicle
N	Investigate the Crashed Vehicle
O	Head to Wayne Tower
P	Infiltrate the Miagani Tunnel Network
Q	Rendezvous with the Batwing
R	Rendezvous with Nightwing
S	Follow the Weapons Truck
T	Access the Weapons Cache and Interrogate Penguin
U	Destroy Penguin's Weapon Cache
V	Identify a Way to Infiltrate the Stagg Enterprises Airships
W	Disable the Watchtower Guarding the Airships
X	Collect the Remote Hacking Device

NEW AR CHALLENGES

1	Midnight Fury TT
2	Revive and Shine
3	Tower Defense
4	Untouchable

CHAPTER 03 BLEAKE ISLAND

N

ARKHAM KNIGHT'S ROUTE

FROM ACE CHEMICALS

Start

Panessa Studios

1

Clock Tower

D
E   B
C

G F
  H
  I

Sionis Industries

A

L

Mercy
Bridge

GCPD

AVAILABLE SIDE MISSIONS

The Line of Duty	Campaign for Disarmament
The Perfect Crime	Gotham on Fire
Riddler's Revenge	Heir to the Cowl

Creature of the Night	Occupy Gotham
GunRunner	
Armored and Dangerous	

A MEET GORDON OUTSIDE GCPD PRISONER DETENTION

The drive to GCPD is more dangerous with the increased numbers of militia tanks. Take out the Rattler Drones along the way. Drive down to the Prisoner Detention where Commissioner Gordon awaits Batman's arrival.

THREAT LEVEL

The threat from Arkham Knight's Militia steadily increases throughout the story. Various drones, watchtowers, checkpoints, and bombs pop up everywhere. The Threat Level is indicated on the map screen in the upper-right corner with numbers of each threat. Most of these are eliminated as the player progresses through side missions. Be careful when on foot, as they can quickly take out Batman once spotted.

B ESCORT GORDON TO ORACLE'S CLOCK TOWER

Allow Gordon to lead the way as you drive toward the Clock Tower. A couple of Militia Armored Vehicles attempt to apprehend the Commissioner. Take them out with the Immobilizer or by running into them. Press toward an enemy car plus the Run button to perform a Side Swipe. Once they have been taken care of, Gordon pulls to the side of the road. Move into the marker just ahead, wait for him to get into the Batmobile, and continue to the destination.

C TAKE OUT THE ARKHAM KNIGHT MILITIA FORCES OCCUPYING THE CLOCK TOWER

Twelve Rattler Drones attempt to stop Batman as the objective nears. Dodge their attacks while taking them down with the Heavy Cannon. Once the tanks are out of the way, grapple to a high Vantage Point to survey the militia soldiers who occupy the Clock Tower. Six hostiles, including a Medic, patrol the outdoor area. A gargoyle, floor grates, railings/ledges, and many corners offer enough locations to perform Silent Takedowns on all of them.

IT IS DANGEROUS
OUT THERE

MINES

During predator fights, listen to the hostiles. They communicate how things are going, including when mines are placed on Vantage Points or in floor grates. Use Detective Mode to find the locations of these explosives and avoid them, though there is time to get away if you trigger one.

D INVESTIGATE THE CLOCK TOWER FOR CLUES TO HELP LOCATE ORACLE

Grapple to the top of the Clock Tower and enter through the secret entrance. Pick up the wheelchair once the option appears. After Gordon leaves, use the computer to search for clues. With footage from four surrounding CCTV cameras on screen, Batman should be able to find an indication of who has taken her. Use the move controls to select a camera, while look allows for scrubbing of the video. Rotate the stick clockwise or move the mouse right to go forward and vice versa to rewind. Select the upper-right camera and when the guy emerges from the tower zoom in. Now select the section of the image where he is located and scan for evidence to find out who has her. Wait for him to get in the Armored Vehicle and scan one of the sections of the car.

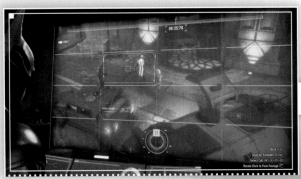

E TRACK THE ARKHAM KNIGHT'S VEHICLE TO LOCATE ORACLE

Initiate Shutdown Procedure, exit the tower, and call the Batmobile. Starting from the tower exit, use the Forensics Scanner to reveal the tire tracks and the route the Arkham Knight's vehicle took.

FORENSICS SCANNER

The Batmobile is equipped with a Forensics Scanner that enables Batman to track the route of the militia vehicle's unique tire tread. Enable Battle Mode and press the Scan button to toggle the scanner, which reveals the tracks as the device pulses. Switching to Pursuit Mode or firing a shot switches the device off, requiring it to be reactivated. Simply follow the route as it appears ahead of the vehicle.

F INVESTIGATE THE MILITIA DEVICE

Just outside Sionis Industries, the militia buried a device into the ground. Exit the car and investigate to find out it is a bomb. Batman decides to use the Batcomputer to hit it with multiple viruses and detonate it with a controlled explosion.

G DEFEND THE VIRUS UPLOAD

The militia sends 16 Rattler Drones to stop Batman. Activate Battle Mode and defend the virus upload from the tanks. With that many drones, enemy shots are incoming almost constantly. Stay on the move while taking the vehicles out with the Heavy Cannon.

H DEFUSE THE BOMB WITH A CONTROLLED EXPLOSION

With the drones out of the way, attach the Power Winch to the bomb, and lightly hold the accelerator to rev the engine. Keep the needle in the orange until the bomb detonates. This registers as the first bomb removed in the Campaign for Disarmament side mission.

IT IS DANGEROUS
OUT THERE

CAMPAIGN FOR DISARMAMENT

Find and defuse all explosive devices deployed by the militia.

Fourteen bombs are scattered throughout the three islands. Hit each one with the virus and then defend it from the militia onslaught until it can be detonated. Each device defused earns a WayneTech Upgrade Point.

THE DARK KNIGHT RETURNS:
GAME PLAY

ENEMIES OF THE BAT

WAYNETECH ARSENAL

STORY MODE

MOST WANTED: SIDE MISSIONS

AR CHALLENGES

■ TRACK THE ARKHAM KNIGHT'S VEHICLE TO LOCATE ORACLE

Return to the tire tracks and use the Forensics Scanner to follow the vehicle's route south to Mercy Bridge. The Batmobile is unable to proceed, though, as the militia has hacked into the Transport Control System, raising the bridge and locking Batman out.

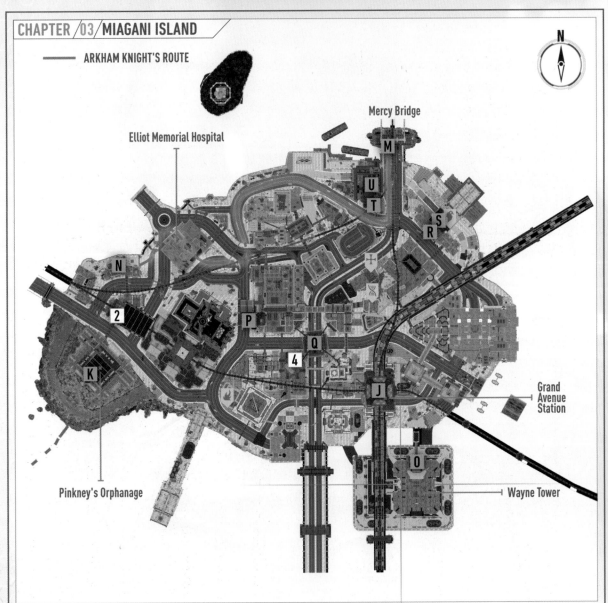

CHAPTER /03/ MIAGANI ISLAND

—— ARKHAM KNIGHT'S ROUTE

N

Mercy Bridge

Elliot Memorial Hospital

Pinkney's Orphanage

Grand Avenue Station

Wayne Tower

J PROCEED ON FOOT TO THE MILITIA ACCESS POINT AT GRAND AVENUE STATION AND REGAIN CONTROL OF MERCY BRIDGE

A waypoint is placed at Grand Avenue Station straight ahead on Miagani Island. Glide over to the new island and proceed to the station, landing on the railing just above the militia uplink terminal. Eight armed soldiers occupy the large depot, including one Boa Sentry Drone operator. Two hostiles are easy pickings from the start as they guard the laptop below. The others can be picked off from floor grates, Vantage Points, behind walls, upper floors, and more. If spotted or heard, flee the immediate area and continue to take down the militia soldiers. With the area clear, use the computer to gain access to Mercy Bridge.

BOA SENTRY DRONE

The Boa Sentry Drone is a remote control surveillance device used in predator situations. It is flown around by one of the hostiles, adding an extra set of "eyes" in the sky. Avoid its field of vision, which is indicated by lights on the front. Enable Detective Mode to spot the drone's operator, who is connected to the device by a line. Take this guy out to cause it to crash.

MORE RIDDLER'S REVENGE

Rescue Catwoman from the Riddler at Pinkney's Orphanage.

Technically, Riddler's Revenge has already started with the investigation of the villain at the Train Yard and the collectibles. Now Edward Nigma clues you into the main event of the side mission. He has kidnapped Catwoman, who he is holding at the abandoned Pinkney's Orphanage. You must solve a mix of combat and puzzle challenges found both inside and outside the building to set her free. The trials held inside the orphanage require Batman and Catwoman to work together. Refer to the Most Wanted chapter for more information.

IT IS DANGEROUS OUT THERE

K HEAD TO RIDDLER'S ORPHANAGE TO RESCUE CATWOMAN

After a lengthy announcement from the Riddler and while Alfred works on getting the bridge accessible, glide and grapple over to the orphanage, located on the west side of the island. Avoid the ground as militia drones litter the roads. Five of Riddler's thugs greet you at the entrance, including an informant. Take them down and interrogate the highlighted foe before entering the building and rescuing Catwoman.

Edward Nigma introduces the duo to his automated combatants. These robots learn from the fight, allowing the Riddler to build better opponents for the next battle. The first challenge for Batman and Catwoman requires them to defeat 10 of these fighters. The first version of the androids is easily taken care of with melee attacks and counters. Take advantage of the assistance from your partner and dispose of the metal thugs. After the skirmish, talk to your teammate.

DUAL TEAM

This bout is the first of a number of dual team fights. When teamed up with a partner, press the Switch Character button to toggle between them. A circular meter builds on the left side of the HUD to a bat symbol. Press the Switch Character button to perform a Dual Team Takedown on the current target.

CATWOMAN

PROFILE

REAL NAME	**Selina Kyle**
OCCUPATION	**Professional Thief**
BASED IN	**Gotham City**
EYE COLOR	**Green**
HAIR COLOR	**Black**
HEIGHT	**5 Ft. 7 In.**
WEIGHT	**125 Lbs**
FIRST APPEARANCE	*Batman* #1 [Spring 1940]

ATTRIBUTES

-Trained gymnast and athlete
-Expert hand-to-hand combatant
-Highly skilled with whips
-Unrivaled stealth capabilities
-Obsessed with stealing famous and well-protected items

An orphan who learned to survive on the mean streets of Gotham City, Selina Kyle turned to thievery to survive. Determined to do it with style, she learned martial arts and trained in gymnastics to perfect her skills.

Her criminal activities are tempered by a reluctant altruism, making her an inconstant villain and occasional hero. She maintains a complicated, adversarial relationship with Batman that frequently turns flirtatious and occasionally romantic.

Little is known about her movements since the closure of Arkham City, but a string of high-profile burglaries suggests she is still at large in Gotham City.

L   RETURN TO MERCY BRIDGE TO RESUME TRACKING THE ARKHAM KNIGHT'S VEHICLE

Once ready to return to the main story, head over to Mercy Bridge to use the Batmobile's Forensics Scanner where the tracks left off.

M   TRACK THE ARKHAM KNIGHT'S VEHICLE TO LOCATE ORACLE

Mercy Bridge is lowered, revealing six militia drones on the other side: two Mamba Drones, a Diamondback, and three Rattlers. Stay back and pick off each one with the Heavy Cannon. The Mamba Drones launch guided missiles that can be knocked down with the Vulcan Gun. The Rattlers can be taken out instantly with a direct shot at the sensory array with the Vulcan Gun. With the bridge safe to navigate, scan the tracks across the bridge, to the right, past the Gotham Mall and Elliot Memorial Hospital, to a row of bollards that block the road. Rattler Drones litter the island, so feel free to take a break from forensics and eliminate these foes.

MAMBA DRONE

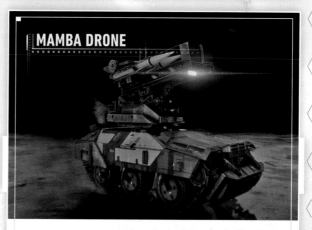

The Mamba Drone launches two guided missiles at its target. A red arc from the launcher to the Batmobile indicates that missiles are ready to deploy. Red squares on the HUD identify their location in flight. Once locked on, a message informs the player. Listen for the warning beeps and quickly target the projectiles with the Vulcan Gun. Take the drone out with the Heavy Cannon.

IT IS DANGEROUS OUT THERE

N INVESTIGATE THE CRASHED VEHICLE

Investigate the crashed SUV ahead to discover that Arkham Knight must have taken Oracle and moved on. Enable the Evidence Scanner to investigate the scene. Move the circular reticle around the vehicle and surroundings to search for evidence. Once found, hold the Run button to scan it in. Scrub through the playback to follow the clues.

Scan in the right part of the vehicle and then rewind to reconstruct the scene. Take it all the way back to the start and let it play. It shows the car veering off the road and the driver being launched out the windshield.

Walk around the planters to find the driver lying on the ground. Scan him to find out he was hit with pepper spray.

Scan the passenger seat and reconstruct the scene again. The passenger-side door is sent flying when the SUV impacted the planter. Rewind the scene and follow the door over the railing. Scan it in to reveal more of the scene.

Reconstruct the scene again and watch as Oracle rolls out of the SUV before impact. Follow her path as she breaks the pallet and attempts to crawl away. Batman deduces that a shot was fired at her.

Rewind the scene and follow the trajectory of the bullet as it hits just to the right of Barbara—a warning shot. There must be a reason for her to cause the crash. Investigate further to find out why.

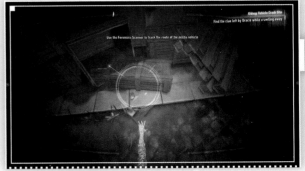

Scrub backward again and carefully watch Oracle as she crawls away. She tosses something into the crates on her left. Trace the path and scan the nearest box to find a scrambler device.

⓪ HEAD TO WAYNE TOWER AND ANALYZE THE ARKHAM KNIGHT'S ENCRYPTION PROTOCOLS

It will take a while for Lucius Fox to decrypt the data on the device, so it's a good time to see what's going on with Gotham's Most Wanted. Alfred informs Batman of two new cases, an interloper who stands on a rooftop next to a burning bat symbol and a fire at the Bristol fire station. These are optional at this point, but well worth the WayneTech Upgrade Points you earn by completing them.

GOTHAM ON FIRE

Investigate reports of an arsonist loose in Gotham.

The Bristol fire station is ablaze and arson is suspected. The suppression system needs to be powered up to stop it from spreading and then the arsonist must be taken in. Refer to the Most Wanted chapter for full details.

HEIR TO THE COWL

Investigate reports of a masked vigilante in Gotham.

A vigilante stands atop a building on Miagani Island. Batman needs to investigate the suspicious, masked man and see what he wants. Refer to the Most Wanted chapter for more information on this side mission.

CREATURE OF THE NIGHT

Obtain a blood sample from the winged creature for analysis.

As Batman grapples to the next rooftop, a new creature appears out of nowhere and belts the vigilante. This bat-looking monster is worth investigating before he causes too much trouble. The Most Wanted chapter holds full details on how to find out who he is and how to capture him.

IT IS DANGEROUS OUT THERE

Drive or glide to Wayne Tower in the southeast corner of the island and grapple up to the highest balcony. The shutters open, allowing access to Bruce Wayne's office. Talk to Lucius Fox and then access the computer on the desk to find out the Arkham Knight is in the Miagani Tunnel Network. Before leaving the office, Lucius gives Batman a choice between two Batmobile upgrades. The one you select is delivered shortly.

- **CPU Virus** – Overrides the friend or foe identification system of militia drones. An infected drone targets other drones instead of the Batmobile. When deployed at higher weapon energy levels, this infects multiple enemy targets.

- **Weapon Generator MK III** – Allows a user to overcharge secondary weapons, increasing their offensive capability.

SNEAK PEEK

While inside Wayne's office, use the bust on the bookshelf to reveal two Batpods with works in progress inside. Lucius shows off a new version of the Disruptor, but it's not ready for deployment yet.

P INFILTRATE THE TUNNEL NETWORK UNDER MIAGANI ISLAND

Hop in the Batmobile and drive into the waypoint near the Miagani Botanical Gardens to access the tunnel system. Continue inside, stop short of the dead end, and fire the Power Winch at the fan above. Pull it down and grapple inside.

Bust through the weak walls ahead, pry the vent cover off to the left, and crawl inside. Select the Line Launcher and slide over the fan to the next platform. Look to the right to spot a switch on the wall. Toss the Remote Controlled Batarang and guide it into the button to open the gate on the right. Use the Line Launcher again to move through the new opening.

At the next fan, throw the Remote Controlled Batarang into the air and guide it through the hole on the left wall. Maneuver it down to the left and hit the button on the panel ahead to open another gate. Aim the Line Launcher at the far wall and fire to start a slide. About half way, look to the left and fire another line through the opening.

Follow the path to a big room where numerous militia soldiers gather below. Swing over to the beam, turn around, and continue to another girder. Proceed along the beams until a wall vent to the right becomes accessible. Swing inside to drop into the floor grate and follow the path into a side room.

Exit the grate to get the attention of the Arkham Knight himself. When the brute kicks Batman, counter the move to push him away. Stun and take him down with a Beat Down. This attracts the attention of 12 soldiers, four Combat Experts, one Medic, and two Brutes. Be ready to redirect whenever you're unsure of what to do next, while taking down the big pack of thugs.

Find the box in the corner and use it to open the access gate. Select the Batmobile Remote, bring down the wall, and take out the Diamondback and Rattler Drones. Enter the vehicle and continue along the path. At the next gate, hop out and use the gate access to just miss the APC.

IT IS DANGEROUS
OUT THERE

Chase the vehicle through the city. When the Armored Vehicles get in the way, use the Immobilizer to remove them. Perform Side Swipes when an enemy drives up beside the Batmobile. Once you've taken out the APC, hop out and interrogate the soldier. Press the accelerator when prompted to do so, to intimidate the thug and find out about Penguin's involvement and North Refrigeration.

RENDEZVOUS WITH THE BATWING TO EQUIP A NEW SECONDARY WEAPON FOR THE BATMOBILE

The new Batmobile upgrade is ready for deployment. Meet it at the waypoint on Grand Avenue. With help from the new upgrade, take care of the attacking drones.

PENGUIN

PROFILE

REAL NAME	Oswald Chesterfield Cobblepot
OCCUPATION	Black Market Racketeer
BASED IN	Gotham City
EYE COLOR	Blue
HAIR COLOR	Black
HEIGHT	4 Ft. 10 In.
WEIGHT	175 Lbs
FIRST APPEARANCE	*Detective Comics* #58 [December 1941]

ATTRIBUTES

-Criminal and financial mastermind
-Expert hand-to-hand combatant
-Mercilessly cruel
-Various underworld connections

The Penguin is an eccentric criminal mastermind known for his shady business dealings. Born into the wealthy Cobblepot family, Oswald was sent overseas for school as a boy. When his family hit hard times, Cobblepot immersed himself in criminal education on the streets of London.

Years later, he re-emerged as the Penguin, a black-market arms dealer in Gotham City, facilitating the illegal financial activities that fund much of the city's underworld.

Since his humiliating defeat in Arkham City, Penguin has resurfaced, supplying arms to Gotham's occupying forces via a front company called North Refrigeration.

ARMORED AND DANGEROUS

Find and neutralize all of the militia's APCs

Armored Personnel Carriers carrying the militia's senior command have been mobilized throughout the city. Three of these vehicles on each island need to be tracked down and immobilized. Check out the Most Wanted chapter for more information.

R RENDEZVOUS WITH NIGHTWING TO GET INTEL ON PENGUIN'S WHEREABOUTS

Meet up with Nightwing atop the entrance to Ranelagh Ferry Terminal in the northeast corner of Miagani Island. He has been tracking the North Refrigeration trucks out of Blüdhaven, which is why Nightwing chose to meet at this location. He hands over a new Disruptor prototype as a van pulls up below. Six thugs appear, including two who are armed, as well as a brute. Fire the Disruptor at each of their guns and then hit the gun locker, so they cannot grab another without getting a shock. Once the firearms are disabled, drop down and take out the crew.

NIGHTWING

PROFILE

REAL NAME	Dick Grayson
OCCUPATION	Crimefighter
BASED IN	Blüdhaven
EYE COLOR	Blue
HAIR COLOR	Black
HEIGHT	6 Ft.
WEIGHT	180 Lbs
FIRST APPEARANCE	*Tales of the Teen Titans* #44 [1984]

ATTRIBUTES

-Trained to fight crime by Batman
-Skilled acrobat and master martial artist

The youngest of a family of acrobats known as The Flying Graysons, Dick Grayson watched his parents die at the hands of a mafia boss extorting money from the circus.

Bruce Wayne adopted the young orphan as his ward and subsequently trained him to become his crime-fighting partner, Robin.

Determined to prove himself, and growing weary of living in Batman's shadow, Grayson moved to Blüdhaven to fight crime under his new name—Nightwing.

IT IS DANGEROUS OUT THERE

DISRUPTOR

The new and improved Disruptor allows Batman to sabotage weapons, gun locker, equipment, and more. Upgrades allow for more uses. The device can also be used for tracking vehicles, such as in the GunRunner side mission. Simply aim at the weapon or piece of equipment and fire to disable it.

S FOLLOW THE WEAPONS TRUCK TO LOCATE PENGUIN'S SECRET HIDEOUT

Fire the Disruptor at the van and then knock on the back. As they speed away, immediately follow them, keeping them in view. Don't use the Batmobile, as it spooks the thugs. The truck's position is shown when it's behind buildings, as long as it doesn't get too far away. Grapple and glide to keep up with the vehicle.

T ACCESS THE WEAPONS CACHE AND INTERROGATE PENGUIN

Eventually, they lead Batman right to the weapons cache, just down the street from where the chase originated. The shutter is locked behind the thugs and soldiers guard the only way in from the rooftop. Grapple to a high vantage point and survey the scene. You must deal with six armed hostiles and two Sentry Guns. Go ahead and use the Disruptor to sabotage one of the closest firearms, and take out the other two, before proceeding. Disable each turret from behind when the area is clear. Eliminate the remaining guards and enter the hatch inside the roof access.

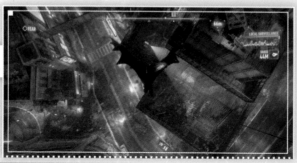

Twenty hostiles and Penguin himself guard the weapon cache below. Fortunately, they are all unarmed. Find the vent on the wall and slide down into the floor grate. Move behind the boss and interrogate him. Counter the optimistic soldiers when they strike, including the two who grab guns from the weapon crate. Nightwing joins Batman, starting the brawl with the remaining thugs. Switch between the two vigilantes and use the Dual Team Takedown whenever possible.

U DESTROY PENGUIN'S WEAPON CACHE

Once everyone has been dealt with, enter the vault and spray Explosive Gel on the highlighted crate in the back. Exit the room and interact with the door. With the vault closed up tight, move away from the blast area and detonate. Talk to Nightwing and exit the building. On the roof, hostiles have set up an ambush for Batman. Pull out the Batmobile Remote and drive the vehicle up to the top level of the parking garage across the street. Take out the Sentry Guns and soldiers that block the vigilante's escape.

GUNRUNNER

Find and destroy all of Penguin's weapon caches.

Contact Nightwing for more Penguin truck locations and track them back to the weapons caches in the same manner as here. The Most Wanted chapter gives all locations of Penguin's trucks and weapons caches.

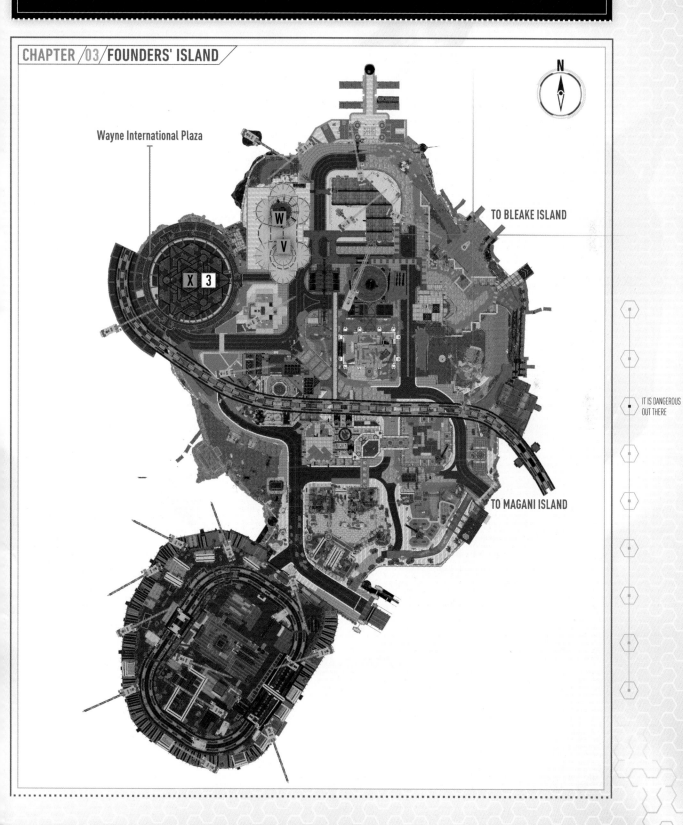

CHAPTER /03/ FOUNDERS' ISLAND

N

Wayne International Plaza

TO BLEAKE ISLAND

W

V

X 3

TO MAGANI ISLAND

IT IS DANGEROUS
OUT THERE

V IDENTIFY A WAY TO INFILTRATE THE STAGG ENTERPRISES AIRSHIPS

Penguin divulged information about Simon Stagg and his airships, so that's the next objective. He's on Founders' Island, which is guarded by the militia's long-range radar and missile launcher. That means Batman must go in on foot. Grapple to the top of a tall building and glide toward the waypoint on Founders' Island.

SIMON STAGG

PROFILE

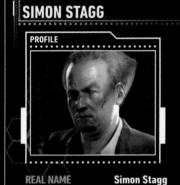

REAL NAME	Simon Stagg
OCCUPATION	CEO of Stagg Enterprises
BASED IN	Central City
EYE COLOR	Blue
HAIR COLOR	White
HEIGHT	5 Ft. 11 In.
WEIGHT	170 Lbs
FIRST APPEARANCE	*The Brave and the Bold* #57 [January, 1965]

ATTRIBUTES

-Cunning negotiator
-Unscrupulous
-Sound business mind

A wealthy scientist, philanthropist, and entrepreneur, Simon Stagg is the founder and CEO of Stagg Enterprises, a company specializing in advanced biomedical research.

A self-proclaimed visionary, Stagg has been developing clean energy solutions and a revolutionary airborne inoculation technology onboard his airship laboratories.

In recent years, Stagg Enterprises has been accused of human rights violations in regards to medical testing on humans. Simon Stagg vehemently refuted the accusations and his company was cleared of all charges.

SERPENT DRONE

This aerial drone flies around the island with one purpose—find Batman. These vehicles do not play into any side mission, but they do earn you a little XP and getting them out of the way is a nice bonus. A red cone shows its current field of view. Avoid this or get shot down. Glide onto the top of the surveillance aircraft and Batman automatically sprays some Explosive Gel. Detonate it to take the drone down.

W DISABLE THE WATCHTOWER GUARDING THE AIRSHIPS

A watchtower has been stationed just outside the airships. A Sentry Gun hangs on the outside and five armed soldiers patrol below. A central command point controls the turret and must be taken out before entering the airships. One hostile operates a Boa Sentry Drone while another holds a device that can track Batman's Detective Mode. A meter appears in the middle of the screen that shows the thug's progress toward detecting the vigilante whenever Detective Mode is used. Be sure to disable it before being found. Use the circular beams to get the drop on the soldiers. Watch out, as they place mines on vantage points to deter their use. Once you've taken care of the five enemies, approach the computer, spray Explosive Gel, and detonate. This destroys any connected Sentry Guns, allowing access to the airship.

OCCUPY GOTHAM

Seek out the militia watchtowers and destroy the command points.

More watchtowers are set up around the three islands. Avoid getting spotted by the Sentry Guns as you eliminate the soldiers and destroy the command point to earn WayneTech Upgrade Points. Refer to the Most Wanted chapter for their locations and how to defeat each one.

X COLLECT THE REMOTE HACKING DEVICE FROM THE TOP OF WAYNE INTERNATIONAL PLAZA

Lucius has readied the Remote Hacking Device for pickup at Wayne International Plaza. Glide to the southwest toward the skyscraper and grapple to the very top. Activate the vault to find a Batpod inside, which reveals the device when opened. This arrives just in time as a service hatch on top of the airship is locked tight and requires hacking into a nearby security console to get inside.

REMOTE HACKING DEVICE

The Remote Hacking Device is a powerful gadget with many uses. It descrambles equipment, hacks into security consoles, and triggers environmental objects and traps. It is used often to bypass security protocols and is vital in getting past the upcoming objectives.

IT IS DANGEROUS
OUT THERE

Line Launcher Perch [LineLauncherStop]

PREY THAT NO LONGER FEARS YOU

THE CHAPTER AT A GLANCE

❗ OBJECTIVES

A Track Down Scarecrow in Airships

B Destroy the Weapon Turrets on the Second Airship

C Pursue Scarecrow Across to the Second Airship

🔱 NEW AR CHALLENGES

- None

🚩 AVAILABLE SIDE MISSIONS

 The Line of Duty

 Heir to the Cowl

 The Perfect Crime

 Creature of the Night

 Riddler's Revenge

 GunRunner

 Campaign for Disarmament

 Armored and Dangerous

 Gotham on Fire

 Occupy Gotham

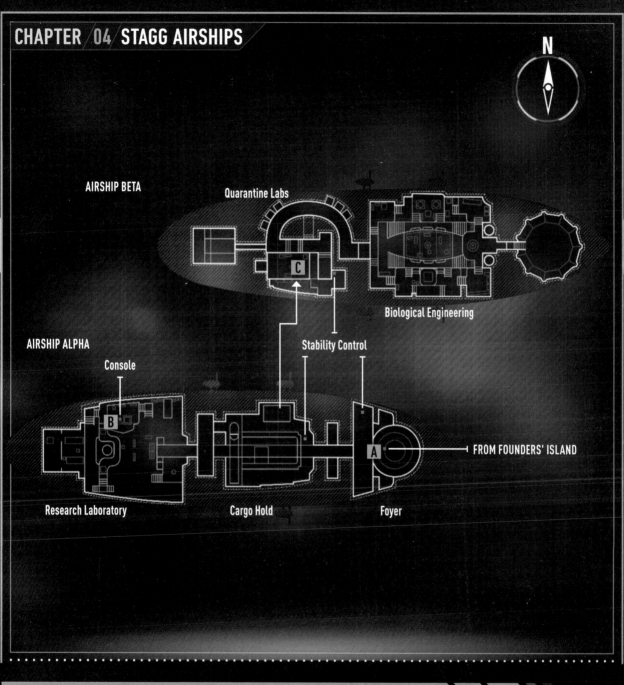

AIRSHIP BETA

Quarantine Labs

C

Biological Engineering

Stability Control

AIRSHIP ALPHA

Console

B

A · FROM FOUNDERS' ISLAND

Research Laboratory

Cargo Hold

Foyer

N

A · TRACK DOWN SCARECROW IN THE STAGG ENTERPRISES AIRSHIPS

Hop onto the north railing to spot the airships ahead. The nearest one, Alpha, is accessible through a service hatch on top. Glide down, pull out the Remote Hacking Device, and aim it at the security console inside, located just south of the entrance. Start the hack and enter BIOCHEMISTRY as the passcode using the move and look controls. Descend into the zeppelin to reach the foyer.

- Use Remote Hacking Device

Three armed guards, including a Boa Sentry Drone operator, can be seen below. Rip the vent cover off the nearby wall, enter the next room, and drop through the grate to land on the same level as the hostiles. Aim the Remote Hacking Device at the drone operator and download the control codes. Next, press the Strike button to incapacitate all three targets. Take advantage of this feature of the hacking device when a drone is present in a predator situation.

Step to the left to find another security access panel beyond the glass wall. Enter PROTEINS as the password to open the door. Proceed through the opening and enter the small room to the left. Access the computer to override the airship stability controls. This gives Batman the ability to tilt the ship, though only within range of this terminal. The graphic on the right side of the HUD shows whether this feature can be used. Press the Call Batmobile button to access the stability controls. At that point, the move controls rotate the zeppelin, moving obstacles that are not secured—such as the crate that blocks the trap door in the previous room. Move the crate and drop down through the trap door. Climb down the ladder to reach the storage area below.

INSECT CRATES

Look out for Insect Crates throughout the airships, often hiding in corners. Melee attack it if possible or use the Batclaw to pull it down when out of reach. This counts toward Riddler's Collectibles.

Tilt the airship to the left to clear the containment boxes out of the way. Drop down and move to the opposite side of the room. Turn to face three more crates in the center of the room. Some of these boxes have magnetic locks that can be toggled with the stability controls active and the Remote Hacking Device equipped. The lock turns green and now the crate can be moved. Use the stability controls to tilt the ship and slide the crate to the right. Use the hacking device to lock the box in place by once more targeting the lock. Tilt the ship to the left to clear the exit.

WATCH YOUR STEP

Be careful when moving crates around on the airships. If caught in its path or standing on top, Batman takes damage, possibly to the point of death.

Proceed to the end of the next corridor and grapple through the hatch above as a dual bladed brute narrowly misses getting a piece of the vigilante. Avoid his blade attack, stun him, and take him down with a Beat Down. Use the Remote Hacking Device to open the gate, entering ELEMENTS as the password.

BLADE DODGE

The Blade Dodge carries over from *Arkham City* and *Origins* and is performed in the same manner. When a thug attacks with a blade or two, yellow markings appear overhead. Pull away from him and hold the Counter button to avoid getting hit. An upgrade becomes available that allows you to counter the attacker after the dodge.

Twenty-six unarmed hostiles, including a brute, mill about in the cargo hold below. They have captured Simon Stagg and are currently interrogating him. Start the fight with a Glide Kick and continue to combo between the soldiers. Watch out for the brute and his blade attack. Performing an Environment Takedown on him makes this guy much easier to deal with—though you do miss out on the added combo count from the Beat Down. Charge attacks are easy to miss if you're not paying attention. Quick toss a Batarang to knock him down. With the pack out of the way, talk to Stagg before he's taken away to the second airship.

PREY THAT NO LONGER FEARS YOU

Hack the security panel next to the exit with the Remote Hacking Device and enter NUCLEICACIDS as the password. This provides access to the second airship, but gun turrets keep you inside the first. Batman must find a way to disable the weapons before proceeding across.

B   DESTROY THE WEAPON TURRETS ON THE SECOND AIRSHIP

Use the computer at the end of the cargo hold to override the airship stability controls. Drop into the nearby hatch, where containment boxes block the path ahead. Activate stability control, tilt the ship to the right, and lock the first container on the right. Shift them back to the left and sneak through on the right.

Release the container that blocks the path, then tilt all the way to the left and lock it on the other side along with the next crate. Shift the

containers back to create a corridor. Move forward three boxes, shift left, and exit out the other side. Climb through the grate above and continue up the steps.

Use the Remote Hacking Device on the panel at the other end of the hall and enter CARBOHYDRATE to access the elevator shaft. Grapple through the hatch above and approach the next corner. To the left, entering LIPIDS into the security console opens up an exit back to the Cargo Hold. Go right toward the Research Laboratory, grapple into the venting above, and follow it onto a vantage point inside the lab.

Eight armed hostiles litter the spacious room, including a Boa Sentry Drone operator, a Medic, and a soldier with a Detective Mode detector. The next objective is at the computer on the right, but you must dispose of the thugs before you can access it. Easily eliminate the two men on the right by dropping behind them from the beam above. Perform Silent Takedowns on them before retreating back to a vantage point. From there, the options are numerous. Focus on getting rid of the Medic next. Vents on the side of the room lead down to the floor grates, giving Batman an easy escape if spotted.

With the laboratory clear, use the console to reveal that Stagg's fingerprints are required to shut down the turrets. In the same manner used at the Clock Tower to find out who took Oracle, CCTV feeds of Simon Stagg fleeing from danger are available to reconstruct his prints.

Scrub through the video until Simon touches the floor or railing with his hand. Scan that section of the image to see if prints are present. Watch for Stagg to steady himself on the railing, look near the exit, and on the floor. The fourth location is on the floor after he is thrown down the stairs. Next, find all four locations and use Detective Mode to scan the prints. This allows Batman to reconfigure a full handprint.

Use the console with Stagg's handprint to gain control of the turrets on airship Alpha. Batman destroys the guns on the second ship, allowing for the pursuit of Scarecrow.

C PURSUE SCARECROW ACROSS TO THE SECOND AIRSHIP

PREY THAT NO
LONGER FEARS YOU

Exit the Research Laboratory through the venting or biometric gate on the east side of the room and return to the Cargo Hold. Ten soldiers have reoccupied the room, including two Medics. Upon entry, a Medic shows off a new ability with his stun gun. When fired at another combatant, the second guy's suit temporarily holds the electric charge. Batman is unable to attack the target straight on. Quickfire the Batclaw at the charged enemy to dissipate the electricity, making him safe to strike. Clear out the hostiles.

BIOMETRIC GATES

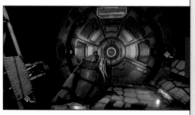

The circular, biometric gates in the airship have been ignored up to this point, as access has not been possible. Now that you've acquired Simon Stagg's fingerprints, these doors can be used, which offer quicker movement between the different sections of the airship.

After the fight, Lucius Fox offers up a second upgrade for the Batmobile. This time, choose between the upgrade not chosen before and an EMP for the vehicle.

- **EMP – An electromagnetic pulse is designed to temporarily scramble drone weapon targeting and divert incoming missiles. Successive blasts also temporarily immobilize enemies in the immediate vicinity. Don't worry, the Batmobile is immune.**

Enter NUCLEICACIDS into the security console to open up the gate. Just inside the second airship, eight unarmed enemies await Batman's arrival. Glide Kick through the window to knock an unaware hostile down. Continue the combo, keeping an eye out for blade attacks from the combat experts. Once the room is clear, spray Explosive Gel on the weak wall on the east side and detonate it.

Continue through the newly opened hallway and follow the path to the left and then right to Quarantine Labs. Accessing the computers affords more insight into Stagg's involvement. At the other end of the corridor, continue through the door to Biological Engineering.

Around to the left, another console provides stability controls on the west side of airship Beta. Turn to the left to spot a containment box inside the glass corridor. Tilt the ship right to dislodge the crate and then move it the other way so that it crashes through the two panes of glass and exits the zeppelin.

Ten hostiles, highlighted by a minigunner, are scattered throughout this large, multilevel room. Steer clear of the big guy while picking everyone else off with Silent Takedowns. If detected, escape into the floor or to a perch above. Stay on the move until the enemy loses the vigilante. If you remain stationary for too long, a soldier will pick you off. Take advantage of the multiple floors, rooms, and corners to sneak up on the thugs. Disrupting three guns helps improve the odds.

THE MINIGUNNER

The minigunner is a big soldier with a big gun, who requires a lot of force to knock out. Because of the noise generated during the takedown, this guy should be left for last. Pick off the other soldiers while keeping him at a distance. Once the big guy is alone, strike him to begin the takedown and follow it up with a Beat Down. He swings his massive weapon back and forth at Batman. Press Counter each time to avoid being knocked out and continue the punches in between. After evading the fourth attempt, the vigilante finishes him off.

ENVIRONMENT

Look out for items around the room to help in the predator challenge. Using the Remote Hacking Device on a Power Cell produces a blast that incapacitates nearby enemies. Activate a Robotic Arm with the device to startle surrounding foes. Detective Mode highlights these items with descriptions of how they can be used, so thoroughly scan the room upon arrival.

With the guards out of the way, talk to Stagg before proceeding through the biometric gate on the east side. Approach one of the "Scarecrows" ahead and perform a takedown, only to be taken down instead. Once Batman recovers, eliminate the small group of unarmed soldiers before striking the boss. Scarecrow manages to escape the vigilante as he blows a piece of the airship clean off the end.

PREY THAT NO LONGER FEARS YOU

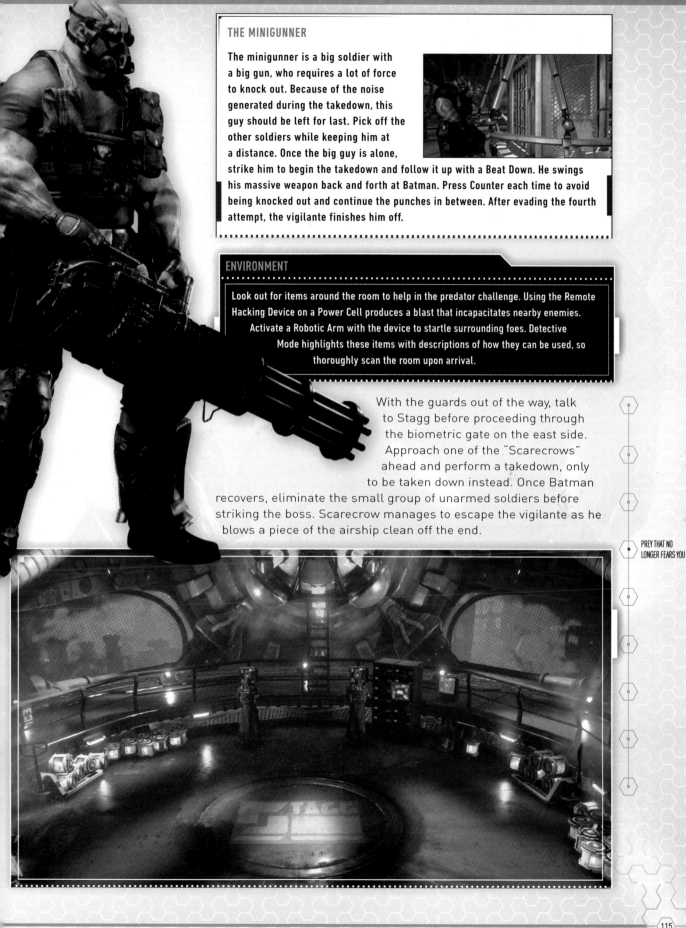

TONIGHT ENDS WITH GOTHAM'S FALL

THE CHAPTER AT A GLANCE

⚠ OBJECTIVES

A	Rescue Oracle from Scarecrow's Safe House
B	Meet with Ivy at the GCPD
C	Scan the Arkham Knight's Cobra Drone
D	Destroy the Arkham Knight's Cobra Drone
E	Equip a New Secondary Weapon for the Batmobile
F	Take Ivy to the Botanical Gardens
G	Destroy the Cobra Tanks
H	Head to the Wayne Tower Parking Garage
I	Use the Batmobile Sonar
J	Protect Ivy's Plant from the Militia
K	Head to Panessa Studios
L	Glide onto the Relay Drone
M	Destroy the Arkham Knight's Radar Network
N	Take Out the Arkham Knight's Missile Battery
O	Lower the Barriers Around the Missile Battery
P	Return to Oracle's Clock Tower

NEW AR CHALLENGES

1	David & Goliath
2	Drone Zone
3	Gotham Knights
4	Seek and Destroy
5	Terminal Velocity

N

TO FOUNDERS' ISLAND

GCPD

TO MIAGANI ISLAND

AVAILABLE SIDE MISSIONS

- The Line of Duty
- Gotham on Fire
- Armored and Dangerous
- The Perfect Crime
- Heir to the Cowl
- Occupy Gotham
- Riddler's Revenge
- Creature of the Night
- Two-Faced Bandit
- Campaign for Disarmament
- GunRunner

A RESCUE ORACLE FROM SCARECROW'S SAFE HOUSE

Make your way to Scarecrow's Chinatown safe house on Bleake Island to arrive just in time for a show.

B MEET WITH IVY AT THE GCPD

In the hopes that Poison Ivy's immunity to the fear toxin can help the city, drive to GCPD and talk to the inmate. She agrees to assist the vigilante and willingly climbs into the passenger seat.

C SCAN THE ARKHAM KNIGHT'S COBRA DRONE TO IDENTIFY A WEAKNESS

On the way out of GCPD, Batman comes to a stop before the closed shutter. Cash informs him of a big tank patrolling just outside. He lifts the door just enough for the vigilante to crouch underneath. Once outside, he automatically grapples to a vantage point and scans the Cobra Tank ahead. A closer look is necessary to find a weakness. Swing and glide to the vehicle. Scan the back and each side while avoiding its sensor. It scours the area in front and to the sides giving the player plenty of space to analyze the tank without being detected. Once you scan all three sides, you find a weakness at the rear exhaust port.

COBRA DRONE

This militia heavy tank is too well-armored to take down directly and its weaponry can overpower the Batmobile. Based on Batman's scans, there is a weakness through the rear exhaust port. The drone constantly scans side to side, but occasionally it stops and performs a 360-degree scan. You should always try to avoid its sensors, but if you do get caught, quickly duck behind cover or speed away. A Cobra Drone becomes more aggressive once its prey has been detected. The icon on the radar turns red when it's in this state. Constantly check the radar and note the locations of the Cobra Drones. Sneak behind one in Battle Mode and the Batmobile aims at the exhaust port. Once targeted, fire the Heavy Cannon to instantly take the drone out.

TONIGHT ENDS WITH GOTHAM'S FALL

D DESTROY THE ARKHAM KNIGHT'S COBRA DRONE

Head back to GCPD and call the Batmobile just outside the building. Get behind the Cobra Drone and allow the exhaust port to be targeted. Once ready, release a shot from the Heavy Cannon to destroy the tank.

E EQUIP A NEW SECONDARY WEAPON FOR THE BATMOBILE AT CLOCK TOWER FACILITY

Lucius Fox has the next Batmobile upgrade ready for installation. Drive to the Clock Tower and enter the garage on the northwest side. The vehicle is modified with the chosen upgrade.

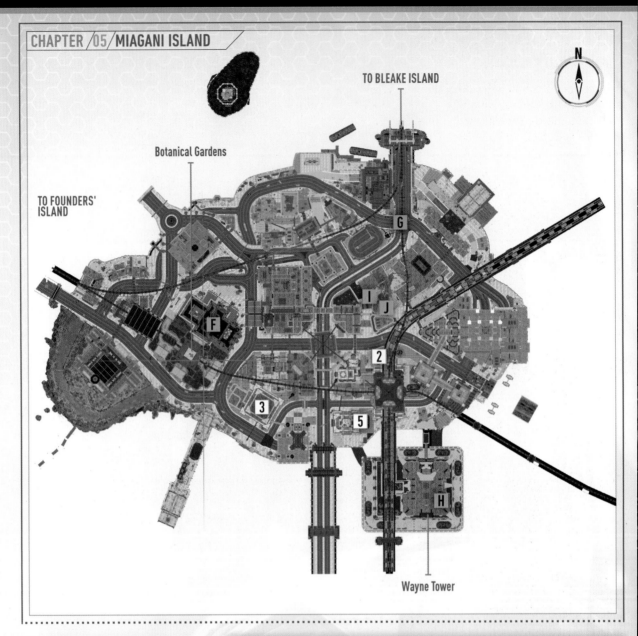

CHAPTER /05/ MIAGANI ISLAND

N

TO BLEAKE ISLAND

Botanical Gardens

TO FOUNDERS' ISLAND

G

I
J

F

O

2

3

5

H

Wayne Tower

F TAKE IVY TO THE BOTANICAL GARDENS

Drive Ivy to Miagani Island where Arkham Knight has called in a squadron of Cobra Drones to take on the Batmobile.

G DESTROY THE COBRA TANKS ON MIAGANI ISLAND

Three Cobra Drones patrol nearby on Miagani Island. Take them out in the same manner as the lone tank. Use the radar to isolate each one, being careful a second vehicle doesn't sneak up behind you.

F TAKE IVY TO THE BOTANICAL GARDENS (CONT.)

Once the area is safe again, drive to Miagani Botanical Gardens and drop off Poison Ivy.

TWO-FACED BANDIT

Stop Two-Face and his men from robbing Gotham's banks.

After Poison Ivy enters Miagani Botanical Gardens, Two-Faced Bandit Most Wanted becomes available. Two-Face takes advantage of the chaos and attempts to rob the Chinatown Branch of Bank of Gotham. Use your predatory skills to stop the villain and his henchmen. All three banks must be protected before the villain is taken to GCPD. Check out the Most Wanted chapter for details on the three predator fights.

H HEAD TO THE WAYNE TOWER PARKING GARAGE AND COLLECT IVY PLANT TRACKING DEVICE

Lucius prepares a device for the Batmobile that can track Ivy's plant. Drive south under the Grand Avenue Station and turn into the Wayne Tower parking garage. Pull into the spot next to the elevator just as a squad of militia drones show up and immediately assault your vehicle. Rattlers, Diamondbacks, and Mambas attack from all sides. Stay alert for incoming projectiles and destroy the tanks before returning to the parking spot. Sonar is installed that allows the Batmobile to scan below ground.

I USE THE BATMOBILE SONAR TO LOCATE AND RELEASE IVY'S PLANT

More militia have been deployed around the city. Fire the Sonar to reveal the plant roots on the radar. Follow the roots with the radar. A reddish dot shows the plant's center. Drive onto the spot, located southwest of the Bank of Gotham. Use a sustained sonar pulse to break the plant free.

TONIGHT ENDS WITH
GOTHAM'S FALL

J PROTECT IVY'S PLANT FROM THE ARKHAM KNIGHT'S MILITIA WHILE IT MATURES

A pack of thugs along with a medic and brute attack the plant. Glide over their rooftop and take them all down. Remember to use the Batclaw to dissipate the electricity from a charged enemy. Batman checks in with Ivy and Alfred once it is safe to do so.

K HEAD TO PANESSA STUDIOS TO ANALYZE THE ARKHAM KNIGHT'S FORCES

Go to the Panessa Studios rooftop and use the V.I.P. elevator. Enter the Quarantine Cells room and grab the Freeze Blast Grenade that sits on a table next to the left cell. Access the Batcomputer to analyze the Arkham Knight's militia forces. Two Radar Towers protect a Missile Launcher on Founders' Island, preventing the Batwing to scan that island for the Cloudburst. The Batmobile is also unable to get close to the equipment. A Relay Drone manages the communications between the devices. Batman should be able to reverse engineer its security protocols to give him some time to take out the radar towers.

FREEZE BLAST GRENADE

The Freeze Blast Grenade can be quickfired during combat to temporarily incapacitate an enemy. This allows you to remove a hostile from the fight for a short period. Outside of a skirmish, the device is used to solidify gas outlets, allowing access to new areas in the game.

CHAPTER /05/FOUNDERS' ISLAND

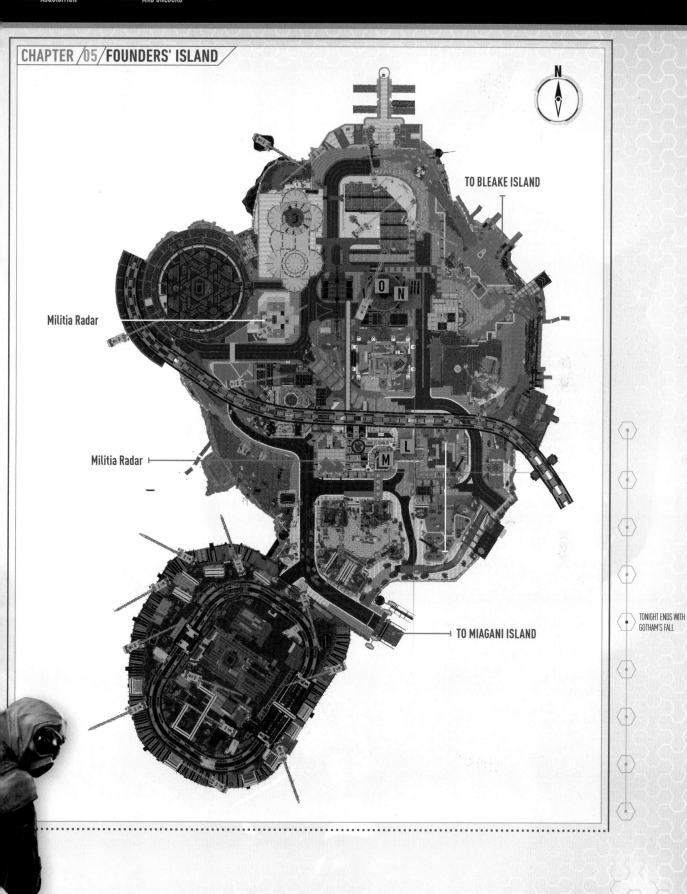

N

TO BLEAKE ISLAND

Militia Radar

Militia Radar

TO MIAGANI ISLAND

TONIGHT ENDS WITH
GOTHAM'S FALL

35m

Line Launcher Perch (Hold)

L GLIDE ONTO THE RELAY DRONE AND EXAMINE IT TO FIND A WAY TO DEFEAT THE DRONE FORCES

Glide to Founders' Island and spot the Relay Drone that flies around Otisburg. Get some height and land on top of the aircraft. Batman manages to snag the communications chip from inside and adds it to the Remote Hacking Device, giving it the ability to temporarily blind a drone.

DRONE HACKER WITH THE REMOTE HACKING DEVICE

By applying the relay chip to the Remote Hacking Device, you can blind drones for sixty seconds. Aim at any drone and use the device to make Batman invisible to the militia vehicle. Hitting it again resets the timer to 60. Only one can be disabled at a time, so by blinding a second drone, the original returns to normal.

M DESTROY THE ARKHAM KNIGHT'S RADAR NETWORK

A Dragon Drone patrols above the rooftop to the west, guarding the first Militia Radar. Aim the Remote Hacking Device at the chopper and blind it. Glide to the now accessible rooftop and approach the Radar Console. Place Explosive Gel on the computer and detonate to destroy the first radar. Be sure to keep an eye on the Dragon Drone's timer. You need to get off the rooftop before it reaches zero or hit it again with the hacking device.

The Militia Radar monitors the air and roads for any signs of the Batmobile or Batwing. To get the Batwing operational in the area, Batman must go in on foot and eliminate the radar towers.

The second radar is located on the Lex Corp rooftop to the northwest. Grapple to the highest point of the roof and observe the group of militia below. Four soldiers, four combat experts, and a brute pose a challenging skirmish before the radar can be destroyed. Line up a Fear Multi-Takedown to quickly eliminate a few of the hostiles. Target the combat experts since they are tougher to deal with than the soldiers.

With the threat removed, interact with the yellow electric box, to reveal the Radar Console below. Two Gun Turrets protect the computer. Drop down to the west to reach a lower roof. Duck behind cover to avoid taking damage from the automated weapon. Equip the Remote Hacking Device, peek around the corner, and blind the turret for 15 seconds. Quickly run behind the gun and destroy it from behind.

TONIGHT ENDS WITH
GOTHAM'S FALL

N   TAKE OUT THE ARKHAM KNIGHT'S MISSILE BATTERY

The radar units are out of the way, but the long-range missile launcher must be disabled. Glide east to the incomplete Queen Industries building and land on the upper level. Activate Detective Mode and survey the predator zone. Eight armed soldiers guard the launcher. Multiple levels and rooms allow for isolating of the hostiles. There are rooms that can be closed off by using the Remote Hacking Device on a remote switch. Look for lone enemies and perform Silent Takedowns on them. If a small group of thugs forms, use a Fear Multi-Takedown to eliminate them at once. Be sure to flee from the area, since the commotion does attract attention. With the militia out of the way, approach the launcher. Batman realizes the armor is too thick to penetrate on his own.

THERMOBARIC GRENADES

After taking down an enemy from a floor grate, the opposition may use thermobaric grenades to flush Batman out. Clear out of the floor when the Arkham Knight commands their use. Grapple up a chute or to an upper floor.

O   LOWER THE BARRIERS AROUND THE MISSILE BATTERY

A defense shield protects the missile battery on the east side. Grapple up to the top floor and enter the double doors to find the control room. Use the laptop on the right to lower the barrier, making it reachable for the Batmobile's Heavy Cannon.

N   TAKE OUT THE ARKHAM KNIGHT'S MISSILE BATTERY (CONT.)

Five Cobra Drones now patrol the area as you take control of the Batmobile. They are major nuisances if they are not dealt with first. Work your way behind each one and destroy them with the Heavy Cannon. With the area clear of drones, drive to the Queen Industries building and find the adjustable bridge on the south side. From the west, fire the Power Winch at the anchor point and pull back to create a ramp.

RANGE OF BATMOBILE REMOTE

Be careful wandering too far away as you fight the drones. The remote does not have infinite range and, if you drive out of this area, you lose control of the Batmobile.

At that moment, Arkham Knight and a group of his soldiers show up at the control room. Use a Fear Multi-Takedown on a few of them, including the medic. Then, aim the next attack at the villain. After a bit of a struggle, the Arkham Knight makes a hasty escape. Watch out for soldiers who have been electrically charged by the second medic and finish off the remaining hostiles in the room.

O LOWER THE BARRIERS AROUND THE MISSILE BATTERY

One of the soldiers managed to raise the barrier, so use the laptop again to get it back down.

N TAKE OUT THE ARKHAM KNIGHT'S MISSILE BATTERY

Back at the Batmobile, continue to pull back with the winch. Accelerate toward the ramp and hit the Afterburner to jump onto the building across the street. The Missile Launcher begins to fire at your vehicle once in range. From the upper floor, dodge to the side to avoid incoming cannon fire while shooting down the missiles with the Vulcan Gun. Get in shots from your Heavy Cannon whenever possible to destroy the missile battery.

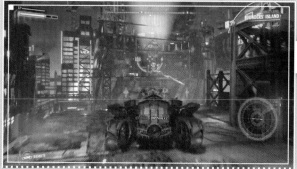

P RETURN TO ORACLE'S CLOCK TOWER TO REVIEW THE BATWING SCANS FOR THE CLOUDBURST DEVICE

With the skies safe again for the Batwing, scanning can continue for the Cloudburst. Drive to the Clock Tower and drop through the secret entrance. Use the bust on the shelf and access the Batcomputer to check on the Batwing. It has not found anything yet, but an emergency call comes in from Panessa Studios that requires Batman's immediate attention.

TONIGHT ENDS WITH
GOTHAM'S FALL

SOME KIND OF BAT TRICK

THE CHAPTER AT A GLANCE

! OBJECTIVES

A Investigate Panessa Studios

B Stop Harley Quinn from Taking The Joker Infected

C Return the Escaped Joker Infected to Their Cells

D Apprehend Christina Bell in Sound Stage B

E Apprehend Albert King in Sound Stage A

F Apprehend Johnny Charisma in Sound Stage C

G Apprehend Harley Quinn

H Equip a New Secondary Weapon

NEW AR CHALLENGES

- None

AVAILABLE SIDE MISSIONS

 The Line of Duty

 The Perfect Crime

 Riddler's Revenge

 Campaign for Disarmament

 Gotham on Fire

 Heir to the Cowl

 Creature of the Night

 GunRunner

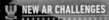 Armored and Dangerous

Occupy Gotham

Two-Faced Bandit

Panessa Studios

A   INVESTIGATE PANESSA STUDIOS

Harley Quinn has taken over Panessa Studios and threatens to free the prisoners. Grapple to the Panessa rooftop and drop down to the railing just south of the V.I.P. elevator. Line up a Fear Multi-Takedown on the two-armed thugs and continue to eliminate the group. Interact with the gate to find out Harley Quinn has changed the voice activation. Use the device to calibrate the sample and then use it on the panel to open the door. When Harley's actual voice is heard through the door, Batman grapples to safety.

CALIBRATING A VOICE SAMPLE WITH VOICE SYNTHESIZER

The current Harley Quinn voice sample must be calibrated with the Voice Synthesizer before it can be used. The Pitch and Wave Modulation can be modified using the Look and Move controls, respectively. Note the vertical and horizontal bars are adjusted when changes are made. The altered sample is played over and over during the process, so use the sound to determine how close it is. Readings on the screen can also be used to determine the accuracy. This image shows the final settings. Once you feel that it is ready, press Run to verify the voice print for accuracy, which is indicated by a percentage. This must reach 100% to complete the calibration. Don't worry; there is no penalty for multiple attempts.

HARLEY QUINN

PROFILE

REAL NAME	Dr. Harleen F. Quinzel
OCCUPATION	Professional Criminal
BASED IN	Gotham City
EYE COLOR	Blue
HAIR COLOR	Blonde
HEIGHT	5 Ft. 7 Inches
WEIGHT	140 Lbs
FIRST APPEARANCE	*Batman: Batman Adventures* #12 [September, 1993]

ATTRIBUTES

-Surprising strength and stamina
-Superior gymnastic skills
-Total disregard for human life

An Arkham Asylum psychiatrist assigned to treat The Joker, Dr. Harleen Quinzel instead became obsessively fixated on her patient, believing herself to be in love with him.

She helped him escape and took on her own criminal identity as Harley Quinn, a violent and unpredictable felon whose only motivation was achieving The Joker's approval.

Because of his cruel and mercurial nature, this in some ways made her just another of his victims, albeit a very dangerous one.

Since her ill-fated attempt to avenge her lover's death in Arkham City, Harley is rumored to have assumed control of Joker's criminal gang and begun plotting another attack on the man she holds responsible—Batman.

VOICE SYNTHESIZER

The Voice Synthesizer allows Batman to imitate vocal signatures and use them during combat to order enemies and create disarray. More voices are obtained as you progress through the game, but for now Batman can only imitate Harley Quinn. Hold Aim Gadget and select the desired enemy with the Crouch button. Place the reticle where you wish to move the target and press Crouch again to give the order. Press Grapple to deselect the thug. Only one hostile can be ordered around at a time. Once the command has been given, the Voice Synthesizer icon in the lower-left corner of the HUD is highlighted before it begins to count down a cool down period. The device cannot be used until the icon is clear again.

Barking orders with the Voice Synthesizer is a great way to remove an enemy from a group and isolate him for an easy takedown. Use this new ability often to reduce clusters of hostiles, allowing for easier Silent Takedowns.

B STOP HARLEY QUINN FROM TAKING THE JOKER INFECTED

Eleven armed hostiles now occupy the rooftop, including a minigunner. Test out the new gadget by selecting one of the guys below and sending

him to the landing pad in the corner. Glide behind him and silently take him down. Use the floor grates, high vantage points, corners, and multiple levels of the environment to eliminate the remaining thugs—leaving the big guy for last. With the roof clear, enter the studio and ride the elevator down to the basement.

GENERATOR

Generators on the studio rooftop are used as an emergency power supply. Overloading the motor using the Remote Hacking Device can cause a small-scale blast and incapacitate nearby enemies.

SOME KIND OF BAT TRICK

CHAPTER /06/ PANESSA STUDIOS

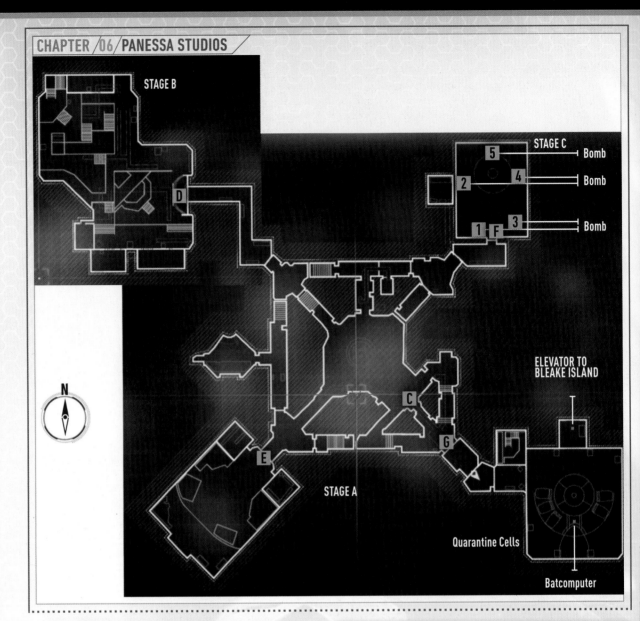

A brawl is already underway between a large group of Harley's men and Robin at the Quarantine Cells, but a locked gate prevents entry. Use the Voice Synthesizer to gain access. Eliminate 3 to 5 guys right away with a Fear-Multi Takedown. Then, team up with Drake to finish off the group of thugs and brutes. Join your partner in the middle of the room and interrogate the thug about the location of Harley and the infected. Next, access the Batcomputer to find the three prisoners, who each have their own plans for Batman.

THUGS WITH SHIELDS

Use the Aerial Attack to take out thugs using shields. Hit him with a Cape Stun and then double tap Run to perform the maneuver, knocking the hostile to the ground.

C RETURN THE ESCAPED JOKER INFECTED TO THEIR CELLS

Run past Henry Adams and enter the doors ahead. Waypoints appear at Sound Stages A, B, and C. These represent the locations of the three infected. Stage B must be first, but the other two can be done in either order. Albert King presents a challenging brawl for Batman and Robin. Christina Bell has a predator scenario for the dynamic duo. Johnny Charisma's offering is more of a puzzle.

JACK IN THE BOXES

Look out for small Jack in the Boxes lying around Panessa Studios. Toss a Batarang at the items to destroy them. This counts toward Riddler's Collectibles.

D APPREHEND CHRISTINA BELL IN SOUND STAGE B

Take the corridor straight ahead, enter the door alongside Robin, and team up against the small pack of thugs inside. Proceed into Stage B. A minigunner blocks the path to the right. Grapple up to the vantage point in the corner and swing behind him. Drop down, sneak up from behind, and perform a Dual Team Takedown on the big guy. Follow the hallway through another door, where a group of Harley's hooligans protect Christina Bell.

Find a good vantage point and survey the situation. Ten hostiles in all defend her, six in the immediate area and four more in a separate room with Christina. Only one minigunner joins the first group, while two remain back with the others. Disrupt their weapons before pursuing any enemies. Use the vantage points, railings, and various levels of the stage to eliminate the thugs before going after the minigunner. With the first six defeated, the second group enters. When taking down a minigunner, make sure no other hostiles are nearby. Once everyone has been taken care of, climb the steps in the corner and enter the final room. Counter Christina's attack to apprehend her. Exit the stage as Robin carries her back to her cell.

SOME KIND OF BAT TRICK

ALLOW ROBIN TO HELP

Robin joins Batman in this predator zone. The player can switch between the two with the Call Batmobile button. When the dual team symbol fills up on the left side of the HUD, your partner is available for a takedown. A press of the button calls the other vigilante in for a takedown against your current target.

E APPREHEND ALBERT KING IN SOUND STAGE A

A group of Harley's thugs hang out just beyond a security gate at the entrance to Stage A. Enter the floor grate opposite Stage B and move toward the enemies. Use the Voice Synthesizer to order one of the hostiles to push the button. Once the gate is open, jump out with a Fear-Multi Takedown and eliminate the thugs. Finish off the brute with a Cape Stun and Beat Down before pushing the button on the right wall. Interact with the figure in the middle of the room.

Enter Sound Stage A to find Albert King and eight thugs on a western-themed stage. Watch out for the boss, as his punches cannot be countered. Avoid him at all costs while using the smaller foes to build up the Dual Team meter. Hit Albert with a Dual Team Takedown once it is available. Repeat this process three times to reduce the boss' health to 50%. The next time the takedown is executed, rapidly tap the Strike Button to strike him in the mid-section. Counter his punches while continuing the Beat Down, much like fighting a minigunner. One last team-up, just like the previous one, is required to finish the boxer. Again, Robin has the tough task of returning him to his cell. Exit the way you came in.

F APPREHEND JOHNNY CHARISMA IN SOUND STAGE C

Enter the corridor marked Stage C and stop before the corner. A minigunner stands guard on the other side. Turn around and grapple into an open vent above. Follow it until Batman drops behind a structurally weakened wall. Spray Explosive Gel on the backside. Select the Voice Synthesizer, activate Detective Mode, and tell the minigunner to investigate the weak wall. Trigger the detonation as soon as he is within range. Press the button on the other side of the hall. Go through the door and investigate the figure ahead.

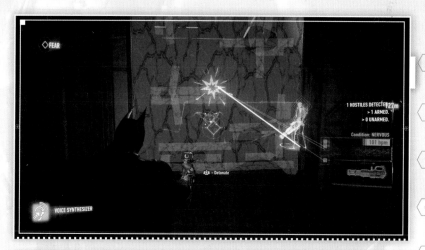

Enter the Stage C door and approach the vent on the left. Batman directs Robin to take that route to reach the next room. Approach the keypad next to the door ahead and with help from Henry Adams, CCTV footage appears on Batman's screen. Zoom in on the keypad and scrub the scene forward. Note the first digit that Johnny enters. As he steps in front of

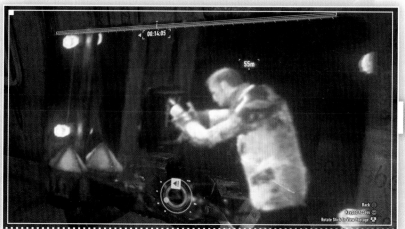

SOME KIND OF
BAT TRICK

the panel, zoom out and change your focus to the keypad in the mirror. Now the rest of the access PIN can be figured out as he punches the numbers—remembering that the image is mirrored. Press the Keypad Access button and enter 0539 to unlock the door. Step inside to find the performer on stage wearing a bomb vest along with five other bombs around the room, each resting atop two barrels.

As the camera focuses toward the entrance, Robin drops in from the vent on the right. Now you control him as he attempts to disarm all five bombs. Note which way Johnny Charisma is facing. If Robin is in his view, the explosives are detonated. Quickly move to the first bomb and hold the Run button to disarm. Then, as the stage rotates around, move to the next objective on the right. Return to the top and head to the bomb sitting on the bleachers to the left. Carefully, continue down the left side of the room and take care of the fourth bomb and then the final one at the back of the stage. Robin is vulnerable as he disarms the last bomb, so be sure to move from the previous dynamite once out of view, quickly defuse it, and return to the barrels on the right. There is just enough time to get it done. Next, move behind the infected singer and perform a takedown to remove the vest and apprehend him.

BE CAUTIOUS

There are tarp-covered tables and boxes all around the room that offer shelter for Robin. If not confident about reaching the next bomb, take refuge at these locations to avoid being spotted. It is a long song, so there is time. The number of explosives left is tracked in the upper-right corner of the HUD.

Run back toward the Quarantine Cells before getting stopped at a security gate and a group of Harley's men. Move back toward Stage A and drop into the floor grate out of view of the thugs. Order one of them to push the button, but this time it doesn't work as Harley Quinn shows up.

G APPREHEND HARLEY QUINN

Robin convinces her to open the gate. Wait for her to move in close and take her down from the floor grate. With help from your partner, take down the thugs and brutes. If things start to get rough, retreat into a corridor for extra room. After clearing the hostiles out, take the prisoners to the cells. Once the excitement is over, interact with the left quarantine cell. When the door opens, move into the room. After the flashback, return to the cell and interact with Robin.

H EQUIP A NEW SECONDARY WEAPON FOR THE BATMOBILE AT THE PANESSA STUDIOS FACILITY

Take the elevator back outside, glide off the north side of the rooftop, and call the Batmobile. Drive into the nearby garage to get the remaining Batmobile upgrade.

SOME KIND OF
BAT TRICK

NATURE ALWAYS WINS

THE CHAPTER AT A GLANCE

! OBJECTIVES

- **A** Investigate the Seismic Activity
- **B** Work with Poison Ivy
- **C** Pick Up Poison Ivy and Return Her to GCPD
- **D** Interrogate Simon Stagg
- **E** Track Down Simon Stagg
- **F** Use the Nimbus Power Cell
- **G** Use the Batmobile Sonar to Locate Ivy's Plant
- **H** Gain Access to the Subway Network
- **I** Use the Batmobile Sonar to Locate Ivy's Plant
- **J** Protect Ivy's Plant
- **K** Destroy the Arkham Knight's Cloudburst Tank
- **L** Investigate What Has Happened to Poison Ivy
- **M** Speak to GCPD Communications Officer to Investigate Possible Lead

NEW AR CHALLENGES

- **1** City Heat TT
- **2** Under the Pale Moonlight
- **3** Knight Time Strike

AVAILABLE SIDE MISSIONS

 The Line of Duty

 The Perfect Crime

Riddler's Revenge

Campaign for Disarmament

Gotham on Fire

Heir to the Cowl

Creature of the Night

 GunRunner

 Armored and Dange

 Occupy Gotham

 Two-Faced Bandit

 Own the Roads

 Friend in Need

N

TO BLEAKE ISLAND

TO FOUNDERS'
ISLAND

1

L C
B
F

A

46m

Powerslide (Hold) R2

A INVESTIGATE THE SEISMIC ACTIVITY ON MIAGANI ISLAND

After receiving the Batmobile upgrade, Alfred informs Batman of seismic activity on Miagani Island and that contact with Lucius Fox has been lost. The former pertains to the main story path while the latter begins the Friend in Need Most Wanted. Drive to the waypoint near Miagani Botanical Gardens to investigate the seismic activity.

FRIEND IN NEED

Investigate the loss of contact with Lucius Fox.

Alfred has not been able to get ahold of Lucius for some time and he feels it should be investigated. Drive to the basement elevator of Wayne Tower to begin. The Most Wanted chapter has full details for this short side mission.

OWN THE ROADS

Wipe out the militia checkpoints deployed around the city.

Temporary walls surround a group of soldiers and/or drones at each checkpoint. These must be disposed of through combat, predatory means, or by solving a puzzle. Full details on each checkpoint are given in the Most Wanted section.

B WORK WITH POISON IVY TO DEFEAT THE MILITIA FORCES ATTACKING THE BOTANICAL GARDENS

The Arkham Knight sends in 24 drones to deal with Poison Ivy including Rattler Drones, Diamondbacks, and Twin Rattlers. Help her defend the Botanical Gardens from the onslaught of militia vehicles. The drones surround the area, making for some tough situations with shots coming from all directions. Stay on the move, using the Vulcan Gun and Heavy Cannon to wipe out the forces.

BATMOBILE UPGRADES

At this point the Batmobile has received all three upgrades. The Virus and EMP can be extremely helpful in vehicle combat, so take advantage of their abilities. Be careful when using them in close proximity, as the EMP will shut down friendly drones.

WATCH THE RADAR

Glance at the radar often to keep track of the Cobra Drone positions. The triangular icon points in the direction that the drone does. If it's on a different level than you, a chevron points up or down. The icon turns red when the tank breaks from its regular patrol pattern. It is important to stay out of sight from these tanks. Checking their locations keeps them from sneaking up on the Batmobile unexpectedly.

Next, five Cobra Drones are sent to the area. Remember, to take this drone out, sneak up behind it and, once the target has been acquired, fire the Heavy Cannon at the weak point to destroy it instantly. Maneuver around the buildings to get behind a drone. As the Batmobile nears an intersection, check the radar to verify that it is safe to continue. The tanks occasionally perform a 360-degree scan, where they stop and spin their sensor all the way around to detect anything nearby. Quickly duck behind cover if you're caught in their field of view.

C PICK UP POISON IVY AND RETURN HER TO GCPD

With the area clear of drones, return to Miagani Botanical Gardens and eject from the Batmobile. Land on the top level of the structure and interact with the plant to pick up Poison Ivy, but she insists on remaining at the gardens. Meanwhile, Alfred interrupts with information on the Cloudburst. The Arkham Knight mans the Cloudburst Tank as it drives across Perdition Bridge to Bleake Island. An explosion rocks the city, causing chaos throughout and making the Batmobile inoperable.

SIDE MISSIONS ARE UNAVAILABLE

Note that the toxin disables all of the side missions. You must wait until the air is safe again before pursuing the Most Wanted.

NATURE ALWAYS WINS

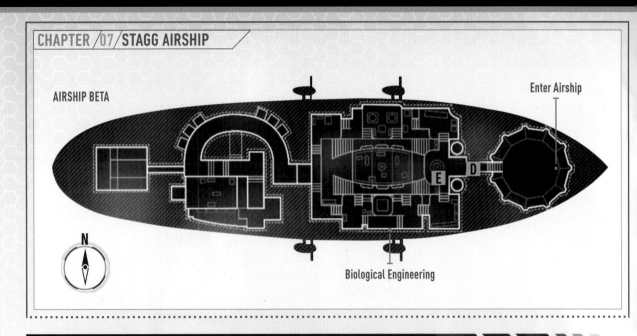

CHAPTER /07/ STAGG AIRSHIP

AIRSHIP BETA

Enter Airship

E D

Biological Engineering

N

D INTERROGATE SIMON STAGG TO FIND A WAY TO DEFEAT THE CLOUDBURST TANK

Glide and grapple back to Stagg's airships on Founders' Island, sticking to the rooftops to avoid the toxin. Enter Airship Beta through the hole on the front, targeting one of the hostiles ahead. Seven unarmed-soldiers, including a medic and a brute, must be taken down before proceeding inside. Step up to the door as Batman equips the Voice Synthesizer. Stagg's voice must be used to gain access to the zeppelin and fortunately, a sampling has already been recorded. Use the device to calibrate the sample and then use it on the panel to open the door.

Proceed through the biometric gate ahead to reach Biological Engineering, where eight militia soldiers also search for Simon Stagg. Two Boa Sentry Drone operators and two medics highlight this predator zone. The room should be familiar as it was used in a similar fight earlier in the story. The Arkham Knight's voice has already been synthesized, so use the Voice Synthesizer to order the combatants around. A good way to start the fight is to command a medic to investigate the area around Stagg's cage, allowing Batman to scoop him up from the vantage point. Work your way around the area and silently take the rest down, paying particular attention to the remaining medic.

BOA SENTRY DRONES

Note that the Remote Hacking Device can be used on the Boa Sentry Drone to turn its anti-personnel weaponry against the enemy or to temporarily disable its optics. Use the Remote Hacking Device directly on the operator to download the codes, making the drone fight for Batman. Aim the device at the drone to instruct it to fire at nearby soldiers. Hacking the drone first causes it to temporarily go blind.

E TRACK DOWN SIMON STAGG USING HIS FINGERPRINT TRAIL

Approach Stagg's cage on the near side of the room and activate Detective Mode to pick up his fingerprints. Follow the trail down the steps to the lower level and through the corridor with the primate cages. This leads to a handprint on a floor panel. Open it to find Stagg, cowering inside. Batman interrogates the scientist to find out about the Nimbus Power Cell that is required to drive through the toxin.

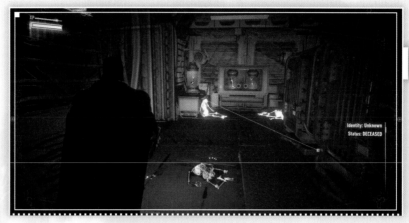

F USE THE NIMBUS POWER CELL TO REPAIR THE BATMOBILE

Exit the airship and return to the Batmobile on Miagani Island. Land at the waypoint on the nearby rooftop. Press the Call Batmobile button to start the repair.

Slowly remove the power core from the vehicle. When attacked, press Counter to counter the thug. With the Nimbus Power Cell inserted, slowly push it back in.

CHAPTER /07/ FOUNDERS' ISLAND

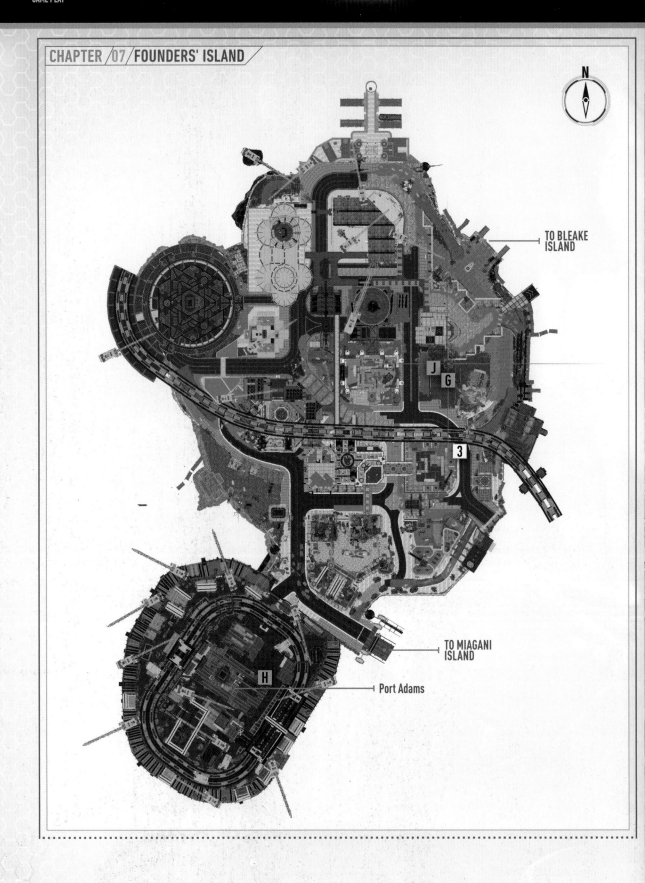

N

TO BLEAKE
ISLAND

J
G

3

TO MIAGANI
ISLAND

Port Adams

H

G USE THE BATMOBILE SONAR TO LOCATE AND RELEASE IVY'S PLANT ON FOUNDERS' ISLAND

Behind the wheel of the Batmobile, accelerate away from Botanical Gardens and drive to Founders' Island, where Ivy knows of a buried tree that might help. Be on the lookout for tanks still roaming the island. Fire the sonar to reveal the tree's root system on the radar. Head east and then south and hit the sonar again to display the tree, represented by the dot on the radar. Drive onto that spot and hold the button to fire a Charged Seismic Sonar Blast, but it is not strong enough to release the tree. Batman must find a way to get closer.

H GAIN ACCESS TO THE SUBWAY NETWORK VIA THE ELEVATOR AT PORT ADAMS TO GET DEEP ENOUGH UNDERGROUND TO RELEASE IVY'S PLANT

Follow the waypoint to a gate on the south side of the island. Once opened, drive inside where the Arkham Knight has placed a number of drones in defense, including a Python, Diamondbacks, and Rattlers. Stay on the move along the tracks and take them all down with the Heavy Cannon and Vulcan Gun, remembering to use the special abilities when available. On the southwest end of the port, a ramp offers entry into the container yard. Hit the Afterburner and jump inside.

DRAGON DRONE

This rapid assault aircraft flies around the battlefield firing its machine gun and rockets at the Batmobile. It is easily shot out of the air with the Vulcan Gun or part of a Missile Barrage, but combine this pest with a group of drones and it can eat away at a vehicle's armor. Look out for circles on the ground, as this is where it targets its projectiles.

PYTHON DRONE

Much like the Mamba Drone, this static missile platform fires guided missiles that must be shot out of the air with the Vulcan Gun. That is where the similarities end though. This well-armored drone does not move and it fires a low-and-straight-flying rocket along with the missiles. Listen for the warning beeps and dodge to the side while taking out the projectiles.

More Rattler Drones must be dealt with before finding the elevator. Strafe around the containers  for protection and pick off the remaining tanks. Once the area is secure, find the freight lift in the northeast quadrant of the yard and pull off the door with the Power Winch. Fire the winch at the motor inside, drive inside, and rev the engine to power it up.

NATURE ALWAYS WINS

CHAPTER /07/ IVY TUNNELS

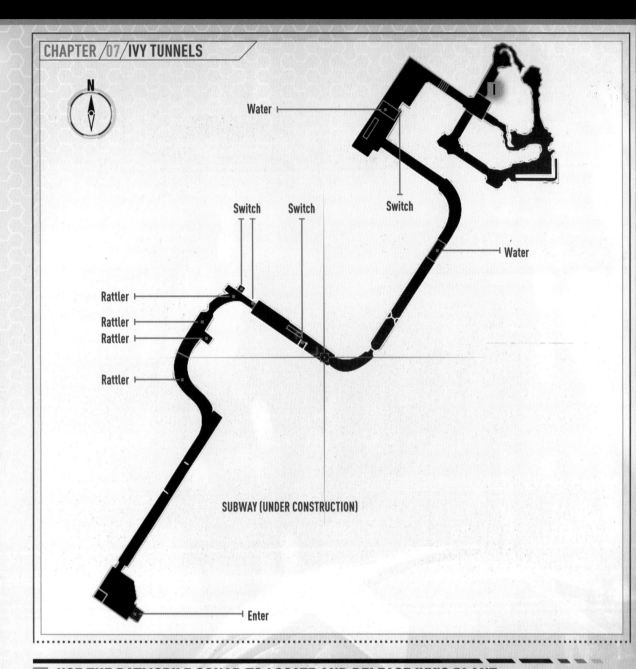

N

Water

Switch   Switch   Switch

Water

Rattler

Rattler
Rattler

Rattler

SUBWAY (UNDER CONSTRUCTION)

Enter

▌ USE THE BATMOBILE SONAR TO LOCATE AND RELEASE IVY'S PLANT ON FOUNDERS' ISLAND

Follow the subway tracks and drive up the right side to avoid the first gate. Keep the speed up and continue to the top, hitting the Afterburner to clear the second. Hop out at the closed gate ahead and drop into the floor grate. On the other side of the obstruction, a Rattler stands guard. Blind it temporarily with the Remote Hacking Device before exiting the floor. Note that only one drone can be disabled at a time. Run past the tank, duck behind the right wall, and wait for a patrolling Rattler to turn around. Note the blue light that represents the Rattlers' field of vision.

Step around the corner to find a third Rattler tucked in a cubbyhole. Quickly, disable the gun as it scans to your left. Continue forward and hit the Rattler Drone ahead with the hacking device. Run past the tank and grapple up to the beam above. Four more Rattlers occupy the corner ahead. Swing to the next girder, glide behind the tanks, and enter the control room. Throw the switch to unlock the security gate that blocks the Batmobile.

Bring your vehicle to Batman's location, destroying the militia's Rattler Drones along the way. Around the corner, the Batmobile is blocked again. Toggle to Batman and throw the switch that sits next to the gate. Enter the vehicle and continue to load zone A, where a raised platform prevents going any further. Eject from the car, enter the control room ahead, and unlock the ramp. Use the remote to drive the Batmobile up the new path as the vigilante hops inside.

NATURE ALWAYS WINS

Round the corner and pick up speed as the Batmobile approaches a gate ahead. Drive up the side and squeeze through the opening on top. Continue around to the bottom to slip underneath a fan. Stay on the gas and drive along the left side to avoid a pool of water. Slow up after the dip in the road and drive up the path on the right to reach another ramp and a gap full of water. Exit the vehicle, grapple over to the control room ahead, and find the switch inside. Unlock the ramp to lean it toward Batman and then drive the Batmobile onto it. Drive to the other side, switch back to Batman, and lock the ramp. Now it can be used to clear the water. Punch the Afterburner to reach the other side.

J PROTECT IVY'S PLANT FROM THE MILITIA FORCES WHILE IT MATURES

Before you know it, 40 drones descend on the area. A wide variety of vehicles take part, including Diamondbacks, Rattlers, Twin Rattlers, Dragons, Mambas, and a Python Drone. Poison Ivy gets assistance from her plants, so don't worry if something emerges from the ground. Stay alert for incoming projectiles. Dodge the rockets and shoot down the guided missiles. It is important to use your special abilities when available, but it also helps to have a Missile Barrage ready when surrounded.

Drive up the steps to the right and mow over the bollards. Use the Sonar to find the plant. Drive through the weak wall to the left to find the spot. Fire a charged Seismic Sonar Blast to loosen the ground. This releases the plant as it deposits the Batmobile above ground in Divinity Churchyard on Founders' Island.

AVOID BEING SURROUNDED

With 40 militia drones, things can get pretty chaotic. Stay on the move and use the entire space to avoid being surrounded. Poison Ivy lets Batman know if he is wandering too far away. At that point, return to the churchyard.

CHAPTER /07/ BLEAKE ISLAND

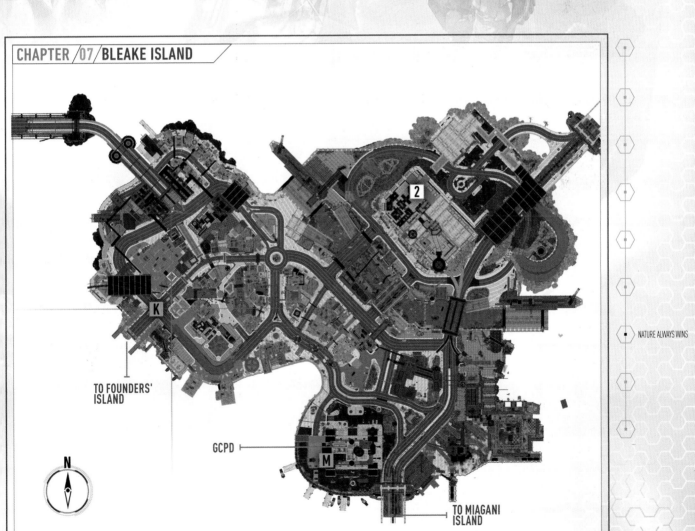

K

TO FOUNDERS'
ISLAND

GCPD

M

TO MIAGANI
ISLAND

2

N

■ NATURE ALWAYS WINS

K DESTROY THE ARKHAM KNIGHT'S CLOUDBURST TANK

With the Batmobile's telemetry functional again, it is now time to go after Arkham Knight and his tank. Drive to Bleake Island where Batman instructs Alfred to raise the bridges. This confines the tank battle to the one island. Six Cobra Drones guard the Cloudburst Tank. Avoid the boss while concentrating on the Cobras. The big tank's location is noted on the radar with a vehicle-looking icon as opposed to the generic pointer of the Cobra Drones. Taking care of the drones first allows time for Alfred to find a weakness.

CLOUDBURST TANK

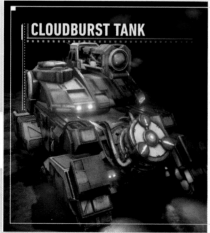

Arkham Knight's assault vehicle is a well-armored tank with a powerful energy weapon. It is constantly scanning 360-degrees around his vehicle. Steer clear of this guy as much as possible as the Batmobile takes considerable damage if you directly take on the Cloudburst Tank.

Touch the drone and the player takes damage. When spotted, the boss attempts to lock on to his target. A horizontal bar, in the middle of the HUD, expands outward. Once full, a strong energy shot is fired. As long as you remain targeted, he continues to discharge his gun. He eventually fires guided missiles like the Mamba and Python Drones. Listen for the warning and use the Vulcan Gun to shoot them out of the air.

With the guards out of the way, get in close to the Cloudburst Tank, keeping a wall in between you so he doesn't notice the Batmobile. Scan to analyze the coolant lines. These four spots are the weak points, located on each side near the ground. The Batmobile is no match for this tank when taken straight on. Once its sensor passes your location, peek out from cover, lock on and fire the Heavy Cannon at the coolant lines, and fall back. This sends its core temperature to critical. A horizontal meter appears in the top middle part of the HUD and steadily lowers. Once depleted, the drone has cooled down. Simply run away from the boss during this aggressive period. Repeat this process on the coolant lines on the other three sides.

At this point a health bar appears in the upper-right corner as the Cloudburst becomes vulnerable. This is the entire bottom of the drone. The tank now begins to launch guided missiles and rockets at the Batmobile. Concentrate fire on the lower body of the tank while backing away from the irate boss. Dodge away from the circular targets on the ground to avoid the rockets and knock the missiles out of the air with the Vulcan Gun. Do not let up on the attacks until the enemy blows up. When given the opportunity, pummel the guy before he slips away.

L INVESTIGATE WHAT HAS HAPPENED TO POISON IVY

Return to Poison Ivy at Miagani Botanical Gardens and interact with the tree to check on her.

RETURN TO THE MOST WANTED

With the toxin cleared out, it is possible to pursue the Most Wanted once again.

M SPEAK TO GCPD COMMUNICATIONS OFFICER TO INVESTIGATE POSSIBLE LEAD

Drive to GCPD, enter the Communications Room behind Aaron Cash, and speak with Sergeant McAllister to learn more about a broadcast over a SWAT channel. This gives Batman a way to track down Scarecrow.

NATURE ALWAYS WINS

CRIPPLED
BY FEAR

CHAPTER AT A GLANCE

OBJECTIVES

A Collect the Remote Electrical Charge

B Track the SWAT Radio Signal

C Destroy the Arkham Knight's Excavator

D Confront and Apprehend Scarecrow

NEW AR CHALLENGES

None

AVAILABLE SIDE MISSIONS

 The Line of Duty

 The Perfect Crime

 Riddler's Revenge

 Campaign for Disarmament

 Heir to the Cowl

 Creature of the Night

 GunRunner

 Armored and Dangerous

 Occupy Gotham

 Two-Faced Bandit

 Own the Roads

 Friend in Need

N

TO FOUNDERS' ISLAND

GCPD A

TO MIAGANI ISLAND

A COLLECT THE REMOTE ELECTRICAL CHARGE FROM THE GCPD EVIDENCE ROOM

Before leaving the GCPD, enter the Evidence Room and find the Remote Electrical Charge prototype all the way in the back of the Archive section. It may be useful at your next destination, since it seems to be without power at the moment.

REMOTE ELECTRICAL CHARGE

The Remote Electrical Charge can be quickfired during combat to shock enemies, stopping them in their tracks. It can also be used to activate or deactivate generators and other electrical equipment. This comes in handy in and out of combat.

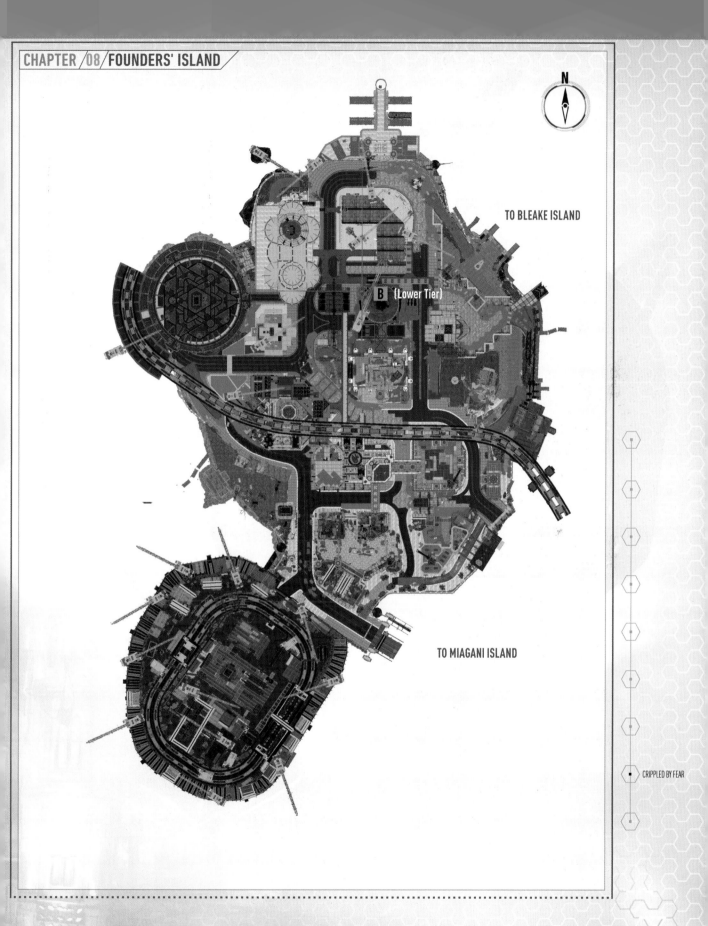

N

TO BLEAKE ISLAND

B (Lower Tier)

TO MIAGANI ISLAND

CRIPPLED BY FEAR

B TRACK THE SWAT RADIO SIGNAL TO LOCATE COMMISSIONER GORDON

Exit the GCPD and drive to The Ryker Heights district of Founders' Island. Use the access next to the Queen Industries building to reach the lower tier and approach the north side of Killinger's Department Stores. Drop into the manhole to reach a maintenance hallway.

Around the corner, a generator rests in water, making the path too dangerous to cross. Select the Remote Electrical Charge, aim at the equipment, and turn it off. Cross to the water, turn around, and turn the generator back on. Grapple into the venting at the end of the corridor.

Batman arrives below a big group of armed soldiers, just in time to watch Gordon being taken away. There are too many foes to take on directly. Instead, pull out the Voice Synthesizer and turn around. Order an enemy to push the button on the east wall. This opens the shutter on the north side, revealing the Batmobile. Take control of the vehicle and take down the pack of hostiles. Exit the floor grate.

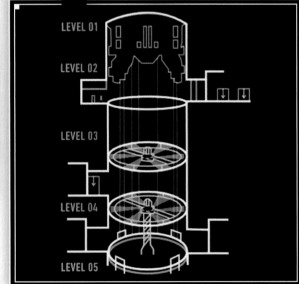

CHAPTER /08/ HIDEOUT

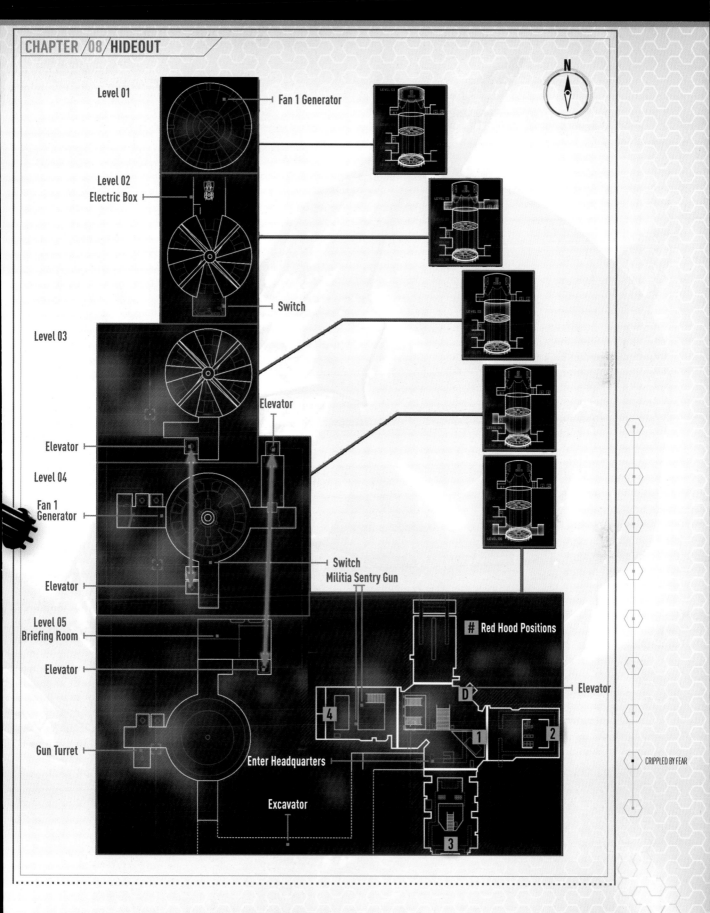

N

Level 01 — Fan 1 Generator

Level 02
Electric Box

Switch

Level 03

Elevator

Elevator

Level 04

Fan 1
Generator

Elevator

Switch
Militia Sentry Gun

Level 05
Briefing Room

Elevator

Gun Turret

Enter Headquarters

Excavator

Red Hood Positions

Elevator

D

4

1

2

3

CRIPPLED BY FEAR

ACCESS TO THE HIDEOUT

Enter Killinger's lobby and interact with the electric panel in the far corner to open the nearby gate. This gives access to the hideout, which descends five levels underground. You start out at level 02, but the bottom floor (Level 05) is the goal. This is where Commissioner Gordon has been taken. Two fans block direct access, so they need to be shut down. First, take control of the Batmobile and fire the Heavy Cannon at the weak wall below the 02. Switch back to Batman and enter the new hole in the wall. Throw the switch on the left wall to lower the bollards, giving access to the hideout for your vehicle.

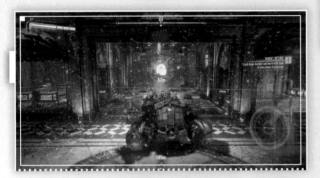

SPIDER DRONES

Look out for Spider Drones that hang out on the walls and ceilings in the Hideout. Shoot them with the Remote Electrical Charge. This counts toward Riddler's Collectibles.

LOWER CAR AND REACH LEVEL 01

Move the Batmobile inside and fire the Power Winch at the Winch Access Point that hangs from the lobby ceiling. Turn around, drive backwards into the hideout, and lower the vehicle to the 03 on the wall—staying clear of the fan blades. Fire a cannon shot at the weak wall straight above, leave the car hanging, and grapple into the opening.

SHUT DOWN FAN 1

Pull out the Remote Electrical Charge, aim at the generator just right of the door, and fire several times in between the protective shield. It speeds up with every shot, so you must be quick. This overloads the machine and powers down the first fan.

LOWER CAR BELOW FIRST FAN

Drop through the hole and glide to the girder that runs across the structure. Pull out the Batmobile Remote and lower the car below the stopped fan to level 04. Aim across the structure at another weakened wall and take it out with the cannon. Use the Riot Suppressor on the soldiers who show up before switching to Batman.

GRAPPLE TO LEVEL 03

Glide down to the stopped fan and swing into the new opening or enter the Batmobile and eject boost to glide over the gap. Look right and grapple up to the ledge, which overlooks an elevator. Drop into the cage, equip the Remote Electrical Charge, and lower it to the bottom.

THE REMOTE ELECTRICAL CHARGE ON AN ELEVATOR

Anytime Batman has access to an elevator motor, the Remote Electrical Charge can be used to raise and lower the lift.

Aim the device at the motor and press the given buttons to move it the desired direction. To use an otherwise inaccessible elevator, simply find a spot where a shot can be made at the electric engine.

ACCESS LEVEL 04

Spray Explosive Gel on the weakened wall and detonate it. Two soldiers with Stun Sticks wait inside the next room. Quickfire an Electrical Charge at both of them and quickly take them down. Throw the switch on the far wall and proceed through the gate. This puts Batman under the second fan.

ACCESS LEVEL 05

Enter the right corridor, grapple onto the left ledge, and observe the hostiles in the next room. Pull out the Remote Electrical Charge, aim at the Industrial Motor on the right shelf, and toggle it on to fry the four soldiers. Flip the switch on the left wall, step inside the elevator, and use the REC to ride it down to level 05.

DEFEAT THE MILITIA SOLDIERS

Climb onto the right shelf and raise the elevator out of the way. Drop down to the now accessible vent and pry off the cover. Inside the briefing room, a pack of 20 unarmed hostiles gets instruction on how to defeat the Dark Knight from their leader, who is wearing a bomb. Follow the beams to the back of the room and drop behind the screen. Start the brawl by disarming the explosive vest. Make the two medics a priority as you eliminate the group of soldiers.

SABOTAGE WEAPONS CRATE

Fire an Electrical Charge at a Weapons Crate to sabotage it. The electric shock incapacitates the next soldier attempting to access it.

RETURN TO LEVEL 04 AND SHUT DOWN FAN 2

Interact with the yellow box to open the exit and follow the corridor back to the main shaft, below a big drill and the Batmobile. Drop to the bottom and enter the corridor on the right. Before moving too far in, blind the Gun Turret in the far corner. Quickly move in to the shaft across from the automated gun and grapple up to level 04. Just as before, fire the Remote Electrical Charge at the generator several times to shut down the second fan.

CRIPPLED BY FEAR

LOWER BATMOBILE AND DRILL

Batman must be rescued from the sentry gun before proceeding. Switch to the Batmobile Remote and lower the vehicle onto the drill, disconnecting from above. Fire the Power Winch at one of the anchor points on the side wall and back up to the left—causing the drill to rotate clockwise, lowering the platform all the way to the bottom of the shaft. Move into the opening and destroy the sentry gun with the Heavy Cannon or Vulcan Gun. Take control of Batman, drop down a level, and

hop into the car. Reattach to an anchor point, but this time, back up right of center. This causes the drill to rise. Stop at the weakened wall and destroy it with another blast from the cannon.

DRIVE BATMOBILE INTO HIDEOUT

Drive into the new opening, being careful to avoid the mining explosives that have been placed around the sides of the tunnel. Interact with the control box on the right wall and drive the Batmobile inside. Weave right, left, and then up and over the obstacles. Boost at the ramp around the corner to clear another barricade. The Arkham Knight pulls in behind Batman in a huge Excavator.

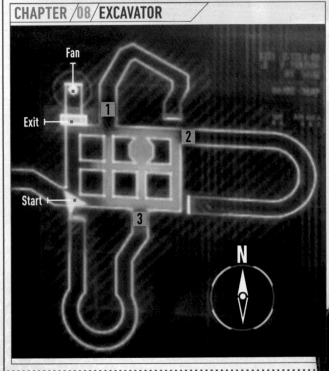

CHAPTER /08/ EXCAVATOR

C DESTROY THE ARKHAM KNIGHT'S EXCAVATOR

There is obviously no taking on this huge mining equipment head to head. Take note of its health that shows up in the upper-right corner of the HUD. Spin around and speed away from the monstrosity, riding up the side of the tunnel to avoid the obstacle. Lead the Excavator into the mining explosives ahead to knock off 25% of its health. It can only withstand three more hits. Conveniently there are three tunnels that have been rigged with the explosives. Lead the Excavator through each one to take away another 25% health. All three lead back into the original area.

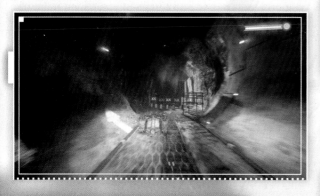

USE THE MINING TUNNEL MAP

A map appears in the lower-right corner of the HUD when facing the Excavator. The Batmobile is shown as the white icon while the enemy appears as a red blip whenever detected. He does not show up until you find him. The three red marks represent locations of mining explosives. The idea is to lead the big guy into each of these tunnels. Note that a red, hexagonal pattern appears around the Batmobile when the Excavator is tailing it.

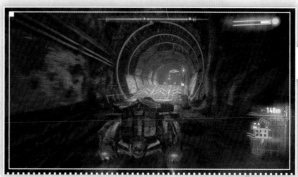

1 Get the Arkham Knight's attention and lead him into the north tunnel. Keep your speed up over the jumps even as you round the tight turn. Hit the Afterburner on a ramp if it seems like you won't make it over the next short barricades. Continue through the explosives to damage the boss.

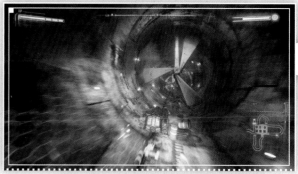

2 Lead the Excavator into the east tunnel. Quickly drive around the beams and scaffolding, between the fan blades, and through the explosives.

3 With the Excavator on your tail, turn into the south tunnel. As you approach the yellow barricades, ride up the left side and stay there around the entire bend. Avoid the stationary fan blade and drive through the mining explosives.

CRIPPLED BY FEAR

If the Batmobile is taken out while facing the Excavator, the player does not lose progress against the boss. Once its health is reduced to zero, exit out the northwest corner. Fire the Power Winch at the fan above and pull it down. Quickly exit the Batmobile before it is destroyed.

Grapple to the ledge above, run down the corridor, and climb into the flooring. An armed soldier, two medics, and eight combat experts hold James Gordon captive just above. Start the fight with a Fear Multi-Takedown. Watch out for incoming combat experts while eliminating the group, then attempt to release the Commissioner from the chair.

RED HOOD PREDATOR ROOM 1

Red Hood takes a sniper position on the perch above and his health bar appears in the corner of the HUD. Red lines show his current field of vision. Avoid this area or it is game over! Stealthily, move between cover until you can get under his position and grapple to him to take away a chunk of his health.

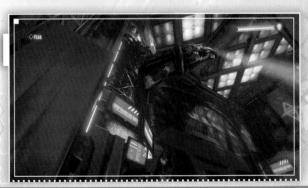

GENERATOR AND ESCALATOR OVERRIDE

The generator motor can be overloaded with the Remote Hacking Device, causing a small-scale blast and incapacitating nearby enemies. Use the Remote Hacking Device on an escalator to overload the motors. This can potentially incapacitate targets depending on the distance they fall.

RED HOOD PREDATOR ROOM 2

The villain changes positions as a new room is opened up. Five armed soldiers patrol the floor as Red Hood scans from a vantage point at the other end. One enemy has a special device such as a Detective Mode detector or Boa Sentry Drone. There are floor grates around the entire room, allowing for Silent Takedowns from below. Use the sizeable area to eliminate the soldiers and then use the floor grates to move underneath the boss. Grapple through the glass to his post to damage him some more. He releases a harmful gas. Batman has 27 seconds to swing through the opening on the far wall or the predator room must be replayed.

RED HOOD PREDATOR ROOM 3

Red Hood moves to a new perch in the adjacent room with six hostiles patrolling the area. This time, the boss controls the Boa Sentry Drone. Work your way around the room, eliminating the soldiers before moving toward the villain. Avoid his detection while positioning yourself directly underneath him. Grapple to his vantage point to take his health down even further. Gas is released again, giving you another 27 seconds to get through the small window.

RED HOOD PREDATOR ROOM 4

Another shutter rises, revealing a new wing as Red Hood takes position at the other end. Again, he controls a Boa Sentry Drone while two Sentry Guns survey the area below. This time, there are no extra soldiers. The drone and automated guns can be blinded with the Remote Hacking Device, but only one at a time. Use the crates in the middle of the room as cover from one gun while moving past the other when it looks the other way. Quickly get underneath the boss and grapple once more to finish him off.

Free Commissioner Gordon, but he gets knocked out as attempt to board the elevator. Take out the four soldiers and brute.

D CONFRONT AND APPREHEND SCARECROW

Join Gordon in the elevator and push the button to ride it to the top, where Scarecrow must be confronted.

CRIPPLED BY FEAR

THE DIE IS CAST

THE CHAPTER AT A GLANCE

! OBJECTIVES

A Protect Oracle

B Destroy the Rattler Tank Drones

C Take Oracle to the GCPD

D Stop Scarecrow's Militia from Destroying Oracle's Servers

E Meet with Oracle at GCPD

F Stop the Assault on GCPD

G Investigate Power Generator

H Access GCPD Parking Garage

I Stop the Assault on GCPD

J Stop Militia from Disabling Security Systems

K Investigate Gordon's Appearance at the Studios

L Surrender to Scarecrow

NEW AR CHALLENGES

- None

AVAILABLE SIDE MISSIONS

 The Line of Duty

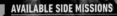 Occupy Gotham

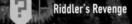 The Perfect Crime

 Two-Faced Bandit

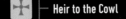 Riddler's Revenge

 Own the Roads

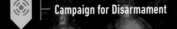 Campaign for Disarmament

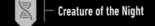 Friend in Need

 Gotham on Fire

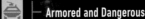 Lamb to the Slaught

Heir to the Cowl

Creature of the Night

GunRunner

Armored and Dangerous

N

TO BLEAKE ISLAND

A

B

TO MIAGANI ISLAND

A PROTECT ORACLE

The Batmobile was destroyed in the tunnels, but fortunately Lucius has made a spare. Call the new ride to have it dropped off nearby.

B DESTROY THE RATTLER TANK DRONES

Test its abilities on the 24 drones that surround Batman and Oracle, including Twin Rattlers, Mambas, and Diamondbacks.

CHAPTER /09/ BLEAKE ISLAND

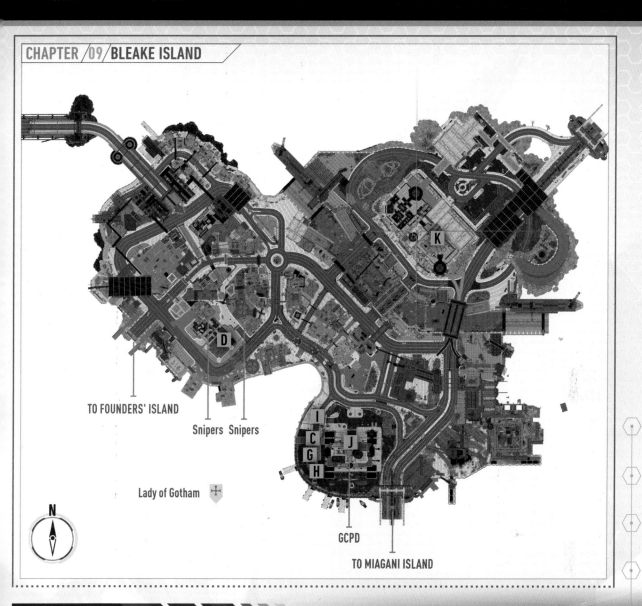

TO FOUNDERS' ISLAND

Snipers Snipers

Lady of Gotham

N

GCPD

TO MIAGANI ISLAND

C   TAKE ORACLE TO THE GCPD

Once the area is safe, put Oracle in the back of your vehicle and drive to GCPD, where she sets up at one of the station's computers. In an attempt to connect to the Clock Tower, they discover Scarecrow's men destroying the server room.

THE DIE IS CAST

D STOP SCARECROW'S MILITIA FROM DESTROYING ORACLE'S SERVERS

Drive to the Clock Tower and grapple to a high vantage point, overlooking the north. Two snipers survey the area and must be taken care of first. Glide Kick each one before turning your focus to the predator zone in and out of the Clock Tower.

Eight soldiers, a medic, and a minigunner patrol the zone. Save the big guy for last while eliminating the others with Silent or Fear Multi-Takedowns. Target the medic first so he doesn't bring a previous victim back into the fold. Once taken care of, climb to the top floor of the Clock Tower and interact with the control consoles to reconnect the servers.

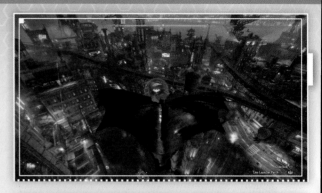

LAMB TO THE SLAUGHTER

Investigate the Lady of Gotham and bring Jack Ryder to safety.

Jack Ryder went to Lady of Gotham to follow up on a lead. Glide to the small island, west of GCPD, to find out what kind of trouble the reporter has gotten into. A complete walkthrough of the short side mission can be found in the Most Wanted chapter.

CHAPTER /09/ GCPD LOCKUP

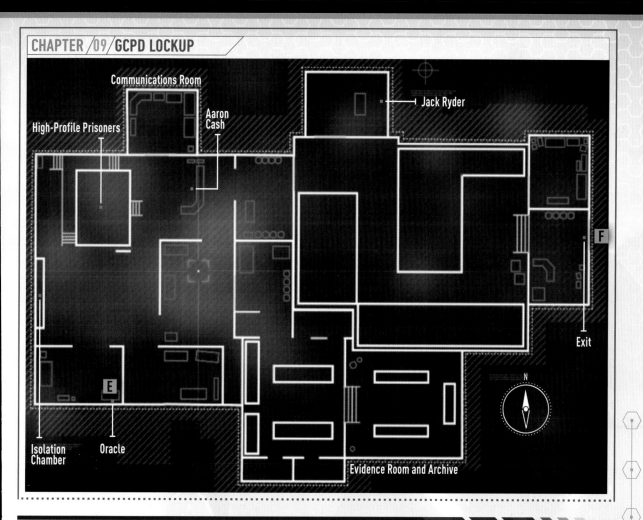

Communications Room

Jack Ryder

Aaron Cash

High-Profile Prisoners

F

Exit

N

Isolation Chamber

Oracle

E

Evidence Room and Archive

E MEET WITH ORACLE AT GCPD TO ANALYZE THE DATA FOR LEADS ABOUT WHERE SCARECROW HAS TAKEN GORDON

Return to GCPD and talk to Oracle, who is still working in the far corner office. As she reports on what she has found, the militia assault the GCPD.

7m

THE DIE IS CAST

F STOP THE ASSAULT ON GCPD

Militia drones and soldiers surround GCPD. Batman must rid the area of the enemy before Scarecrow razes it to the ground. Exit the building as two APCs drop off 14 soldiers and three medics. Target the medics early in the fight and perform a Batmobile Assisted Takedown whenever available. After eliminating the first threat, Cash informs Batman the shutter doors will not open due to the power outage.

G INVESTIGATE POWER GENERATOR TO RESTORE POWER TO GCPD

Power must be restored with an external generator, but first Batman must find a way there. Take control of the Batmobile and fire the Power Winch at the fan, left of the GCPD entrance. Pull it down and grapple inside. Climb into the venting and follow it through the cover at the other end. Step into the lift ahead and grapple into another vent. Follow the dark path until you reach the rooftop, where Batman gets a better view of the militia assault. Run to the west and drop down to the generator, which rests on the lower roof. Unfortunately, it has been destroyed.

H ACCESS GCPD PARKING GARAGE TO POWER UP BACKUP GENERATORS

Backup generators are located in the underground parking garage below. Approach the north end of the roof and use the Remote Hacking Device to blind the Dragon Drone that guards the entrance. Quickly drop down and crouch under the shutter. The generator is just ahead, but another group of militia soldiers must be dealt with first—15 hostiles, including Stun Sticks, a shield, and a brute. Finish them off before firing the Remote Electrical Charge at the three generators.

I STOP THE ASSAULT ON GCPD

Vulnerability in the militia network allows Oracle to hack into the drones, which means she will be fighting alongside Batman. Hop into the Batmobile and drive outside to take on sixty drones. Diamondbacks, Rattlers, Twin Rattlers, Dragons, Mambas, and Pythons all join the vehicle battle. It can get pretty overwhelming in front of GCPD. A back alley on the west side takes you around back with fewer drones to deal with. However, you must eliminate them all.

ORACLE'S HELP

Listen carefully to Oracle's chatter. She clues you in on what she is doing out there. A circular target indicates her target. When a drone's power core is overloaded, fire at it to trigger an EMP blast—freezing any nearby tanks. She may also take over a drone and join the fight, much like using the CPU Virus. Try to keep track of her position, especially when you decide to deploy an EMP.

Stay on the move to avoid being surrounded. An EMP Blast works well when it happens. Use Vulcan fire on the Dragon Drones and incoming missiles, while destroying the ground drones with the Heavy Cannon. The Vulcan Gun can also be used on the Rattler's weak spot just below the cannon. This is a pretty nasty fight. Be sure to take advantage of all the Batmobile abilities, Missile Barrage, CPU Virus, and EMP, and destroy them all. Once the militia tanks have been taken care of, infantry are dropped on the GCPD roof in an attempt to bypass the security.

J STOP MILITIA FROM DISABLING THE GCPD SECURITY SYSTEMS

Grapple to the highest part of the GCPD roof on the right to face the enemies, including eight soldiers, a medic, and a brute. Before the soldiers notice Batman, perform a Fear Multi-Takedown on the nearby hostiles. The Remote Electrical Charge can be used to disable Stun Fist Brutes.

MORE HELP FROM ORACLE

Oracle has control of the security and utility systems on the roof, giving Batman the ability to do Oracle Assisted  Takedowns. Look for the blue items around the roof, such as the electrified fence, HVAC vent, and gas pipes. Press the Environment Takedown button configuration to perform the maneuvers.

With the initial group out of the way, a second squad is dropped on the roof, which includes four soldiers, two medics, and two brutes. Target the medics early on and eliminate the group. Using the Oracle Assisted Takedowns on the brutes is ideal.

THE DIE IS CAST

K INVESTIGATE GORDON'S APPEARANCE AT PANESSA STUDIOS

After the fight, Oracle informs Batman that Gordon's voice was used to access Panessa Studios. Glide over to that location and enter via the V.I.P elevator. The perpetrators are gone, but the vigilante is filled in on the happenings.

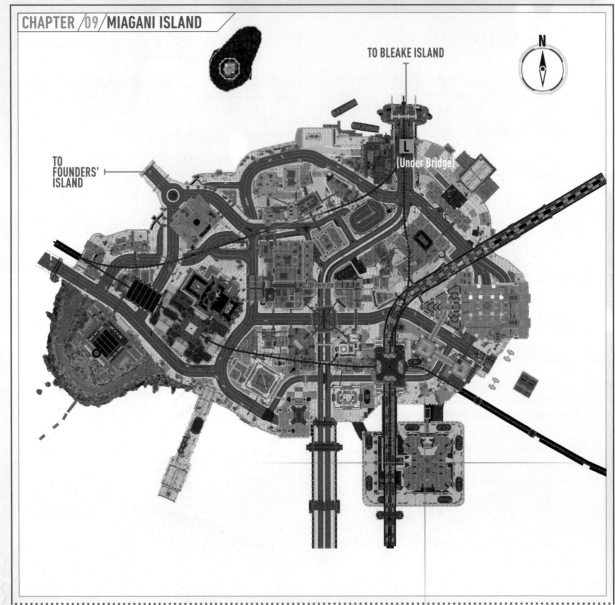

CHAPTER /09/ MIAGANI ISLAND

TO BLEAKE ISLAND

TO FOUNDERS' ISLAND

L (Under Bridge)

N

L SURRENDER TO SCARECROW TO SAVE ROBIN AND GORDON

A message from Crane informs Batman to show up at a storage depot in Kingston, alone. This is it, the endgame. Exit the building and drive to Miagani Island. Hop off the left side of the bridge and enter the storage facility. Inside, Scarecrow has a message for Batman. Approach the monitors to hear him out. Move over to the table and give up the utility belt and gadgets. Approach the truck on the right and step inside to surrender to the villain.

The truck begins to move through the city. After a short time, the vehicle is knocked over. As Batman emerges from the rear, he finds himself in Crime Alley, behind the Monarch Theatre. Climb onto the dumpster and hop over the fence and attempt to open the theater door. Pay your respects to the man and woman who lie on the ground. The vigilante's past demons are getting the better of him. They climb over the fence and begin to attack. With no utility belt and gadgets, use counters and strikes to knock them out. Takedowns can be performed when available. When prompted, rapidly tap the Strike button to finish them off.

When you regain control, jump into the Batmobile and take out the soldiers that surround the room. Hop out and enter the door on the right. Follow the corridor around its twists and turns, taking down any enemies that stand in the way.

Activate the flashlight after the lights go out and make your way down the hallway. Destroy the chairs that block the path to the left and continue onward. When the room appears to trap you inside, wait a short while and another door appears. Obliterate the statues that show up and when light appears through a weakened wall, destroy the plaster. Follow the walkway to the other end and throw the switch labeled Exit. When the foe comes at Batman, counter and strike him until you can finish him off with an Environment Takedown. An ending cinematic follows.

With Scarecrow finally apprehended and the story complete, New Story + becomes available. Also, finish eight Most Wanted missions to unlock a new ending. Complete all of these activities to get the full ending.

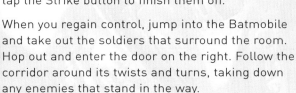

THE DIE IS CAST

MOST WANTED
SIDE MISSIONS

After locking Poison Ivy up in GCPD during Chapter 1, talk to Commissioner Gordon at the maximum-security desk, where Aaron Cash fills Batman in on three cases. This starts the first three side missions: The Line of Duty, Riddler's Revenge, and The Perfect Crime. These incidents can be investigated anytime Batman has free rein of the city, earning WayneTech Upgrade Points as objectives are completed.

Press the Mission Select button to bring up the Mission Select wheel. This allows the player to choose the next objective. Down checks the Most Wanted status and up returns to hunting down Scarecrow. Side Missions fill up the rest of the slots around the wheel, as Alfred introduces them to Batman.

Eleven villains make up the Most Wanted list across 14 side missions. As these quests are finished, the bosses are taken to GCPD Lockup. After completing the story, the Knightfall Protocol becomes available. Complete seven of the Most Wanted side missions and activate Knightfall protocol to watch an ending beyond that of the story. Complete all of the Most Wanted side missions and activate the Knightfall protocol to receive the full ending.

The Most Wanted chapter has everything needed to complete the missions with unlock criteria, detailed maps, and full objective coverage. Note that Campaign for Disarmament, Occupy Gotham, and Own the Roads must be completed before facing the boss for these militia quests. He is covered within the Campaign for Disarmament section.

ARMORED AND DANGEROUS

FIRST AVAILABLE: Chapter 3 after receiving first upgrade for Batmobile

MAIN OBJECTIVE: Find and neutralize all of the militia's APCs

LOCATION: Random, 3 on each island

MOST WANTED VILLAIN: N/A

REWARD: 9 Upgrade Points, 1 per immobilized APC

FIND AND NEUTRALIZE ALL OF THE MILITIA'S APCS

The Arkham Knight mobilizes his senior command throughout the city in armored personnel carriers. Nine APCs in all, three on each island, must be tracked and immobilized to complete the mission.

Alfred informs Batman of this development just after the Batmobile receives its first upgrade in Chapter 3. The APCs do not spawn at specific locations, but instead appear near the Batmobile when the side mission is selected—assuming all three have not been immobilized on the current island.

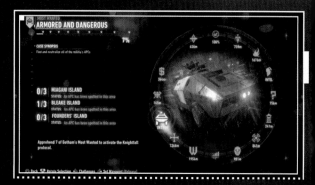

The following table shows specific details about the APCs and escorts for all nine chases. They always appear in this order, no matter which island they are found on.

- APC Speed – The speed at which the APC travels, rated from 1 to 4, where 4 is the fastest.

- Of Escorts – Number of Military Vehicles escorting the APC. Beyond the third APC, reinforcements appear when an escort is taken out. The number of SUVs in reserve is given within the parenthesis. In other words add the first number with the reserve number for the total Escorts possible.

- Fire Type – The Escorts are either equipped with a rocket launcher or a double rocket pod.

- Rocket Fire Rate – The speed at which the APC fires rockets at Batman, where 3 is the slowest.

ARMORED AND DANGEROUS MOST WANTED

	1	2	3	4	5	6	7	8	9
APC Speed (1–4)	1	1	2	2	3	3	3	4	4
# Of Escorts (Reserve)	3	3	0	3(1)	3(1)	3(2)	3(3)	3(4)	3(5)
Fire Type	RPG	RPG	RPG	RPG	Double Rocket Pod	Double Rocket Pod	Double Rocket Pod	Double Rocket Pod	Double Rocket Pod
Rocket Fire Rate	3	3	3	5	5	5	7	7	9

When you're first informed of a nearby APC, the vehicle's health is shown in the upper-right corner of the HUD. Just below the health meter, the number of remaining escorts is shown. Signal strength is just above the radar. Signal Decaying means that the carrier is too far away. The orange meter decreases from the left to right. Once it depletes completely, the signal is lost and must be found again.

Signal Lock signifies that the militia truck is fairly close. A full green bar is shown when it is next to the Batmobile, decreasing as it moves further away.

Immobilize, Side Swipe, or run directly into the vehicles to take them out. The Batmobile Ram Charge upgrade is very useful here. The objective is to take down the APC in front, but XP is earned for each SUV eliminated along the way. After the lead vehicle takes a few hits, it crashes, earning a WayneTech Upgrade Point each time.

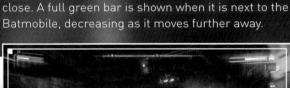

Starting with the third APC, it fires rockets at the Batmobile. The Military Vehicles have rocket launchers. Watch out for incoming projectiles, weaving back and forth to avoid taking damage.

CAMPAIGN FOR DISARMAMENT

FIRST AVAILABLE: Chapter 3 while tracking the Arkham Knight's vehicle

MAIN OBJECTIVE: Find and defuse all explosive devices deployed by the militia

LOCATION: Bleake Island (4), Miagani Island (6), Founders' Island (5)

MOST WANTED VILLAIN: Unknown

REWARD: 14 Upgrade Points, 1 per bomb defused
3 Upgrade Points for delivering Deathstroke to GCPD

The militia begins burying bombs around the city, as Batman tracks the Arkham Knight's vehicle in Chapter 3. Flashing beacons indicate their positions. The first explosive device must be defused as part of the story. The rest appear at different points during the campaign and can be completed at any time thereafter. Refer to the table on page 181 for when each one appears.

As Batman nears one of the explosive devices, it shows up on the map and intel is added to the Mission Select screen. When viewing the Campaign for Disarmament icon on the map, a scale on the right represents the difficulty of the militia protection. Just one marker lit up represents the easiest, while all five means very challenging. The difficulty for each device is given in the table below as Very Low, Low, Medium, High, or Extreme. These Batmobile

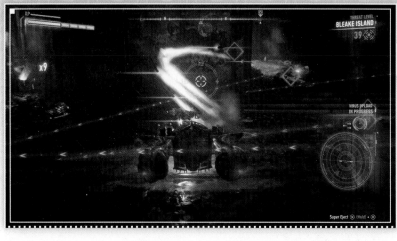

battles become very challenging as the game progresses with bigger squads, higher variety, and more aggressive drones. Be sure to improve the vehicle as WayneTech Upgrade Points become available.

The steps for each explosive device are:

■ **Upload Virus:** Once one is found, fire the Power Winch and start the virus upload.

■ **Detonate bomb:** Attach the Power Winch to the device again and rev the engine to detonate it with a controlled explosion.

■ **Defend:** A squad of militia drones attacks. The selection of tanks becomes increasingly more difficulty to deal with as these bombs are defused. Use the Batmobile's Battle Mode to clear the area of the threat. Note the number of remaining drones

Watch out that you do not stray too far away from the virus upload. A 10-second timer counts down as soon as you exit the area. Quickly re-enter the zone to continue the objective.

MILITIA EXPLOSIVE DEVICE LOCATIONS

MAP LOCATION	CH. FIRST AVAILABLE	LOCATION	SECURITY LEVEL
A	3	Bleake Island – Cauldron, next to Sionis Industries	Extreme
B	3	Bleake Island – Cauldron, train yard	Very Low
C	3	Miagani Island – Bristol, north of Botanical Gardens	Very Low
D	3	Miagani Island – North of Grand Avenue Station	Low
E	5	Miagani Island – Miagani Botanical Gardens	Low
F	5	Founders' Island – Otisburg	Medium
G	5	Founders' Island – Ryker Heights, Urbarail Station	Low
H	5	Founders' Island – Ryker Heights	Extreme
I	7	Bleake Island – Chinatown, north side of traffic circle	High
J	7	Miagani Island – Kingston at base of parking garage	Medium
K	7	Founders' Island – Drescher, near Perdition Bridge	High
L	9	Bleake Island – Cauldron, southwest of Panessa Studios	Extreme
M	9	Miagani Island – Kingston, next to Bank of Gotham	High
N	9	Founders' Island – Port Adams, just inside Entrance	Extreme

CAMPAIGN FOR
DISARMAMENT

◘ DEATHSTROKE HAS ASSUMED COMMAND OF THE MILITIA

OBJECTIVE: Confront Deathstroke at Grand Avenue

REQUIREMENT: Complete Campaign for Disarmament, Occupy Gotham, and Own the Roads

LOCATION: Miagani Island – Grand Avenue

After the Cloudburst tank is destroyed in Chapter 7, Deathstroke assumes command of the army and he must be stopped. After eliminating the militia explosive devices, watchtowers, and checkpoints, drive to Grand Avenue to take him on. Five Cobra Drones join Deathstroke as they search for the Batmobile.

Slade's tank looks very similar to the Cloudburst Tank you took on at the end of Chapter 7. It has a 360-degree field of vision, making it nearly impossible to catch off guard. Use the same strategy that you used against the Arkham Knight. Watch the radar and avoid the big tank, while picking off the Cobra Drones. Missile Barrages are particularly useful against Cobras, allowing you to avoid the heavy tank's field of vision. Sneak up behind the weaker drones, target the exhaust port, and fire the Heavy Cannon to destroy the tanks.

Once the five Cobras have been dealt with, change your focus to Deathstroke. Confront the boss from a safe distance, reverse away from him, and bombard him with gunfire. He has three attacks, guided missiles, a direct energy shot, and rockets. Shoot down the missiles with the Vulcan Gun, while strafing back and forth to avoid his other attacks. Circles on the ground indicate incoming rockets, while the horizontal lines represent the energy attack. Avoid getting trapped by fleeing the area if things get too hairy.

FORENSICS SCANNER

The Forensics Scanner can be used to detect the tank's position through buildings. This gives you a more accurate location than the radar.

Once you defeat him, Batman apprehends the villain. Drive him to GCPD to complete the side mission.

CAMPAIGN FOR
DISARMAMENT

DEATHSTROKE

PROFILE

REAL NAME	Slade Wilson
OCCUPATION	Mercenary
BASED IN	Mobile
EYE COLOR	Blue
HAIR COLOR	Gray
HEIGHT	6 Ft. 5 Inches
WEIGHT	225 Lbs
FIRST APPEARANCE	*New Teen Titans* #2 [December 1980]

ATTRIBUTES

-Medically enhanced physical and mental abilities
-Master tactician and combat expert
-Missing his right eye

Originally a soldier in the U.S. Army, Slade Wilson was part of an experimental super-soldier program where he gained enhanced strength, agility, and intelligence.

Deathstroke became a mercenary soon after the experiment and rapidly gained a reputation as one of the world's greatest assassins.

Following his defeat and incarceration at the hands of Batman, Deathstroke escaped from the maximum security wing of Blackgate Penitentiary and continued working as a gun for hire, hoping that one day he'd get another shot at his nemesis, Batman.

CREATURE OF THE NIGHT

FIRST AVAILABLE: Chapter 3

MAIN OBJECTIVE: Investigate the Winged Creature Stalking the Skies

LOCATION: Bleake Island, near ACE Chemicals (Langstrom's Laboratory)

MOST WANTED VILLAIN: Man-Bat

REWARD: 6 Upgrade Points, 1 per Objective, 3 for apprehending Most Wanted

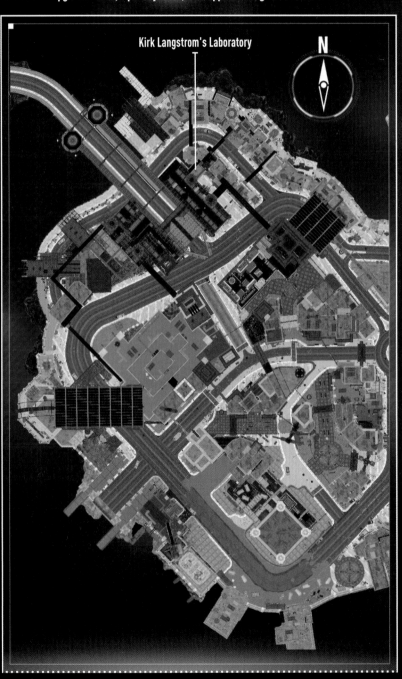

Kirk Langstrom's Laboratory

N

OBTAIN A BLOOD SAMPLE FROM THE WINGED CREATURE FOR ANALYSIS

After hacking into the Transport Terminal, grappling to a rooftop on Miagani Island introduces Batman to an irate, winged creature. While climbing onto the roof, the beast swipes at the vigilante before flying off. This begins the Creature of the Night Most Wanted.

icon appears on the map in the approximate area of a winged creature sighting. Grapple to a high
tage point near this waypoint and scan the area for the flying beast. You can hear a squeal when it
vithin range. Use Detective Mode if you're having trouble spotting it amongst the tall buildings. Once
nd, glide directly at the thing. Batman manages to wrestle it to the ground, taking a blood sample
ore it breaks free. Alfred runs it through the Batcomputer and finds a match, as well as the location
he guy's laboratory in Chinatown.

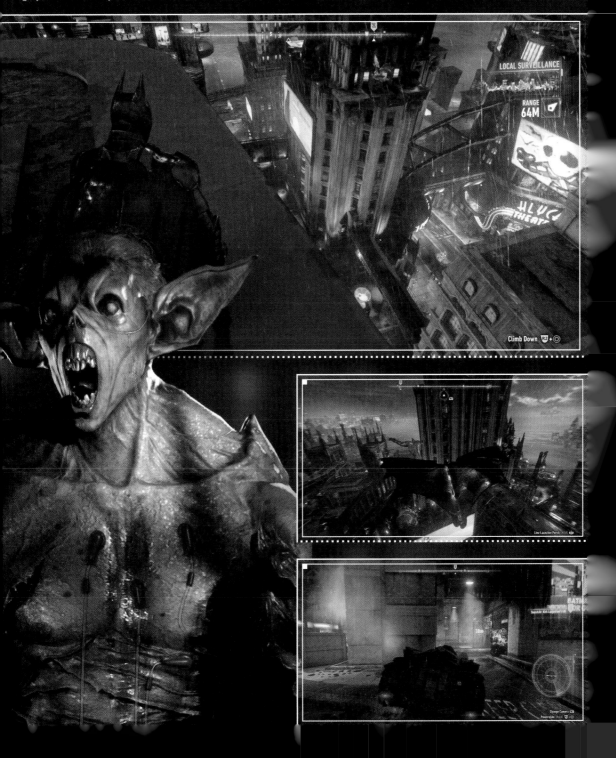

SEARCH DR. KIRK LANGSTROM'S LAB

Drive or glide to the laboratory in Chinatown. The entrance is found on the ground level, tucked underneath a building in a narrow alleyway. Enter the structure, ride the elevator down to the basement, and follow the corridor to Kirk and Francine's lab.

KIRK AND FRANCINE LANGSTROM

PROFILE

REAL NAME	**Kirk Langstrom / Francine Langstrom**
OCCUPATION	**Biologists**
BASED IN	**Gotham City**
EYE COLOR	**Green / Blue**
HAIR COLOR	**Grey / Brown**
HEIGHT	**5 Ft. 9 In. / 5 Ft. 7 In.**
WEIGHT	**170 / 150 Lbs**
FIRST APPEARANCE	***Detective Comics* #400 [June 1970] / *Detective Comics* #402 [August 1970]**

ATTRIBUTES

- Gifted research scientists
- Pioneering gene therapists
- Deteriorating hearing (Kirk)

Kirk Langstrom and Francine Lee met as PhD students, and would go on to publish a joint-research paper on the treatment of human illnesses via gene splicing across species lines.

Marrying soon after graduation, Kirk and Francine continued to work together, despite struggles to find funding and widespread skepticism of their hypotheses.

In recent years their work has become threatened by Kirk's encroaching hearing loss, though the pair believe they have identified an opportunity in his diagnosis.

As you investigates the lab, a homemade video of the couple details their research and the results of the experiment. Use the computer in the corner of the room to access all of the doctor's research. Now Batman must create an antidote by isolating the creature's signature and removing it from Langstrom's DNA.

On the computer screen, Kirk's DNA is shown on the left and the beast is displayed on the right. The yellow sections on the left represent his deafness symptoms. The green on the right shows the foreign genetic material that is causing aggressive changes in the subject. These sections need to be removed to create a clean sample. Press left and right with the Move and Look controls to rotate the resequencer drums and highlight the uncontaminated sections within the windows. A percentage in the middle of the screen shows the DNA sequence integrity. This goes up when clean sections of each sample are highlighted. It drops if the yellow and/or green are selected. Reaching 100% completes the mini-game. With a cure synthesized, Batman must now get the creature to take the injection.

LOCATE MAN-BAT AND ADMINISTER THE CURE

Now you must seek out the creature, who can be found almost anywhere in the city. Glide and grapple through the buildings, listening for the squeal and looking out for the winged villain in the skies. Once found, again glide into the foe to bring him to the ground, where Batman administers the antidote. Unfortunately, not enough was given before he got away. Repeat this process. Track the creature down, knock him out of the air, and administer the rest of the cure.

RETURN MAN-BAT TO THE GCPD LOCKUP

Batman tosses Man-Bat into the back of the Batmobile. You can complete this mission after the battle at the beginning of Chapter 8. Drive to GCPD to place Dr. Langstrom in the isolation chamber and earn the rest of your WayneTech Upgrade Points.

CREATURE OF
THE NIGHT

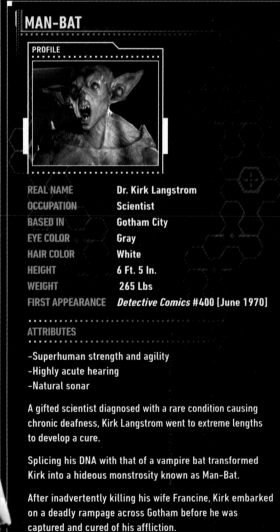

MAN-BAT

PROFILE

REAL NAME	Dr. Kirk Langstrom
OCCUPATION	Scientist
BASED IN	Gotham City
EYE COLOR	Gray
HAIR COLOR	White
HEIGHT	6 Ft. 5 In.
WEIGHT	265 Lbs
FIRST APPEARANCE	*Detective Comics* #400 [June 1970]

ATTRIBUTES

- Superhuman strength and agility
- Highly acute hearing
- Natural sonar

A gifted scientist diagnosed with a rare condition causing chronic deafness, Kirk Langstrom went to extreme lengths to develop a cure.

Splicing his DNA with that of a vampire bat transformed Kirk into a hideous monstrosity known as Man-Bat.

After inadvertently killing his wife Francine, Kirk embarked on a deadly rampage across Gotham before he was captured and cured of his affliction.

FRIEND IN NEED

FIRST AVAILABLE: Chapter 7

MAIN OBJECTIVE: Investigate the Loss of Contact with Lucius Fox

LOCATION: Miagani Island, Wayne Tower

MOST WANTED VILLAIN: Hush

REWARD: 3 Upgrade Points

TO WAYNE
TOWER PARKING

Wayne Tower

N

SEARCH LAST KNOWN LOCATION AT WAYNE TOWER

During Chapter 7, Lucius Fox goes out of contact. Drive toward Wayne Tower on Miagani Island to investigate, but you must access the building from the underground elevator. From the Bank of Gotham, head southeast and enter the tunnel, under the Wayne Tower street sign. Turn left at the parking sign and park at the central elevator. Hop out and ride it up.

Move into the office to confront Thomas Elliot, who has Lucius Fox at gunpoint. Eventually, a prompt appears to Counter the villain, but do not press it yet. He turns his gun on Batman and at that split second is the only chance to take him down. Too early and he shoots the hostage. Too late and he shoots the vigilante. A successful counter earns you three WayneTech Upgrade Points and Hush is enclosed in Wayne Tower. You can continue the game by exiting through one of the doors and gliding off the balcony.

As Bruce Wayne, walk through the lobby and enter the office. Approach the computer on the desk and attempt to use the retinal scanner, to no avail. When Lucius gets close enough, use the scanner again to force him to login instead. Just in time, Batman notices "Bruce Wayne" accessing the computer.

HUSH

PROFILE

REAL NAME	Thomas "Tommy" Elliot
OCCUPATION	Surgeon, Serial Killer
BASED IN	Gotham City
EYE COLOR	Blue (formerly brown)
HAIR COLOR	Black (formerly Reddish-brown)
HEIGHT	6 Ft. 2 In.
WEIGHT	210 Lbs
FIRST APPEARANCE	*Batman* #609 [January 2003]

ATTRIBUTES

-Peak physical conditioning
-World-class surgeon
-Master of disguise
-Determined to destroy Bruce Wayne

Tommy Elliot and Bruce Wayne were childhood friends and, unknown to Bruce, dark reflections of each other.

After a tragic accident claimed one of his parents, the traumatized Tommy developed a pathological hatred for the Waynes.

An incredibly gifted surgeon as an adult, Elliot has spent decades planning an elaborate revenge scheme to destroy Bruce Wayne.

GOTHAM ON FIRE

FIRST AVAILABLE: Chapter 3

MAIN OBJECTIVE: Investigate Reports of an Arsonist Loose in Gotham

LOCATIONS: Bristol Fire Station on South Side Miagani Island
Cauldron Fire Station on Bleake Island
Otisburg Fire Station on West Side Founders' Island

MOST WANTED VILLAIN: Firefly

REWARD: 7 Upgrade Points, 2 per fire, 1 for apprehending Most Wanted

1 MIAGANI ISLAND, BRISTOL FIRE STATION NEAR THE BOTANICAL GARDENS

After investigating the Arkham Knight's crashed vehicle, Alfred informs Batman of a fire that has broken out at the Bristol fire station on Miagani Island. The power has been cut, disabling the fire suppression system—making arson extremely likely. Drive the Batmobile to the fire in southern Miagani Island, next to the Botanical Gardens.

Find the electric panel on the south side, attach the Power Winch, and rev the engine to power the suppression system. As the sprinklers activate, Firefly appears from the third-story window and escapes to the right. Immediately take off after the villain. Use the Afterburner on the straights to close in quickly as he flies around the perimeter of the island.

Watch out for fires that Firefly sets along the way, though they only cover half the road. Stay alert and steer clear of the hazard to avoid taking damage, which can take the Batmobile out if hit too often. A meter on the right side of the HUD displays the arsonist's fuel. As he flies and shoots his flamethrower, this meter is reduced. If it fully drains while Batman is still in contact, Firefly is vulnerable to a takedown. When close enough,

FIREFLY

PROFILE

REAL NAME	Garfield Lynns
OCCUPATION	Serial Arsonist
BASED IN	Mobile
EYE COLOR	Brown
HAIR COLOR	None (Formerly Brown)
HEIGHT	5 Ft. 11 In.
WEIGHT	165 Lbs
FIRST APPEARANCE	*Detective Comics* #184 [June, 1952]

ATTRIBUTES

- Expert in Pyrotechnics and explosives
- Pyromaniac
- Insulated battlesuit equipped with flamethrower

Garfield Lynns was a special effects artist and pyrotechnic expert in the motion pictures industry before he was made redundant and forced into poverty.

Lynns became a petty criminal and serial arsonist, torching huge swathes of Gotham City to feed his pyromania. After setting fire to a chemical plant, Lynns was caught in the blaze and suffered burns to 90% of his body, leaving him hideously scarred.

Upon his recovery, Lynns designed a special flame-retardant, heat-resistant battle suit featuring a military grade flamethrower and jetpack.

2 BLEAKE ISLAND, CAULDRON FIRE STATION NORTH OF GCPD

Look for the smoke billowing out of the Cauldron fire station on Bleake Island, just up the road from GCPD. Repeat the process from the Bristol fire. Use the Power Winch to start up the suppression system and then chase after Firefly. Watch out for tighter turns throughout Bleake Island, designed to throw the Batmobile into Garfield's blazes. Get close enough to take him down, eject from the cockpit, and beat him down to collect a couple more upgrade points. Unfortunately, he slips out of the vigilante's grip, again.

3 FOUNDERS' ISLAND, OTISBURG FIRE STATION SOUTH OF WAYNE INTERNATIONAL PLAZA

Once Founders' Island is accessible with the Batmobile, drive to the fire station in Otisburg. Start up the sprinklers using the Power Winch and then follow closely behind Firefly. Remain alert for his longer flames as the villain leads you through the multi-leveled construction of Founders' Island. Stay close until he runs out of fuel, get within range, and take him down. Finish him off for good with another Beat Down. Batman uses the villain's jetpack to deliver the foe to GCPD, where you collect three upgrade points.

GOTHAM
ON FIRE

GUNRUNNER

FIRST AVAILABLE: Chapter 3

MAIN OBJECTIVE: Find and Destroy All of Penguin's Weapon Caches

LOCATIONS: Miagani Island – Kingston, Harold's Repair
Bleake Island – Sionis Industries
Founders' Island - The Grinning Fishmonger
Bleake Island - Below Chinatown in Sewers
Founders' Island – Otisburg, Amertek Building

MOST WANTED VILLAIN: Penguin

REWARD: 11 Upgrade Points, 2 per Weapons Cache, 1 for apprehending Penguim

During Chapter 3 of the main path, Batman meets up with Nightwing at the Ranelagh Ferry Terminal, where he is informed of Penguin's intent to smuggle weapon caches in from Blüdhaven. Clear out the six thugs before firing the Disruptor at the first van. Knock on the back door and they speed away. The Batmobile cannot be used, as it spooks the thugs, so grapple and glide close behind the vehicle. The truck's position is shown when behind buildings as long as it does not get too far away. Eventually, they lead Batman right to the weapons cache, just down the street from where the chase originated. The shutter is locked behind the thugs and soldiers guard the only way in on the rooftop.

SIGNAL LOCK

When tracking a truck, the signal strength is shown on the right side of the HUD. Signal Decaying means that the van is too far away. The orange meter decreases from the left to right. Once it depletes completely, it is lost and must be found again. Signal Lock signifies that the truck is fairly close, turning green when you're just behind it.

Grapple to a high vantage point and survey the scene. Six armed hostiles and two Sentry Guns must be dealt with. Go ahead and use the Disruptor to sabotage the three closest firearms before proceeding. Disable each turret from behind when the area is clear. Eliminate the remaining guards and enter the hatch inside the roof access.

Twenty hostiles and Penguin himself guard the weapon cache below. Fortunately, they are all unarmed. Find the vent on the wall and slide down into the floor grate. Move behind the boss and interrogate him. Counter the optimistic soldiers when they strike, including the two who grab guns from the weapon crate. Nightwing joins Batman, starting the brawl with the remaining thugs. Switch between the two vigilantes and use the Dual Team Takedown whenever possible.

Once everyone has been dealt with, enter the vault and spray Explosive Gel on the highlighted crate in the back. Exit the room and interact with the door. With the vault closed up tight, move away from the blast area and detonate. Exit the building. An ambush has been set up for Batman. Pull out the Batmobile Remote and drive the vehicle up to the top level of the parking garage across the street and eliminate the Sentry Guns and soldiers.

2 BLEAKE ISLAND – SIONIS INDUSTRIES

The remaining four weapon caches are dealt with in the same manner. After exiting Stagg's Airship, at the start of Chapter 5, select GunRunner from the Mission Select to contact Nightwing. He gives you the next North Refrigeration truck location. Find an unprotected van at the GunRunner waypoint. Hit it with the Disruptor's Tracker Ammo and tap the back door to send it on its way. Follow it to Sionis Industries. Open the door on the southwest corner of the building and use the Remote Hacking Device on the security console to open the main gate. Be careful to not stray too far inside, as two Gun Turrets protect the room. Switch to the Batmobile Remote and use the Heavy Cannon to destroy the weapons.

Move around to the left, grapple through the hatch above, and throw the switch on the wall to open

the rooftop shutters. Return outside and grapple to the roof. Smash down into the room below, where a big group of thugs and a brute await your arrival. With help from Nightwing, take down the group. The Disruptor is useful against the thugs. Plant Explosive Gel on the weapon crate inside, close the vault door, and detonate the cache to earn two more WayneTech Upgrade Points.

Repeat the process again. After dropping Ivy at the Botanical Gardens, select the GunRunner mission to get the next North Refrigeration truck location. Eliminate the group of thugs around the vehicle, shoot it with the Tracker Ammo, and knock on the door. Tail the van to the northwest corner of Founders' Island and down into the old, lower level of the island.

GUNRUNNER

Grapple to the small balcony above the Grinning Fishmonger entrance, but do not climb up. Instead, perform a Silent Takedown on the sniper who guards the exit and step inside.

Move up the steps and slide down the vent to get underneath seven thugs. Continue beyond the weak wall at the other end of the room, place Explosive Gel, and then move next to the other two guys. Detonate the gel and then take out the remaining two soldiers with Fear Takedowns.

Pull the vent cover off the side wall, climb inside, and follow the path to find the weapons cache and more of Penguin's thugs. Move out on the beam and target one of the guys with the Fear-Multi Takedown. Drop as many as possible with the fear and assist Nightwing in taking down the thugs and brutes. Place Explosive Gel inside the vault cage, close the door, and detonate the charge.

4 BLEAKE ISLAND – BELOW CHINATOWN, IN SEWERS

After dissipating the fear toxin, get the next North Refrigeration truck location from Nightwing and proceed to the waypoint. Knock out the thugs who guard the vehicle, tag it with the Disruptor's Tracker Ammo, and knock on the door. On Bleake Island, follow the van into the sewers, just east of the Perdition Bridge and follow the route back to the bollards, which block your path. Take out the soldiers ahead, hop out, and grapple up to the walkway above. Find the control panel and activate the switch to lower the blockade.

Use the remote for the Batmobile and face the right wall. Fire the Power Winch at the anchor point on the wall, pull back to create an opening, and grapple inside. Continue up the shaft and drop through one of the grates to begin a brawl with Penguin's men. Nightwing does not show up for this fight so Batman must take the pack down on his own. Place and detonate Explosive Gel inside the vault. At that point, a monitor reveals that the villain has captured Grayson.

5 FOUNDERS' ISLAND – OTISBURG, AMERTEK BUILDING

With help from Nightwing's tracker, Alfred finds his location in Otisburg and adds it as a waypoint. Find the Amertek building on the east side of Otisburg and grapple to the top of the opening soon sign displayed on the west side of the roof. Seven armed hostiles guard the entrance, including a Detective Mode Jammer. Silently take out the sniper below and then survey the rooftop. Eliminate the rest of the group, rip the cover off the yellow control box, and hop down the elevator shaft. Enter the elevator car and continue to the very bottom of the shaft. Climb down one more level to find Penguin and Nightwing.

Find the opening ahead and step onto a beam in the back room, which is guarded by a Gun Turret. Use the Remote Hacking Device to disable the weapon, hop down, and destroy it from behind. Pull the vent cover off the far wall and follow the vent shaft into the floor. Move past Nightwing, hop out behind the weak wall, and rescue him.

Switch between the two vigilantes as they eliminate the group of thugs and brutes. Spray Explosive Gel inside the final vault and close the door. Penguin has grabbed Nightwing and placed a gun against his head. After the villain questions who the "Flying Graysons" are, perform a Dual Team Takedown on him and then detonate the gel to destroy the last of the weapon caches. Drive Penguin to GCPD to lock him up and collect three upgrade points.

GUNRUNNER

HEIR TO THE COWL

FIRST AVAILABLE: Chapter 3

MAIN OBJECTIVE: Investigate suspicious figure on Kingston rooftop

LOCATION: Starts on Miagani Island, Kingston

MOST WANTED VILLAIN: Unknown

REWARD: 8 Upgrade Points, 1 for Trials 1-3, 2 for Trial 4, and 3 for Completing Finale

After investigating the crashed SUV in Chapter 3, Alfred informs Batman of an interloper who stands on a rooftop next to a burning bat symbol. The suspicious man needs to be investigated. Azrael offers to give up his killing ways and take over the reins of Gotham's savior. Batman decides to test him with four combat trials. Fight as Michael Lane against increasingly more difficult groups of virtual combatants. Defeat each challenge without being hit to move on to the next trial.

KINGSTON

LOCAL SURVEILLANCE

RANGE 164M

Line Launcher Perch (Hold)

A TRIAL 1: JUST THE BEGINNING

LOCATION: Miagani Island, Kingston, rooftop west of Bank of Gotham

REQUIREMENT: Investigate SUV

Travel to Kingston and grapple to the roof of the Gambis building, west of the Bank of Gotham and across the street from the parking garage. Talk to the kneeling man to begin the side mission. Only six thugs need to be defeated for the first trial, though remember, you cannot take a hit. The requirement is only to avoid enemy strikes. It does not matter how you do it. If you only counter and strike the entire fight, while redirecting any charging foes, you succeed. Their melee weapons can be used against them. Completing the challenge unlocks the second trial on Founders' Island.

B TRIAL 2: SHOWING GREAT SKILL

LOCATION: Founders' Island, Otisburg, south of Fire Station

REQUIREMENT: Complete Trial 1

Drive or glide to the lone building in Otisburg, south of the fire station, and grapple to the roof to present the possible successor with his second trial. Seven thugs and a brute appear ahead. Watch out for thrown objects or melee weapons. One hit and the challenge must be repeated. Just as with Batman, a cape stun and beat down takes care of the big enemy. A well-timed special takedown also does the trick.

C TRIAL 3: A COMPETENT WARRIOR

LOCATION: Bleake Island, Chinatown, west of traffic circle

REQUIREMENT: Complete Trial 2

Travel to Chinatown and spot the burning bat symbol on a rooftop, west of the traffic circle. This challenges places Azrael against 10 soldiers and a medic. The use of trained militia is quite the step up from the street thugs. Watch out for the medic to charge a teammate. Use the Remote Electrical Charge to knock him down or use a Counter Throw on him. Watch out for incoming attacks as you pummel the foe.

HEIR TO
THE COWL

D TRIAL 4: THE FINAL CHALLENGE

LOCATION: Lady of Gotham Island

REQUIREMENT: Complete Trial 3

Glide out to Lady of Gotham and speak with Lane to begin his final challenge atop the statue. Six combat experts face off against the crusader. These ninjas attack directly with their sword or in a team-up maneuver where one jumps off another's shoulders. Both can be countered. A third move swings the sword hard to the side and can only be avoided with a Blade Dodge. Defeat the six combatants to complete the last of the trials, collecting another two upgrade points.

E FINALE: RECONSTRUCTING MEMORIES

LOCATION: Bleake Island, Chinatown, Clock Tower

REQUIREMENT: Complete Trial 4

Grapple to the Clock Tower roof and drop through the secret access. Use the console to look into the data on Michael Lane. Batman visualizes his memories with the Batcomputer, but it appears they have been tampered with. Scrub through the video and scan in the four unique Order of San Dumas Lithographs. You are looking for the following at the given timestamps:

00:00:00   Start of the memory sequence

00:05:55   Banner in between baby and child scenes

00:16:44   Shoulder of football jersey

00:28:92   Shield of jouster

00:41:31   Shortly after crime scene tape

HEIR TO THE COWL

With the memory reconstructed, turn around and pick up the sword that sits on a display next to the elevator. Approach Batman where a decision must be made. Depending on the choice made, you are either free to explore Gotham from the Clock Tower or you must drive Azrael to GCPD Lockup.

AZRAEL

PROFILE

REAL NAME	Michael Lane
OCCUPATION	Police Officer
BASED IN	Gotham City
EYE COLOR	Brown
HAIR COLOR	Black
HEIGHT	6 Ft. 2 In.
WEIGHT	210 Lbs
FIRST APPEARANCE	*Azrael: Death's Dark Knight* #1 [March, 2009]

ATTRIBUTES

–The Suit of Sorrows bestows enhanced strength, stamina, and speed
–The Sword of Sins burns with the souls of the damned
–Prone to fits of insanity
–Military- and police-trained tactician

Years ago, Michael Lane was part of a program to create the ultimate crime fighter. Instead, it turned him into an insane criminal.

Thwarted by Batman, Michael confessed his sins to a priest of the secret religious sect, the Order of St. Dumas. They recruited Michael to fight evil as their crusader Azrael, wearing the mystical Suit of Sorrows and wielding the Sword of Sin.

In Arkham City, Azrael prophesized Batman's downfall. Having studied the Dark Knight's fighting style, Azrael sees himself as the Caped Crusader's natural successor.

LAMB TO THE SLAUGHTER

FIRST AVAILABLE: Chapter 9

MAIN OBJECTIVE: Investigate the Lady of Gotham and bring Jack Ryder to safety

LOCATION: Lady of Gotham Island

MOST WANTED VILLAIN: Unknown

REWARD: 3 Upgrade Points

Reporter Jack Ryder hangs out in the Interview Room at GCPD, between maximum security and the holding cells. He can be visited at any time, though he doesn't offer anything really helpful. He is the answer to a riddle though. During Chapter 9, he follows a lead to Lady of Gotham, a small island west of GCPD, and hasn't been heard from since. It is up to Batman to head over there and see what kind of trouble the journalist has gotten into.

INTERVIEW ROOM

JACK RYDER

PROFILE

REAL NAME	**Jack Ryder**
OCCUPATION	**Investigative Reporter**
BASED IN	**Gotham City**
EYE COLOR	**Blue**
HAIR COLOR	**Black**
HEIGHT	**6 Ft.**
WEIGHT	**194 Lbs**
FIRST APPEARANCE	*Showcase* #73 [March, 1968]

ATTRIBUTES

–Determined Reporter
–Known for his aggressive pursuit of stories
–Famous for his controversial talk show
–Utterly lacking in self-awareness

Jack Ryder is an investigative reporter turned controversial talk show host, well-known for his aggressive manner and his relentless determination to get to the truth.

Following his brush with death in Arkham City, Ryder wrote a series of editorials condemning the facility.

By his own admittance, Ryder's testimony proved influential in the state's decision to release a number of falsely imprisoned inmates, many of whom received substantial compensation packages.

A INVESTIGATE THE LADY OF GOTHAM

On the island, Deacon Blackfire oversees a meeting of his followers with Jack Ryder bound in a cage. Land on a beam on the south side or atop the statue. Equip the Disruptor and sabotage the two weapons crates. Glide onto the cage to confront the cult leader, as he calls on his worshippers to defend against the Dark Knight.

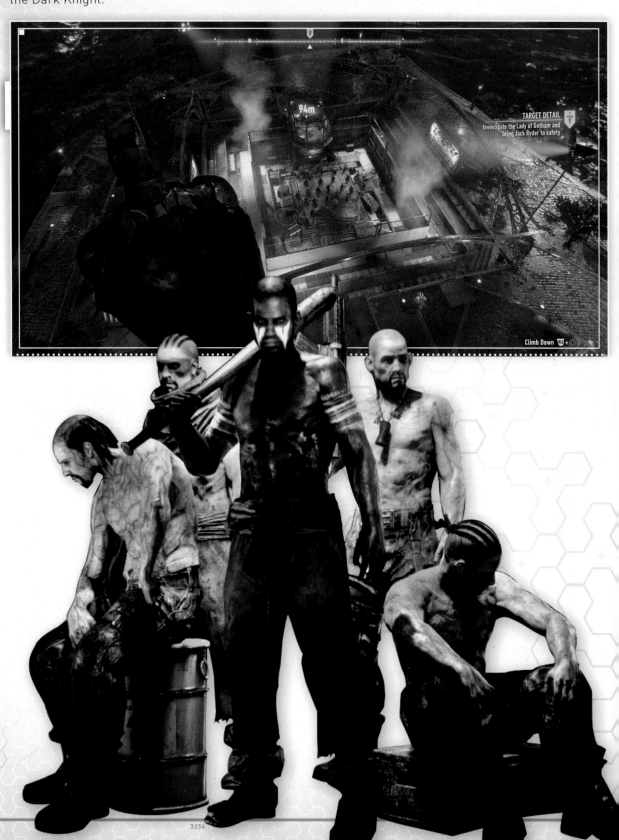

94m

TARGET DETAIL
Investigate the Lady of Gotham and bring Jack Ryder to safety

Climb Down

A timer counts down three minutes. You must defeat all 25 thugs and take down Blackfire within this time or Ryder is dead. Be ready with the counter. With that many brawlers, there is usually an attack coming. Watch out for the blade attacks, otherwise weapons are limited to those in the weapons crates. With the followers knocked out, use the Remote Electrical Charge to shut down the four generators. Now you can grapple to one of the hatches on the front of the cage to apprehend Deacon Blackfire.

LAMB TO THE SLAUGHTER

DEACON BLACKFIRE

PROFILE

REAL NAME	Joseph Blackfire
OCCUPATION	Cult Leader
BASED IN	Gotham City
EYE COLOR	Gray
HAIR COLOR	White
HEIGHT	6 Ft. 1 Inches
WEIGHT	170 Lbs
FIRST APPEARANCE	*Batman: The Cult* #1 [August, 1988]

ATTRIBUTES

-Charismatic cult leader
-Impassioned public speaker
-Claims to be immortal

A power-crazed charismatic conman and cult leader, Deacon Blackfire indoctrinates Gotham's homeless population to serve in his cult and aid him in his quest to control Gotham City.

Blackfire claims to be over a hundred years old, a Native American shaman who was entombed alive after being found guilty of killing a tribal chief and committing heresy.

He claims the secret to his eternal youth is bathing in buckets of human blood, and he uses his charm and powers of manipulation to brainwash an army of devout followers to provide victims for his sacrifices.

THE LINE OF DUTY

FIRST AVAILABLE: Chapter 1

MAIN OBJECTIVE: Locate and Rescue Missing Members of Station 17 Fire Crew

LOCATION: Bleake Island (6), Miagani Island (4), Founders' Island (6)

MOST WANTED VILLAIN: Unknown

REWARD: 18 Upgrade Points, 1 per Firefighter Rescued, 3 for Apprehended Suspect

During Chapter 1, after locking up Poison Ivy, Aaron Cash mentions a missing crew of firefighters. Fifteen members are scattered throughout the city and each one is tied up and protected by a group of hostiles of increasing difficulty. Once the pack of enemies has been taken care of, free the hostage. Each has something to add to the investigation into who is responsible. As each is released, getting close to the next firefighter's location places him on the map and gives an Intel on the Mission Select screen. Only three are available during Chapter 1. Two more are found in Chapter 3. The rest are available as you progress through the fifth chapter. After all 15 are safe at GCPD, the suspect can be apprehended and brought in to the lockup.

1 FIREFIGHTER #1: LEARY-WOOD

LOCATION: Bleake Island - Dixon Dock West

LOCATED: Chapter 1

The first missing firefighter is located at Dixon Dock West in the security office located above the gate. Grapple to the roof and target a hostile through the skylight. If you drove to the location and with the right angle, a Batmobile Assisted Takedown can be performed. Only a few thugs are present inside, so this is a quick fight.

2 FIREFIGHTER #2: ADAMSON

LOCATION: Bleake Island - Chinatown

LOCATED: Chapter 1

Just northeast of the bridge to ACE Chemicals, this hostage is held just past the pier. They are mostly under cover so it is hard to get the jump on them from above. Only a handful of plain thugs guard this firefighter.

3 FIREFIGHTER #3: SCOTT

LOCATION: Founders' Island – Ryker Heights

LOCATED: Chapter 3

In far north Ryker Heights, on the pier, a hostage is held under tight security. A sniper takes aim from the lighthouse. Make him your first victim. A Detective Mode Jammer keeps Batman from getting a good look at the predator zone. He patrols near the trade house on the south side. Make him the second target. Use the beams and floor grates to finish off the other thugs.

4 FIREFIGHTER #4: WYATT

LOCATION: Bleake Island – The Caldron

LOCATED: Chapter 3

In between the lighthouse and Falcone Shipping, this firefighter is held amongst the cranes. Only three armed thugs stand over the guy, but more patrol nearby. This hostage requires predatory skills to free. Stalk the hostiles from the crane and shack rooftop.

5 FIREFIGHTER #5: NORMAN

LOCATION: Bleake Island – The Cauldron

LOCATED: Chapter 3

A firefighter is held northeast of Falcone Shipping, next to the water. Drop onto the line that runs between the building and light post. From there, drop in on the group of thugs. Try to line up an Environment Takedown on the brute, using the overhead light.

6 FIREFIGHTER #6: ASHLEY

LOCATION: Bleake Island – Chinatown

LOCATED: Chapter 3

The thugs have this firefighter tied up on a terrace in Chinatown. Grapple to the rooftop that overlooks the location and start the brawl with a Fear Multi-Takedown, targeting the armed hostiles. Watch out for the guys with knives. Avoid their attacks with a Blade Dodge.

7 FIREFIGHTER #7: CANNON

LOCATION: Bleake Island - Chinatown

LOCATED: Chapter 5

Just across the water from Lady of Gotham island this firefighter is held in southern Chinatown—across the street from the Clock Tower. Strike from the awning above with a Fear Multi-Takedown. Use the Remote Electrical Charge on the thugs with Stun Sticks.

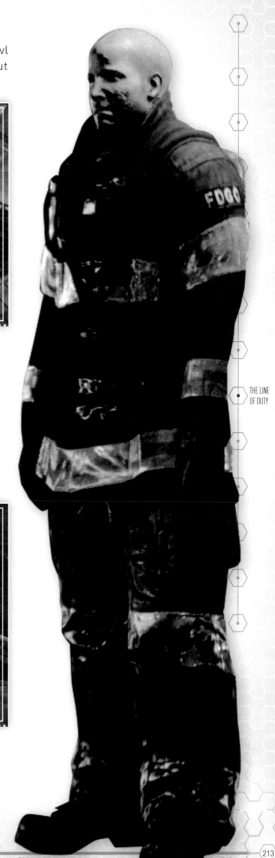

THE LINE
OF DUTY

8 FIREFIGHTER #8: GREEN

LOCATION: Miagani Island – Mercy Bridge

LOCATED: Chapter 3

On the east side of Mercy Bridge, seven armed thugs hold a firefighter at gunpoint. It is possible to get in a Fear Multi-Takedown from the ledge above, but you must be quick with the remaining enemies or grapple away.

9 FIREFIGHTER #9: HILL

LOCATION: Miagani Island – Kingston

LOCATED: Chapter 3

A group of thugs guard this firefighter next to the Gotham Herald building. These normal hostiles do not pose much of a threat for Batman.

10 FIREFIGHTER #10: RICHARDSON

LOCATION: Miagani Island - Kingston

LOCATED: Chapter 3

On the north side of the Grand Avenue Station, six Gun Turrets and four Thugs guard a firefighter. Find the switch on the wall, south of their location. Use the Remote Hacking Device to open it up and then drive the Batmobile inside. Use its firepower to eliminate the automated guns and hostiles before freeing the hostage.

THE LINE
OF DUTY

11 FIREFIGHTER #11: DANIELL

LOCATION: Miagani Island – Wayne Tower, southeast corner

LOCATED: Chapter 3

On the southeast side of Wayne Tower, nine armed thugs guard the eleventh firefighter. Equip the Disruptor and sabotage the three furthest guns. Drop a Smoke Pellet in the middle of the near group and Drop Attack one of the enemies. Continue with a Fear Multi-Takedown to thin out the crowd, being sure to target those with functional weapons. Quickly take care of the rest of the pack.

12 FIREFIGHTER #12: BLISS

LOCATION: Founders' Island – outside Wayne International Plaza, north side

LOCATED: Chapter 3

On the north side of Wayne International Plaza, eight thugs and two brutes watch over the hostage. Drop in on them from above and take them down. No real challenge here.

13 FIREFIGHTER #13: TAYLOR

LOCATION: Founders' Island – Port Adams

LOCATED: Chapter 3

A firefighter is being held hostage in a control room in the middle of Port Adams. Eight armed hostiles guard him, two inside and six patrolling around the exterior. Take them down one-by-one with Batman's predatory abilities.

14 FIREFIGHTER #14: WILSON

LOCATION: Founders' Island - Ryker Heights

LOCATED: Chapter 3

At the Urbarail Station in Ryker Heights, a group of eleven thugs and three brutes holds another firefighter. Scope out the scene from the girders above and then drop in with a Fear Multi-Takedown. Use the Cape Stun on the brutes, followed up with Beat Downs to finish them off.

15 FIREFIGHTER #15: LOZAR

LOCATION: Founders' Island – Ryker Heights, lower tier

LOCATED: Chapter 5

Drive to the old, lower level of Ryker Heights and find Killinger's. Spot a Winch Anchor Point to the northwest on the side of a building. Pull down the wall with the Batmobile's Power Winch and grapple inside. A big group of thugs protects a firefighter in the next room. Swing across to the vantage point to get a better view. Hit the two-armed hostiles with the Disruptor and then start things out with a Fear Multi-Takedown. Finish off the group and free the hostage.

16 MOST WANTED: CHIEF UNDERHILL

LOCATION: Founders' Island - Ryker Heights

LOCATED: Chapter 5, after saving all other Firefighters

Chief Underhill is being held in Ryker Heights on the top floor of the City Vision building. Grapple to a high vantage point and scope out the sixteen-armed hostiles. Use all of the predator skills you've learned up to this point to take down the enemies. The last three guys guard the Chief. Move toward their location and either take them out with a Fear Multi-Takedown or sabotage their weapons and eliminate them with melee attacks.

THE LINE
OF DUTY

CHIEF UNDERHILL

PROFILE

REAL NAME	Raymond Underhill
OCCUPATION	Fire Chief
BASED IN	Gotham City
EYE COLOR	Brown
HAIR COLOR	Black
HEIGHT	6 Ft.
WEIGHT	190 Lbs
FIRST APPEARANCE	*Batman: Arkham Knight* [June, 2015]

ATTRIBUTES

-Extensive knowledge of fire protection
-Driven to help others

Born and raised in Gotham City, Ray Underhill's life began tragically when his mother died in childbirth. It was then left to his father, a highly decorated firefighter and Station 17 Fire Chief, to care for him.

The firehouse became Ray's home and the firefighters who worked there his family. It was a special bond that drove Ray to one day succeed his father as the station chief and become a well-respected firefighter in his own right.

Post Arkham City, facing cutbacks and redundancies, Ray was determined to do whatever he could to protect his family and the station he still calls home.

OCCUPY GOTHAM

FIRST AVAILABLE: Chapter 3, before accessing Stagg's Airships

MAIN OBJECTIVE: Neutralize the militia watchtowers controlling the skies of Gotham

LOCATION: Bleake Island (4), Miagani Island (8), Founders' Island (9)

MOST WANTED VILLAIN: Unknown

REWARD: 21 Upgrade Points, 1 per watchtower

At the end of Chapter 3, the militia set up watchtowers all around the three islands. Gun Emplacements have been placed around the perimeter, while soldiers guard a central Command Console. To take down the watchtower, you must sneak past the automated weapons, eliminate the enemies, and destroy the command point. Each one scores a WayneTech Upgrade Point, with 21 towers in all.

This section covers all 21 towers with location, type of challenge, and a paragraph about what to expect at each.

A WATCHTOWER A

LOCATION: Founders' Island - Ryker Heights, next to Stagg's Airship Alpha

TYPE OF CHALLENGE: Predator

The first watchtower must be completed at the end of Chapter 3 in order to access Stagg's Airships. A Sentry Gun hangs on the outside and five armed soldiers patrol below. One hostile operates a Boa Sentry Drone while another holds a device that can track Batman's Detective Mode.

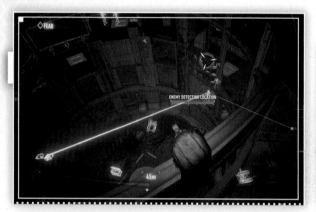

B WATCHTOWER B

LOCATION: Bleake Island – Chinatown, west of Urbarail Station

TYPE OF CHALLENGE: Puzzle

Only two-unarmed thugs man this indoor tower, while two Watchtower Gun Emplacements protect the exterior. The men stand behind a window, accessible from the waterside. Grapple up to the Urbarail track and blind the nearest gun turret. Glide toward the enemies and dive kick the second window. Finish the two guys off before destroying the command point. You can hack the security panel to open the gate and exit toward the street.

C WATCHTOWER C

LOCATION: Bleake Island – The Cauldron, southwest of traffic circle

TYPE OF CHALLENGE: Predator

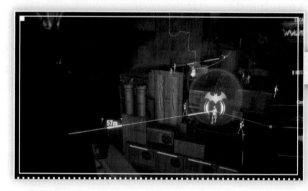

On a rooftop, southwest of the Chinatown traffic circle, seven armed-soldiers and a medic man a watchtower. Two of them operate Boa Sentry Drones. Grapple to a high point on the south side as Sentry Guns hang from the north tower. Though they do point away from the action. Work your way around the zone, taking each guy down with a Silent Takedown. Get a group together and eliminate them with a Fear Multi-Takedown, though this does attract attention.

D WATCHTOWER D

LOCATION: Bleake Island - The Cauldron, opposite police station

TYPE OF CHALLENGE: Combat

A watchtower is stationed opposite the police station, above the gas station. Two brutes and seven thugs patrol the rooftop. Three gun emplacements hang from the tower above. Equip the Disruptor and sabotage the two-armed hostiles' guns. Switch to the Remote Hacking Device and blind the sentry gun directly above the enemies. This gives you sixty seconds to drop in and take them all down. Keep an eye on the timer. If it gets low, hit it again or grapple away.

E WATCHTOWER E

LOCATION: Bleake Island - The Cauldron, roof of Sionis Industries

TYPE OF CHALLENGE: Predator

Five hostiles, including a Boa Drone Operator and Minigunner, occupy the rooftop of Sionis Industries. Save the big guy for last while picking apart the other soldiers with your predatory skills. Strike from the upper roofs and high wire with deadly Silent Takedowns. Be careful relying too much on Detective Mode. Two of these guys wear Stealth Suits, which do not highlight when using Detective Mode.

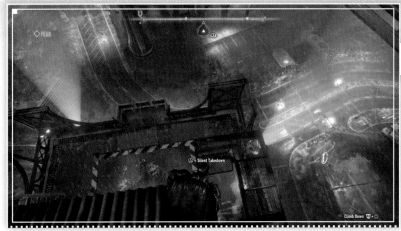

F WATCHTOWER F

LOCATION: Miagani Island - Kingston, roof of Penguin's first Weapons Cache

TYPE OF CHALLENGE: Predator

This watchtower has been set up north of the Gotham smokestack, near Mercy Bridge. A minigunner joins eight-armed soldiers, including a Detective Mode Jammer. This is a sizeable predator zone, with plenty of ways to take down the enemy. Start out by finding the guy with the jammer and taking him down. Continue to eliminate the soldiers while saving the minigunner for last. Once they have all been defeated, enter the central room and destroy the Command Console.

G WATCHTOWER G

LOCATION: Miagani Island - Kingston, roof of Bank of Gotham

TYPE OF CHALLENGE: Combat

The Bank of Gotham rooftop has been taken over by the militia. Two Gun Emplacements surround the northeast corner, leaving plenty of space to glide in untouched. Eight soldiers, two combat experts, a medic, and brute present a challenging combat scenario. One is armed, plus there are three Weapon Crates around the outside. Sabotage the weapons crates and disable the armed foe's gun. This makes the brawl a bit easier. Take care of the medic early on and watch out for the brute.

OCCUPY
GOTHAM

H WATCHTOWER H

LOCATION: Miagani Island - Kingston, north of Wayne Tower

TYPE OF CHALLENGE: Puzzle

East of the Grand Avenue Station, two towers are separated by a walkway, which holds the Command Console for this watchtower. Four Gun Emplacements surround the location, two facing out and two covering the walkway. The combatants are unarmed, but the two turrets eat Batman alive if you take them on directly. Grapple to the east tower to find another console. Destroy it with Explosive Gel to shut down the two automated guns. Now you can drop down and neutralize the soldiers, making the medic a priority.

I WATCHTOWER I

LOCATION: Miagani Island - Kingston, apartment building east of the hospital

TYPE OF CHALLENGE: Predator

East of the hospital, a watchtower has been set up atop an apartment building. Three Gun Emplacements protect the predator zone. Two face west away from the action, while the third overlooks the Command Console. Only five soldiers occupy the tower, but watch out for the mines that have been placed throughout. Perform Silent Takedowns on the western hostiles first and then lure the others to that side, so you can also eliminate them away from the watchful gaze of the turret. Once the soldiers are out of the way, blind the automated weapon and destroy the console.

J WATCHTOWER J

LOCATION: Miagani Island - Kingston, north of Grand Avenue intersection

TYPE OF CHALLENGE: Puzzle

Two Gun Turrets surround a Command Console atop a walkway, just north of the Grand Avenue intersection. Grapple to the middle of the walkway. Destroy the two guns and then the console.

K WATCHTOWER K

LOCATION: Miagani Island – Bristol, roof of hospital

TYPE OF CHALLENGE: Combat

A large pack of combatants have taken over the rooftop of the Elliot Memorial Hospital. The west tower is surrounded by Gun Emplacements, inside and out. Blind one on the outside and grapple to the top to find a console. Blow it up with Explosive Gel to eliminate the two that overlook the hostiles below. Eight soldiers, four combat experts, and two brutes surround the Command Console. Without being spotted, glide down to the tower on the right and approach the open corner on the left. Start the brawl with a Fear Multi-Takedown. Save the Environment Takedowns for the two brutes and finish off the squad.

L WATCHTOWER L

LOCATION: Miagani Island – Bristol, Botanical Gardens

TYPE OF CHALLENGE: Predator

A watchtower has been placed at Miagani Botanical Gardens with a Gun Emplacement hung at each corner. Five soldiers patrol the lower level, including a Boa Sentry Drone operator, who stands near the Command Console. This guy is an easy Silent Takedown from above. Continue to knockout the rest of the hostiles before destroying the console.

MIAGANI
BOTANICAL GARDENS

M WATCHTOWER M

LOCATION: Miagani Island – Bristol, east of Salvation Bridge

TYPE OF CHALLENGE: Combat

This rooftop overlooks Salvation Bridge on the northwest side of Bristol. Gun Emplacements protect from anything approaching from the north as well as from the southwest. Either approach from the southeast or use the Remote Hacking Device to blind one of the turrets. If you glide in from the Lady of Gotham statue, you avoid them altogether. Only five soldiers and a brute man this tower. Save the Environment Takedown for the brute if possible.

OCCUPY
GOTHAM

N WATCHTOWER N

LOCATION: Founders' Island – Drescher, next to Perdition Bridge

TYPE OF CHALLENGE: Combat

Only one of the six soldiers atop this abandoned building, overlooking Perdition Bridge, is armed. A Sentry Gun protects the north side, so make your entrance from the south. Hang from the side undetected and you can start the fight with a Ledge Takedown.

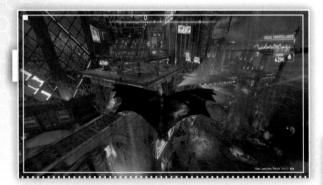

O WATCHTOWER O

LOCATION: Founders' Island – Drescher, docks north of Penitence Bridge

TYPE OF CHALLENGE: Combat

North of Penitence Bridge, a watchtower stands guard on a dock, across the street from the churchyard. Land on the rooftop and examine the seven-unarmed soldiers and two medics below. Start things out with a Fear Multi-Takedown to thin out their numbers and continue to finish them off. Target the medics early on to avoid their healing ability.

P WATCHTOWER P

LOCATION: Founders' Island – Ryker Heights, roof of Cale Anderson building

TYPE OF CHALLENGE: Predator

The militia has established a watchtower on the top of the Cale Anderson Building in Ryker Heights. Grapple to the girders to survey the predator zone. Four minigunners, two medics, and two soldiers in stealth suits occupy the area. This requires predatory skills to clear them out, but combat must be used to take down the big minigunners. Avoid the bigger foes at first, while eliminating the other four. Then, wait for each minigunner to be alone and take him down with counters and a Beat Down. Be careful, as you are extremely vulnerable during the takedown. Flee the area if you get in trouble.

Q WATCHTOWER Q

LOCATION: Founders' Island – Otisburg, south of Penitence Bridge

TYPE OF CHALLENGE: Combat

The next watchtower overlooks Penitence Bridge from the south side. Turrets only protect the southeast side, so approach from the north or west. Only six unarmed combatants guard the wide-open rooftop. Start out with a Glide Kick and finish the pack off. Watch out for the combat experts and their sword attacks.

R WATCHTOWER R

LOCATION: Founders' Island – Otisburg, roof of GothCorp

TYPE OF CHALLENGE: Predator

West of the Bank of Gotham is the GothCorp building, where the militia have set up a watchtower. Seven armed soldiers, including one with a Detective Mode Scanner and a medic, man the rooftop. Gun emplacements guard the south side of the building. Quietly walk between the obstructions or stalk from above, while eliminating the enemy with Silent Takedowns. Once the roof is clear, destroy the command point, located in the northeast corner.

S WATCHTOWER S

LOCATION: Founders' Island – Otisburg, east of Port Adams

TYPE OF CHALLENGE: Puzzle

A militia watchtower has been deployed high atop a building, just east of Port Adams. Two Gun Emplacements protect the northeast side. Only three-armed soldiers are found inside, one operates a Boa Sentry Drone. Use the Remote Hacking Device on the operator to download the control codes and then press Strike to sick it on the hostiles.

T WATCHTOWER T

LOCATION: Founders' Island – Ryker Heights, south of Wayne International Plaza

TYPE OF CHALLENGE: Combat

The militia has taken a high position just south of Wayne International Plaza, with seven soldiers and a brute. Grapple to the crane above to get a good view of the soldiers. Gun Emplacements protect the east and west sides, so either blind one or approach from another direction. Perform a Beat Down on the brute while fending off the thugs. Finish them off before destroying the command point.

U WATCHTOWER U

LOCATION: Founders' Island – Otisburg, abandoned building west of Fire Station

TYPE OF CHALLENGE: Combat

A low watchtower has been spotted in Otisburg atop an abandoned building west of the Fire Station. A Gun Emplacement guards the area from the backside of the station. Three soldiers, two combat experts, and three medics man the tower. Grapple to the building across the street and blind the turret. Quickly Glide Kick one of the hostiles and continue to pummel the group into submission, targeting the medics early on in the fight.

OCCUPY GOTHAM

APPREHEND THE MOST WANTED

Once these watchtowers are destroyed, along with the explosive devices and checkpoints, Batman can confront the new leader of the militia at Grand Avenue in order to take him down and apprehend him. Refer to the Campaign for Disarmament walkthrough for full details.

OWN THE ROADS

FIRST AVAILABLE: Chapter 7

MAIN OBJECTIVE: Wipe out the militia checkpoints deployed around the city

LOCATION: Bleake Island (4), Miagani Island (8), Founders' Island (8)

MOST WANTED VILLAIN: Unknown

REWARD: 20 Upgrade Points, 1 per Checkpoint

Beginning in Chapter 7, checkpoints are deployed across the city. Whereas the watchtowers are placed at primarily high locations, such as rooftops, these posts are located down on the road for the most part. Temporary walls surround a group of soldiers and possibly Checkpoint Drones. These must be disposed of through combat, predatory means, or by solving a puzzle, with the Batmobile out of reach for most of them. Once the soldiers have been taken care of, use Detective Mode to find the commander's body, interact with him to destroy his checkpoint controller—dropping the surrounding walls.

This section covers all 20 checkpoints with location, type of challenge, and what to expect at each.

A CHECKPOINT A

LOCATION: Bleake Island – Chinatown, south of Scarecrow's safe house

TYPE OF CHALLENGE: Puzzle

In Chinatown, approach Scarecrow's safe house from the south side. Hop over the wall to find three Sentry Guns protecting the checkpoint commander. Equip the Remote Hacking Device and blind one of the outside guns. Quietly move to the center turret, throw down a Smoke Pellet, and destroy it. Take out the functional one next before eliminating the third. Sneak up on the commander and perform a Silent Takedown.

B CHECKPOINT B

LOCATION: Bleake Island – Chinatown, next to Perdition Bridge

TYPE OF CHALLENGE: Puzzle

A militia checkpoint has been deployed on the Bleake Island side of Perdition Bridge. Hop over the wall and take out the soldiers and brute. Use the Remote Hacking Device to toggle the security access panel off. This opens an access on the right side of the building. Grapple to the ledge, but do not immediately climb up. Instead, perform a Ledge Takedown on the soldier before finishing off the Commander further inside.

C CHECKPOINT C

LOCATION: Bleake Island – Chinatown, next to Tattoo Parlor

TYPE OF CHALLENGE: Combat

Find a checkpoint in Chinatown, north of the Clock Tower. Two Sentry Guns protect the north wall, but a destructible divider keeps their fire away from the hostiles. Sixteen combatants occupy the area inside the walls, including two medics, two brutes, two Combat Experts, and two with guns. There are a few ways to tackle this challenge. Drive the Batmobile around, destroy the automated weapons, and knock out the guys inside. You can also drop behind the turrets from the wire above and disable them. Soldiers climb over the divider to get to you. Take them out as they do so before finishing off the others inside. Watch out for enemies charged by one of the medics. Knock them back with the Remote Electrical Charge.

RANELAGH FERRY TERMINAL

D CHECKPOINT D

LOCATION: Bleake Island – Chinatown, northeast of hospital

TYPE OF CHALLENGE: Combat

Placed on the edge of the water, the militia occupy a checkpoint northeast of the hospital. Five soldiers and a brute do not pose much of a threat. Start out with a Glide Kick from above and finish off the crew.

E CHECKPOINT E

LOCATION: Miagani Island – Kingston, west of Mercy Bridge

TYPE OF CHALLENGE: Combat

A checkpoint has been set up near the docks, west of Mercy Bridge in Kingston. Seven-unarmed soldiers and a brute man the location. Approach from the west side, gliding down to the side wall. If undetected, perform a Fear Multi-Takedown on the hostiles or grapple to the girder to the south and start from there. Finish off the squad and then destroy the controller.

F CHECKPOINT F

LOCATION: Miagani Island – Kingston, Ranelagh Ferry Terminal

TYPE OF CHALLENGE: Puzzle

At the Ranelagh Ferry Terminal, two Checkpoint Drones guard the main entrance along with five-armed soldiers. A direct attack is suicide, as the cannons would tear Batman apart. Instead, drive up the steps on the northwest side and peek over the wall. Take out the guns with the Heavy Cannon and the soldiers with the Riot Suppressor. Destroy the crates to reveal hiding hostiles.

G CHECKPOINT G

LOCATION: Miagani Island – Bristol, Elliot Memorial Hospital

TYPE OF CHALLENGE: Combat

Underneath the Elliot Memorial Hospital, next to the upper road, the militia has set up a checkpoint with eight-unarmed soldiers and two brutes. Hop onto the north wall and get things started with a Silent or Fear Multi-Takedown. Finish off the squad before taking care of the checkpoint walls.

OWN THE ROADS

H CHECKPOINT H

LOCATION: Miagani Island – Bristol, Urbarail Station

TYPE OF CHALLENGE: Batmobile

The Urbarail Station entrance in Bristol has been taken over by a militia checkpoint. Fortunately, their walls have not gone up yet. Hop into the Batmobile and drive to the southwest or northeast side. Watch out for the Shock Mines and pick off the soldiers who occupy the station. Hop out and finish off any remaining hostiles before destroying the commander's controller.

I CHECKPOINT I

LOCATION: Miagani Island – Bristol, Botanical Gardens

TYPE OF CHALLENGE: Puzzle

Underneath Miagani Botanical Gardens, the militia has closed off the area with a large checkpoint. Eight-armed soldiers surround two Checkpoint Drones. These guns take Batman out immediately if taken on directly. Instead, call in the Batmobile and drive onto the raised road to the northeast. From there, take out the turrets with your Heavy Cannon along with any hostiles you can reach. Grapple onto the far wall and disable three of the armed soldiers. If undetected, sneak up on the group and hit them with a Fear Multi-Takedown.

J CHECKPOINT J

LOCATION: Miagani Island – Kingston, Grand Avenue intersection

TYPE OF CHALLENGE: Combat

Located on the northeast corner of the Grand Avenue intersection, a checkpoint is manned by five soldiers and two medics. Land on the overhang just above and perform a Fear Multi-Takedown on the hostiles below, making the medics a high priority.

K CHECKPOINT K

LOCATION: Miagani Island – Bristol, west of south bridge

TYPE OF CHALLENGE: Predator

A checkpoint has been placed just west of the south bridge. Six-armed soldiers, including a Boa Sentry Drone operator, occupy this predator zone around the west and south sides of the building. Start out on the south side and take the two loners out with Silent Takedowns. Grapple to a wall on the west side and look over the other four hostiles. Eliminate them quietly one at a time or in a flurry with a Fear-Multi Takedown.

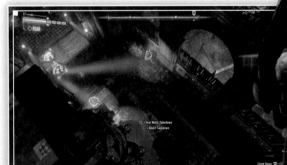

L CHECKPOINT L

LOCATION: Founders' Island – Ryker Heights, base of City Vision Construction building

TYPE OF CHALLENGE: Batmobile Puzzle

Travel to a checkpoint at the base of the City Vision building in north-central Ryker Heights. Inside, a Checkpoint Drone accompanies a group of armed-soldiers. Park the Batmobile south of the drone, exit the vehicle, and run around to the north side. Grapple onto the left side of the wall. Use the Remote Hacking Device on the security access panel in the far corner to allow the Batmobile to destroy the drone. Use the Riot Suppressor on the soldiers before searching for the commander.

M CHECKPOINT M

LOCATION: Founders' Island – Drescher, east of City Vision Construction

TYPE OF CHALLENGE: Combat

From Perdition Bridge, locate the checkpoint on the upper road just in front of the City Vision building. Glide Kick one of the combatants inside the walls and continue to pummel the four soldiers and four combat experts. Be cautious around the Stun Sticks, hitting them with the Remote Electrical Charge when they attack.

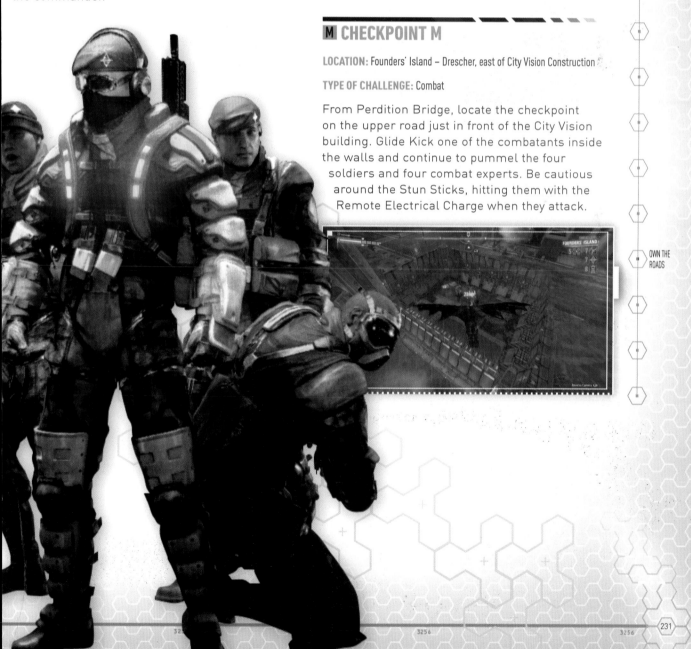

OWN THE ROADS

231

N CHECKPOINT N

LOCATION: Founders' Founders' Island – Drescher,

TYPE OF CHALLENGE: Batmobile Puzzle

Drive to Ryker Heights on Founders' Island and descend to the lower tier. A checkpoint has been deployed underneath the building. From the northwest side, find the Anchor Point on the temporary wall and pull it down with the Power Winch. Drive inside and eliminate all of the Sentry Guns and soldiers. Hop out, find the commander, and destroy his controller.

O CHECKPOINT O

LOCATION: Founders' Island – Drescher, southeast of Perdition Bridge

TYPE OF CHALLENGE: Combat

Southeast of Perdition Bridge, a checkpoint has been deployed next to a raised, partial bridge. This road allows access to Checkpoint T. From above, target one of the hostiles inside the small, walled-off area and perform a Glide Kick to get the brawl started. Finish off the seven soldiers and brute, paying close attention to the two armed men.

P CHECKPOINT P

LOCATION: Founders' Island – Ryker Heights, south of Wayne International Plaza

TYPE OF CHALLENGE: Predator

A deadly checkpoint is situated in between some buildings, southeast of the Stock Exchange. Six Checkpoint Drones and a few armed soldiers occupy the post. Drive the Batmobile just outside the north wall, eject from the cockpit, and grapple to the power cable that spans across the checkpoint. Toggle the remote switch on the east wall with the hacking device to open the way for your vehicle. Equip the remote and use the Heavy Cannon to destroy the drones. Drop inside and eliminate any stragglers before searching for the commander.

Q CHECKPOINT Q

LOCATION: Founders' Island – Otisburg, northeast at T-intersection

TYPE OF CHALLENGE: Combat

Glide to northeast Otisburg and spot the checkpoint that sits next to a pillar for the raised track. Five-armed soldiers occupy the north side of the area. Disable the furthest three weapons from the north wall. Then, drop in with a Fear Multi-Takedown to take care of the pack.

R CHECKPOINT R

LOCATION: Founders' Island – Otisburg, next to Amertek building

TYPE OF CHALLENGE: Combat

A relatively small checkpoint operates at the base of the Amertek building in eastern Otisburg. Eject from the Batmobile and grapple onto the wall. If undetected, perform a Fear Multi-Takedown to get the brawl started. Finish off the squad of nine soldiers and a brute before destroying the commander's controller.

S CHECKPOINT S

LOCATION: Founders' Island – Otisburg, south of Penitence Bridge

TYPE OF CHALLENGE: Combat

Situated on the waterfront, southwest of Penitence Bridge, a checkpoint is manned by just a handful of soldiers, though two do carry firearms. From atop the northern rooftop, sabotage the ballistic weapons before swooping in for a Glide Kick. Be careful around the Stun Sticks and finish the crew off.

T CHECKPOINT T

LOCATION: Bleake Island – Chinatown, southwest of the Clock Tower

TYPE OF CHALLENGE: Puzzle

Checkpoint O must be completed before trying this one.

Two Checkpoint Drones join a group of armed soldiers on the waterfront, southwest of the Clock Tower. The location is well protected, except from a higher spot across the water on Founders' Island. After removing Checkpoint O, lower the partial bridge by firing the Power Winch at the anchor point and pulling back. This snaps the cable, bringing the ramp down. Drive to the other end and take out the cannons and soldiers across the water. Get a running start at the ramp and hit the Afterburner to jump inside the walls. Eliminate any stragglers before finding the commander and destroying his controller.

APPREHEND THE MOST WANTED

Once these checkpoints are destroyed, along with the explosive devices and watchtowers, Batman can confront the new leader of the militia at the Grand Avenue intersection to take him down and apprehend him. Refer to the Campaign for Disarmament walkthrough for full details.

OWN THE ROADS

FIRST AVAILABLE: Chapter 1

MAIN OBJECTIVE: Find and stop the killer displaying bodies throughout Gotham

LOCATION: Bleake Island (2), Miagani Island (2), Founders' Island (3)

MOST WANTED VILLAIN: Unknown

REWARD: 9 Upgrade Points, 1 per Victim, 3 for Apprehending Most Wanted

Pretty Dolls Parlor (Lower Tier)

GCPD

N

During Chapter 1, after locking up Poison Ivy, Aaron Cash mentions an open case with a posed mutilated body found hanging on Merchant Bridge. There are six of these victims in all that must be found and investigated. As the player gets close to a victim, opera music can be heard. Use this clue to find each body. As you progress through the story, Intel is introduced at certain points if bodies haven't been found.

Approach and inspect the body. Since the subject's DNA has been corrupted, the Deep Tissue Scanner must be used to identify the victim. Press the Detective Mode button to use the device. Move the circle around to look for a unique identifier. Once found, hold the Run button to scan it in. Press Aim Gadget and Crouch to switch between the Skin, Bone, and Muscle layers. The player must find one identifier at each level to successfully identify the person.

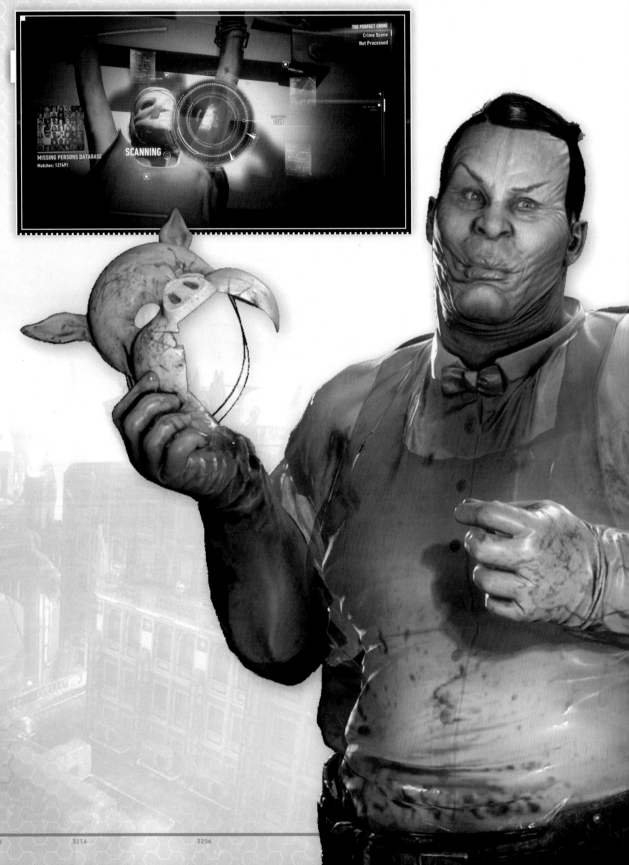

The following table lists the location of the victim along with where to find each unique identifier. Directions are from the victim's view; therefore a left body part is on the player's right.

THE VICTIMS

MAP	LOCATION	VICTIM	SKIN	MUSCLE	BONE
1	Bleake Island: Merchant Bridge	Anthony Lund	Left Ear	Right Abdomen	Left Hip
2	Bleake Island: Gotham Herald building, northwest side	Franklin Accardo	Left Upper Arm	Chest	Left Knee
3	Miagani Island: Heavenly Hotel – east side of roof	Robert Kincaid	Chest	Right Upper Arm	Toes on Left Foot
4	Miagani Island: southeast side of building next to Salvation Bridge	Lisa Mendes	Left Torso	Right Eye	Right Upper Arm
5	Founders' Island: south of Perdition Bridge	Ella Montgomery	Right Thigh	Right Abdomen	Right Skull
6	Founders' Island: north Ryker's Height near docks	Alison Wears	Left Thigh	Left Shoulder	Left Pinky

THE PERFECT
CRIME

With the identities of all six victims, Batman and Alfred figure out that the suspect is located at Pretty Dolls Parlor in Ryker Heights. This small shop can be found on Founders' Island in the underground level.

Enter the parlor and proceed through the unlocked door in the back, as that familiar opera music can be heard. Bust through the soft wood paneling and descend the steps to find Professor Pyg in a circular, surgery room operating on one of his "Dollotrons." When his subject attacks, counter to knock him out. He doesn't stay down though. This time, knock him off his feet and follow it up with a Ground Takedown.

Five of these Dollotrons attack next. Knock them all out, finishing them off with Ground Takedowns. Combo Takedowns, Environmental Takedowns, and Beatdowns also make this fight much easier. Remember that you are vulnerable during this maneuver, so be sure you have enough time to perform the move. An angry Pyg jumps into the room at this point. He throws a series of butcher knives your way as more of his subjects enter the room. Counter each blade to damage the boss. Continue to fight the gowned goons, keeping an eye on the professor. Counter his knife throws to hurt him again.

Whenever a successful counter hits Pyg, he is stunned for a short while. Move in and perform an Environment Takedown with the surgery table. Before picking him up, you must rescue the other victims who are held in suspended cages above. Find the yellow fuse box on the wall and interact with it to bring them down. Pick up the professor to place him in the back of the Batmobile and drive him to GCPD Lockup to earn the last three upgrade points.

PROFESSOR PYG

PROFILE

REAL NAME	Lazlo Valentin
OCCUPATION	Circus Boss
BASED IN	Circus of Strange
EYE COLOR	Blue
HAIR COLOR	Black
HEIGHT	6 Ft. 1 In.
WEIGHT	220 Lbs
FIRST APPEARANCE	*Batman* #666 [July, 2007]

ATTRIBUTES

- Gifted scientist and chemist
- Obsessive perfectionist
- Skilled knife-thrower
- Amateur opera singer

Lazlo Valentin was a gifted scientist who suffered a schizophrenic break causing him to develop a deranged new persona named Professor Pyg.

Pyg formed the Circus of Strange and began touring the country, leaving a string of mysterious missing persons cases in his wake.

An obsessive perfectionist, Pyg uses identity-destroying drugs and invasive surgery on his victims to create genderless lobotomized humans known as Dollotrons.

THE PERFECT
CRIME

RIDDLER'S REVENGE

FIRST AVAILABLE: Chapter 1, Orphanage accessible in Chapter 3

MAIN OBJECTIVE: Defeat Riddler and rescue Catwoman

LOCATION: Pinkney Orphanage
Caves located throughout city

MOST WANTED VILLAIN: The Riddler

REWARD: 25 Upgrade Points, 2 per challenge, 3 for completing Riddler's Revenge

Pinkney's Orphanage

During Chapter 1, after locking up Poison Ivy, Aaron Cash mentions a suspicious looking man milling around the train yard. This begins the most extensive and rewarding side mission in the game. Riddler has set up a series of puzzles for Batman, as well as collectible trophies, destructible items, and riddles to solve. To complete 100% of Riddler's Revenge, you must accomplish all of this. This section covers the six caves and orphanage puzzle rooms set up just for Batman. Riddler Trophies, destructibles, and riddles can be found in the Collectibles chapter.

In Chapter 3, after lowering Mercy Bridge, Edward Nigma announces that he has Catwoman tied up and gives Batman an ultimatum; come to Pinkney's Orphanage on the west side of Miagani Island or she dies. You must solve a mix of combat and puzzle challenges located in and out of the building to set her free. The trials held inside the orphanage require Batman and Catwoman to work together.

You must visit the orphanage as part of the main story path, but beyond that, this side mission can be done at your leisure—though Riddler won't stop pestering you. Glide and grapple over to the orphanage. Interrogate the informant at the entrance before entering the building.

242m

Edward Nigma introduces the duo to his automated combatants. These robots learn from the fight, allowing the Riddler to build better opponents for the next battle. The first challenge for Batman and Catwoman requires them to defeat ten of these fighters. The first version of the androids is easily taken care of with melee attacks and counters. Take advantage of the assistance from your partner and dispose of the metal thugs. After the skirmish, talk to your teammate.

DUAL TEAM

This bout is the first of a number of dual team fights. When teamed up with a partner, press the Switch Character button to toggle between them. A circular meter builds on the left side of the HUD to a bat symbol. Press the Switch Character button to perform a Dual Team Takedown on the current target.

After completing each cave challenge, activate a panel of lights by walking onto the nearby switch. One light is green, the rest are red. This corresponds to the layout of cases at the orphanage. Note which position is green and switch to Catwoman. Walk up to the case in that same position and interact with it to grab the key. If it is the correct one, the counter on Catwoman's collar drops by one. Otherwise the collar detonates, the kitty goes boom, and the choice must be made again. These grids differ between the normal game and New Game +.

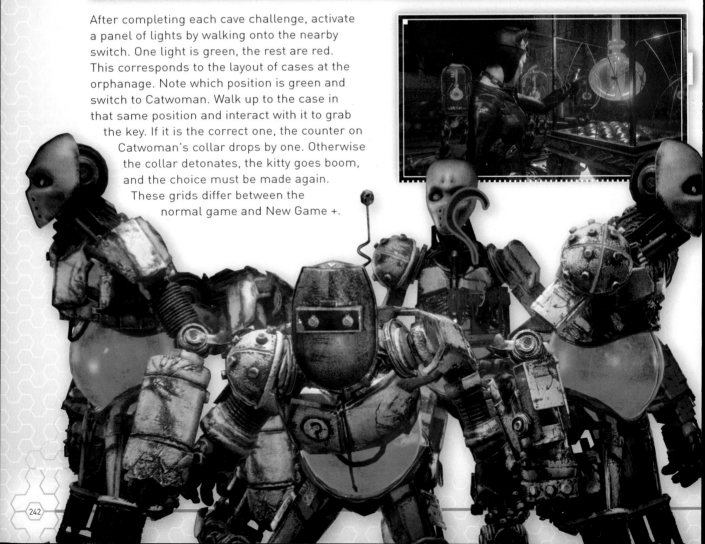

A CAVE 1: MENTAL BLOCKED

LOCATION: Bleake Island – The Cauldron, west of Falcone Shipping

REQUIREMENTS: Talk to Aaron Cash at GCPD during Chapter 1 and complete the Orphanage in Chapter 3

Head to The Cauldron and drive into the Gotham Water Company elevator with the Mental Blocked banner overhead. The Riddler begins his spiel as the player descends into the first of his caves. This challenge gives a taste of what he has in store for Batman, but his bigger plan must wait for now. As the player rolls out of the lift, a red mechanism blocks the path ahead. Batman can jump the gun on the villain by decrypting the codes or he can stay and listen to the rules, which become increasingly entertaining. Press the Immobilizer button to move the contraption out of the way.

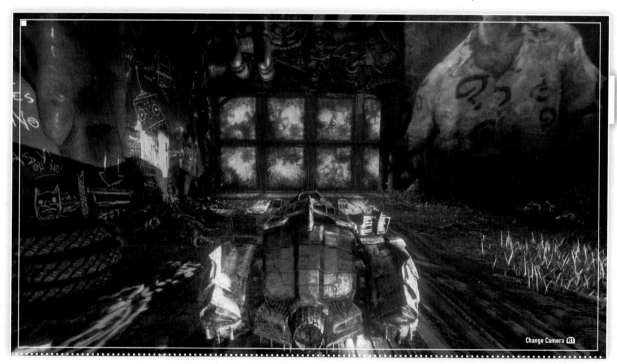

Change Camera R1

The challenge involves racing the Batmobile around a track for three, increasingly more difficult, laps. There are green and red Riddler Blockades that obstruct the road. Tapping Immobilizer toggles between the two. Press once and the red move out of the way and green enter the course. Another tap of the button brings the green into play. These obstructions increase in number as the laps progress.

Complete the first lap and the track switches to the new layout. A timer counts down from the start of each lap and if you don't cross the finish line before it expires, you must repeat that lap. You have 1:20 for the first lap, 1:10 for the second, and a minute for the final.

KEY GRID

Normal

New Game +

RIDDLER'S
REVENGE

B CAVE 2: BALANCING ACT

LOCATION: Bleake Island - Chinatown, near ACE Chemicals

REQUIREMENTS: Complete Mental Blocked

Drive toward the entrance to ACE Chemicals in Chinatown, but turn left just before committing to the bridge. Just around the corner is a garage door labeled Balancing Act. Use it to descend into Riddler's second cave. This challenge requires you to complete the following steps to power up the light board:

- Drive up the ramp, exit the Batmobile and step on the ground switch. Use the remote to drive the vehicle onto the balance board. Activate Riddler's Blockade and drive up to the next platform.

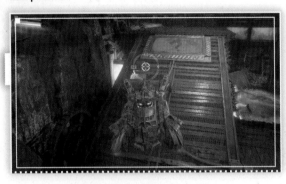

KEY GRID

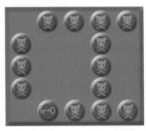

Normal

New Game +

- Press the Immobilizer to bring out the red platform and drive across. Tap the button again and cross the green.

- Drive onto the second balance board and switch the red blockades on and then the green to get the far end all the way up. Hit the Afterburner and jump across to the green platform.

- Drive around to the lift, fire the Power Winch at the switch on the right, and rev the engine—keeping the needle in the orange. This powers the board ahead.

PUZZLE ROOM 1: NUMERACY 101

LOCATION: Miagani Island – Pinkney's Orphanage

REQUIREMENTS: Complete Balancing Act

Enter Pinkney's Orphanage where you must first complete a puzzle before the next challenge. Three question marks hang on the gate ahead. Hitting each one with a Batarang turns a different portion of the big question mark on the floor. The idea is to line up the circles so it is a straight up and down question mark. Then adjust your view until the light in the mirror forms the dot. Scan to solve the riddle.

Join Catwoman and enter the door labeled Numeracy. Maneuver Batman onto the switch on your right and Catwoman to the left. Numbers from 1 to 5 are displayed on a light board in front of each character. Remember the order and switch to the other person. Toss Batarangs or crack the whip at the question marks in that order, where the left one is 1 and the right is 5. Hit them in the following order for both Batman and Catwoman:

Catwoman: 1 3 5 2 4

Batman: 3 1 4 5 2

This releases 10 more Riddler Robots. These combatants are improved fighters over the previous ones, but still not a huge challenge for the two. Have Catwoman walk over to the case against the wall and grab the third key.

RIDDLER'S REVENGE

D CAVE 3: CRUSHONATOR

LOCATION: Miagani Island – Bristol, beneath Elliot Memorial Hospital

REQUIREMENTS: Complete Numeracy 101

Drive to the hospital and find the garage labeled Crushonator underneath. If not completed yet, a militia checkpoint keeps the Batmobile out. Defeat the hostiles and then drive the vehicle into the third cave, where another racetrack has been constructed. Again, red and green Riddler Blockades move in and out with a push of the Immobilizer. This time though, they drop from the ceiling, crushing anything that gets caught underneath. Watch out for bright green obstructions that move on their own. Otherwise, it is the same idea as the first cave. Fail a lap and you must retry it again. Any successful laps remain complete. You have 1:40 for the first lap, 1:30 for the second, and 1:20 for the third.

Memorization of the course is crucial for completing this challenge, but it is possible to finish the first time with very good reactions. Keep your eyes on the course ahead, being ready to stop, hit the Afterburner, or activate the Riddler Blockades at a moment's notice.

KEY GRID

Normal

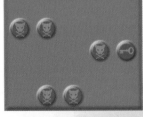

New Game +

E CAVE 4: FLIGHT SCHOOL

LOCATION: Miagani Island – Kingston, under Gotham Casino

REQUIREMENTS: Complete Crushonator

Drive to Kingston and find the Flight School garage behind the casino. Descend into the fourth cave. Three Riddler Pressure Pads must be pressed by gliding into them to complete this challenge. The trick is to get enough air to reach each one. Drive out of the elevator and eject just before hitting the railing. Glide into the button

ahead, push off, and return to the vehicle. If you fail, simply grapple to the chain above the Batmobile and try again.

The switch is around the corner to the right. Again, race toward the railing in the Batmobile and eject just before the end. Get plenty of height and glide to the right. Make a 180-degree turn and continue into the second pressure pad at the end of the corridor. Glide and grapple back to the car.

This time do the same thing to glide toward the second switch before entering a tight, deadly tunnel on the right. Keep as high as possible while avoiding the sharp, spinning blades. Turn right after the death trap and glide down to the third pressure pad. Return to the light board next to the elevator to get Catwoman another key.

KEY GRID

Normal

New Game +

RIDDLER'S REVENGE

C PUZZLE ROOM 2: INTRO TO PHYSICS

LOCATION: Miagani Island – Pinkney's Orphanage

REQUIREMENTS: Complete Flight School

Back at the orphanage, enter the door marked Intro to Physics. This challenge requires Batman and Catwoman to guide an electric charge to its destination. On the stage ahead, there are three pressure pads that control a single horizontal pipe. If Catwoman steps on the switch, it raises a little. Batman alone takes it just beyond half way. When both step on the pad the pipe goes to the top. The idea is to start the charge moving and quickly raise each pipe into the correct spot to help the charge reach the destination in the upper-left corner. Follow the steps below to complete the challenge:

- To start the charge moving, toss a Batarang at the question mark on the left and stand on the left switch.
- Move Catwoman onto the second pressure pad. After the electric charge passes Batman, move him to the third switch.

- Wait for the charge to pass Batman's location and then move him alongside Catwoman on the first pressure pad to complete the puzzle.

- After it passes Catwoman, move her with Batman on the third pad. As the charge switches back the other way, remove Batman from the switch.

An electrified floor prevents you from just grabbing the next key. Have Batman jump onto the pressure pad on the right while Catwoman goes for the key. Riddler introduces ten of his new and improved red and blue robots. Only Catwoman can attack the red while the blue must be left for Batman. Finish them off before finally grabbing the prize.

- Batman should next step on the second pressure pad. With the charge past Catwoman again, move her to the first one.

CAVE 5: DRAIN PAIN

LOCATION: Founders' Island, Otisburg, next to Divinity Church

REQUIREMENTS: Intro to Physics

Drive to Divinity Church on Founders' Island, enter the lower tier, and find the Drain Pain garage. Descend into the fifth cave to find another puzzle. There are holes around the sides of the pit ahead that must be entered to complete specific objectives. The problem is they are blocked at the moment. That is where the Batmobile comes in, as it is used to turn the pit. Follow these steps to complete the challenge:

- Fire the Power Winch at the anchor point above, turn around, and descend down the wall, next to the spinning blades. Move right to cause the wall to move right until the opening is over the hole in the far wall. You know you end up in the right spot if the Batmobile is on top of a Batmobile reserved parking symbol.

- Eject from the car and glide into the new opening. Step onto the pressure pad to lower the water one level. Hop back into the Batmobile and drive it to the right to the number 2.

- Attach the winch to the anchor point above and lower the car to just above the water. Move left until the opening is over the weakened wall and fire the Heavy Cannon to destroy it.

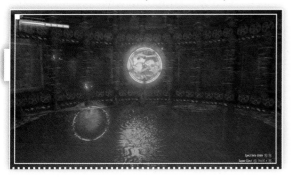

- Eject from the car and glide into the hole, being sure to clear the electrified panels just inside. Step on the pressure pad to lower the water another level. Four Riddler Robots pop up, so take them down.

- Reenter the vehicle, drive right until the spinning blades are next to you and then drive back up the wall. Find the number 3 and lower the Batmobile from the Winch Anchor Point above. This time go down three levels.

- Spin the wall until you are on top of the reserved parking, eject from the car, and glide into the third hole. Step onto the pressure pad around the corner and two Gun Turrets appear where you entered. Equip the Batmobile Remote and destroy the automated weapons.

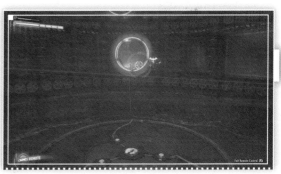

- Glide down to the pressure pad at the bottom of the pit to activate the light board high above.

KEY GRID

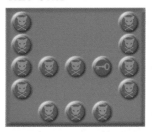

Normal

New Game +

 RIDDLER'S REVENGE

C PUZZLE ROOM 3: ADVANCED DEATHTRAPS

LOCATION: Miagani Island – Pinkney's Orphanage

REQUIREMENTS: Complete Drain Pain

Drop Down Ⓞ

The next puzzle room presents two rooms full of electrified panels and a light board on the wall ahead. Again Bruce and Selina must work together to complete the puzzle. Move Batman onto the pressure pad on the right. Have Catwoman pounce to the ceiling, climb into the adjacent room, and step on another pad.

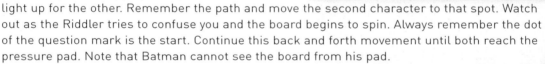

Each character has one light lit up on the board ahead, which represents the other person's first move. Step on the appropriate panel and more light up for the other. Remember the path and move the second character to that spot. Watch out as the Riddler tries to confuse you and the board begins to spin. Always remember the dot of the question mark is the start. Continue this back and forth movement until both reach the pressure pad. Note that Batman cannot see the board from his pad.

This introduces ten more Riddler Robots in red and blue. Note that a robot turns green during a Dual Team Takedown, making it vulnerable to both fighters. Grab the key to get a small step closer to freedom.

G CAVE 6: CONDAMNED

LOCATION: Miagani Island – Kingston, beneath Ranelagh Ferry Terminal

REQUIREMENTS: Complete Advanced Deathtraps

Drive to Ranelagh Ferry Terminal in Kingston and find the Condamned garage on the left side. Descend into Riddler's final cave to find another race. This challenge introduces you to new obstacles, such as the spike poles that move side to side or back and forth. Pressing Immobilizer raises and lowers them or they can be driven between. You have 1:30 for the first lap, 1:20 for the second, and 1:10 for the final lap.

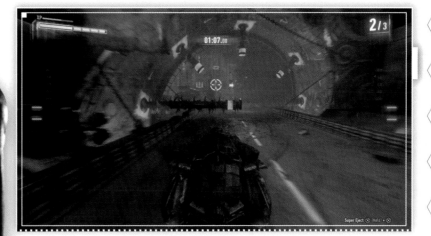

This race gets incredibly tough on the third lap as Riddler takes control of the obstacles. A few of the obstacles require you to learn the timing.

KEY GRID

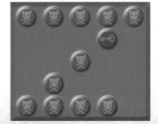

Normal

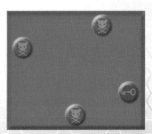

New Game +

RIDDLER'S
REVENGE

C PUZZLE ROOM 4: FINAL EXAM

LOCATION: Miagani Island – Pinkney's Orphanage

REQUIREMENTS: Complete Condamned

At the orphanage, enter the Final Exam door and move past the first room to reach the puzzle. A 5x5 grid of pressure pads lies in the middle of the floor below, but you can't just walk out to them. Instead, have Catwoman pounce to the ceiling and drop down onto the switches. Two spots are missing a pad. Generators sit at the end of each row. Fire the Remote Electrical Charge at a generator lined up with the opening to cause it to either attract or repel the row of pads in front of it. If the row is full, they do not move. A laser is fired from the ceiling at one of the pad positions. You must shift the switches around so that it lines up with the open slot. If Catwoman steps on a pressure pad, it does not move even if in the path of an attracting or repelling generator.

The first time there is only one laser, place Catwoman on a pressure pad and move the rows around with the REC. Once the laser hits an open spot, a light appears on the left wall to indicate a puzzle is complete. At that point, spinning blades sweep across the floor. To avoid them, pounce to the ceiling or watch their movements and duck under the bar. A second laser is introduced in the second and third puzzles. Work the pressure pads around until both hit open spots. The three puzzles must be solved before grabbing the final key in the first room.

There are many ways to solve these puzzles. Here is a quick solution for each one. The diagrams show the view from the left side with the laser placement and starting empty slots, assuming the following solution is used.

PUZZLE 1 (LASER AT B2)

- Catwoman on A1 and repel generator A
- Catwoman on C2 and attract generator 2

	1	2	3	4	5
A	?	?	?	?	
B	?	?※	?	?	?
C	?	?	?	?	?
D	?	?	?	?	?
E		?	?	?	?

PUZZLE 2 (LASERS AT A1 AND D3)

- Repel generator 1
- Catwoman on E2 and attract generator 2
- Catwoman on D4 and attract generator D

	1	2	3	4	5
A	?※	?	?	?	?
B	?		?	?	?
C	?	?	?	?	?
D	?	?	?※	?	?
E		?	?	?	?

PUZZLE 3 (LASERS AT C5 AND E5)

- Catwoman on B3 and repel generator 3
- Attract generator 1
- Attract generator C
- Attract generator E

	1	2	3	4	5
A		?	?	?	?
B	?	?	?	?	?
C	?	?	?	?	?※
D	?	?		?	?
E	?	?	?	?	?※

C FIGHT RIDDLER

LOCATION: Miagani Island – Pinkney's Orphanage

REQUIREMENTS: Complete Final Exam

With the caves and puzzle rooms complete, attempt to exit the orphanage. Riddler shows up in a mech and pushes Batman back inside. Red and blue Riddler Robots pop up from the floor and surround the boss. His health appears in the upper-right corner of the HUD. He fires a green laser across the battlefield, harming anything in its path. He also has the ability to switch the color of the robots, so pay close attention to the color you are fighting. It's no use attacking him directly as he is heavily shielded.

With help from Catwoman, take down the robots while avoiding Riddler's laser attack. Be sure to fight the blue with Batman and the red with Catwoman. Whenever a Dual Team Takedown is available, use it since the color doesn't matter. After the squad of robots has been exterminated, Edward puts up an electrified fence around himself. This completes the first battle. To take him on again, you must collect all of the Riddler Trophies.

C FIGHT RIDDLER PART 2

LOCATION: Miagani Island – Pinkney's Orphanage

REQUIREMENTS: Complete the first Fight with Riddler and collect all Riddler Trophies

Once you've collected all the trophies, return to Pinkney's Orphanage and use the question mark console to fight Riddler's mech again. It is just Batman this time with all blue Riddler's Robots. After a number of them have been taken down, Riddler turns some red. Fire the REC to knock the red ones back until Catwoman has a change of heart and shows up.

Take out the squad of robots and Riddler thrusts the mech's right fist into the ground. It lets off a green glow, so attack the arm with either character to damage the boss. Continue to strike him until Edward retaliates. Continue to pummel the robots, causing Riddler to punch the ground every time the room is cleared out. If the fist glows red, attack with Catwoman. If blue, attack with Batman.

Once his health has been depleted, Batman apprehends the villain. Drive him to GCPD to score the rest of the upgrade points.

RIDDLER'S REVENGE

$ TWO-FACED BANDIT

FIRST AVAILABLE: Chapter 5

MAIN OBJECTIVE: Stop Two-Face and his men from robbing Gotham's banks

LOCATION: Bleake Island - Bank of Gotham: Chinatown Branch
Founders' Island - Bank of Gotham: Drescher Branch
Miagani Island - Bank of Gotham: Kingston Branch

MOST WANTED VILLAIN: Two-Face

REWARD: 7 Upgrade Points, 2 for small and medium banks, 3 for large bank and apprehending Two-Face

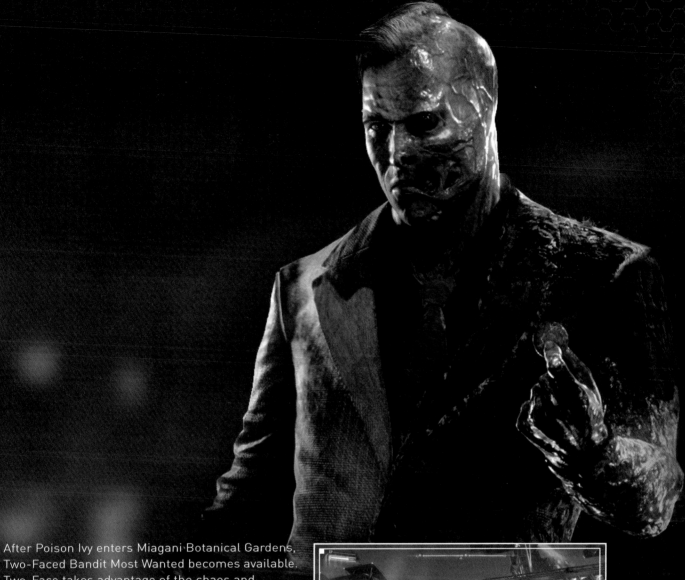

After Poison Ivy enters Miagani Botanical Gardens, Two-Faced Bandit Most Wanted becomes available. Two-Face takes advantage of the chaos and attempts to rob the Bank of Gotham's Chinatown Branch. This requires you to use all the predatory skills you've learned to stop the villain and his henchmen. Three banks of varying size must be protected before the villain is taken to GCPD. From smallest to biggest, he hits the Chinatown Branch, Drescher Branch, and Kingston Branch. After the side mission is introduced during Chapter 5, each of these robberies is discoverable after the previous one is complete.

The alarm sounds throughout the first part of the robbery, so noise isn't an issue. Perform quick, loud takedowns to limit the amount of cash they get away with. A Hostiles Defeated counter in the upper-right HUD shows how many you have taken down out of the total number of robbers. To the left is a bar, showing how much money is left in the vault. Once it reaches zero or all robbers have been taken care of, they switch their focus

to Batman as the alarm is disabled, doors are locked, and more Two-Face Thugs show up. This means you must change your fighting style to preferably Silent Takedowns. The more thugs you can take down during the robbery, the less you must deal with when it goes quiet.

A SMALL BANK: CHINATOWN BRANCH

LOCATION: Bleake Island – Chinatown

 # OF ROBBERS: 8

 # OF THUGS AFTER ALARM SHUT DOWN: 5

CASH: $100,000,000

Eight armed thugs make a path between the vault and the truck, either along the main corridors, or through the far office. Making noise with the takedowns is okay, but being seen still gets Batman in trouble. Try to take out a small group with a Fear Multi-Takedown and continue to eliminate the remaining enemies.

After switching their focus to Batman, 13 thugs join the fight. Eradicate the threat using the vantage points, floor grates, and from above the offices.

B MEDIUM BANK: DRESCHER BRANCH

LOCATION: Founders' Island – Drescher

 # OF ROBBERS: 10

 # OF THUGS AFTER ALARM SHUT DOWN: 8

CASH: $200,000,000

Ten armed thugs rob the Drescher Branch. This bank has three floors, connected by escalators. The thugs grab money from small rooms on multiple floors, so they tend to separate more than the Chinatown branch. Quickly take them down using Detective Mode to find their locations. If you get lucky, a few will group together for a nice Fear Multi-Takedown.

Seven thugs enter the bank with one thing on their mind; kill the Batman. This predator zone has more room and levels than the small bank, giving the player many more options for how to take down Two-Face's men.

C LARGE BANK: KINGSTON BRANCH

LOCATION: Miagani Island – Kingston

 # OF ROBBERS: 15

 # OF ENEMIES AFTER ALARM SHUT DOWN: 8

CASH: $300,000,000

The third bank is huge, requiring two trucks to haul the cash away. Again multiple floors and small vaults spread Two-Face's men out. Aggressively go after the fifteen thugs. If seen, use the Fear Multi-Takedown. Look out for chandelier release override switches that can be triggered with the Remote Hacking Devices, causing a chandelier to fall to the floor.

After losing all of the cash or defeating the 15 thugs, Two-Face enters the bank along with a thug, two medics, three soldiers, and two guys in Stealth Suits. The men carry a Detective Mode Scanner and Detective Mode Jammer. Therefore, there is no using Detective Mode until the jammer has been taken care of. Use all of your gadgets to make the fight easier. Take down Two-Face at any time with the same methods used against the others.

Once the Kingston Branch has been cleared out, Batman apprehends Two-Face. Drive him to GCPD Lockup to collect the last of the upgrade points.

TWO-FACE

PROFILE

REAL NAME	Harvey Dent
OCCUPATION	Professional Criminal
BASED IN	Gotham City
EYE COLOR	Blue
HAIR COLOR	Brown/Grey
HEIGHT	6 Ft.
WEIGHT	182 Lbs
FIRST APPEARANCE	*Detective Comics* #66 [August, 1942]

ATTRIBUTES

- Hideously scarred on half of his face
- Extremely skilled with his twin .45 semi-automatics
- Psychotic obsession with duality and the number two
- Defers to his half-scarred coin in choices of life or death

District Attorney Harvey Dent was one of Batman's strongest allies in Gotham City, until a criminal threw acid in Dent's face, hideously scarring him.

The wounds fractured his psyche, and he was reborn Two-Face, a schizoid criminal mastermind obsessed with duality. His former good-luck charm, a "two-headed" trick silver dollar, was damaged on one side in the attack, and Dent has seized on it as a reflection of his half-scarred visage. He flips it to decide the fates of his victims.

In the wake of The Joker's death, Two-Face is rumored to be working alongside other super villains to bring Gotham to its knees and destroy Batman once and for all.

TWO-FACED
BANDIT

AR CHALLENGES

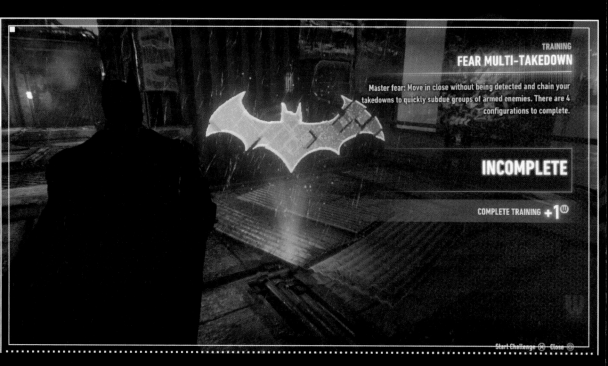

The Challenge Rooms found in previous *Arkham* franchise titles return as Augmented Reality Challenges. These challenges are more expansive than those in earlier games, since they take place in a simulation of the larger city rather than mostly in smaller arenas. AR Challenges allow training in all manner of methods of criminal dispatch, whether via hand-to-hand combat, predatory stealth takedowns, or vehicular mayhem using the Batmobile.

Tutorial Challenges help you practice some new techniques made possible by the Batmobile and the new Batsuit. Combat Challenges push your FreeFlow mastery to the limit, and feature some guest appearances by other crime fighters. In Predator Challenges you strike from the shadows and rooftops, picking off a heavily-armed force one by one. The Batmobile Race Challenges put the Batmobile's Afterburn and power slide abilities from Pursuit Mode to

the test, while Batmobile Battle Challenges call upon Battle Mode against swarms of simulated militia drones. Finally, Batmobile Hybrid Challenges feature a timed mix of both racing and combat, as you zip between different Battle Mode engagements using Pursuit Mode.

BLEAKE ISLAND

FOUNDERS' ISLAND

MIAGANI ISLAND

N

AR CHALLENGE LOCATIONS

1 Throw Counter

2 Fear Multi-Takedown

3 Predator Fundamentals

4 Grapnel Boost Mk II

5 Summon, Eject & Glide

6 Weapon Energy Diagnostics

7 Combo Master

8 Tower Defense

9 Azrael's Atonement

10 Gotham Knights

11 Smash and Grab

12 Terminal Velocity

13 Revive and Shine

14 Under the Pale Moonlight

15 Midnight Fury TT

16 City Heat

17 Crushonator

18 Condamned

19 Mental Blocked

20 Untouchable

21 One Man Army

22 Natural Selection

23 Slumdog Billionaire

24 Seek and Destroy

25 Knight Time Strike

26 Road Rage

27 Big Game Hunter

28 David and Golitath

29 Drone Zone

AR Challenges are unlocked through progress in the game's story. Many unlock naturally through progression, while some require that certain specific actions be performed before a challenge becomes available.

Once AR Challenges are unlocked, they can be accessed from their locations throughout Gotham City, or from the main menu. During story gameplay, press left on the D-Pad to check progress on various AR Challenges, and to view unlock conditions for AR Challenges you haven't yet completed.

Tutorial challenges encountered early on simply need to be completed for a reward, but later challenges require more thoroughness. Completing a tutorial challenge or scoring all three stars in other challenges rewards you with a WayneTech Upgrade Point. If you have points to spend, you can allocate them from within the Batcomputer's menu, improving abilities and unlocking new ones on the fly. Depending on performance in later AR Challenges, you earn one, two, or three stars. The first time you score all three, you earn a WayneTech Upgrade Point. These stars also track overall AR Challenge mastery, and collecting enough of them unlocks Achievements or Trophies (depending on your platform of choice).

TUTORIAL CHALLENGES

1 THROW COUNTER

Send enemies flying and leave them begging for mercy. Use the new Batsuit's increased defensive capabilities to unleash five successful Throw Counters to complete the training.

Unlock Requirements	Acquire new Batsuit

There's no penalty for attempting Throw Counters over normal Counters. The worst that happens is you perform a normal Counter instead.

The would-be attacker you send tumbling away often knocks over one or two of his buddies, as well.

Very early on, you'll acquire a new, updated Batsuit. Lucius has set up some training simulations to acquaint you with the suit's new features. Throw Countering is one of these. When an enemy is about to strike Batman, press toward that enemy plus the Counter button at the last moment to perform a Throw Counter. The enemy will be swept or lifted off their feet and tossed violently aside, more forcefully than by a normal Counter. Not only does this increase damage to the target, but it can also knock over other foes nearby. Throw Counters are also worth twice as many points as standard Counters. This challenge is completed simply by performing Throw Counters repeatedly. Use this simulation to practice timing Throw Counters, and positioning Batman around enemies so his counters hurl them into each other.

2 FEAR MULTI-TAKEDOWN

Master fear: Move in close without being detected and chain your takedowns to quickly subdue groups of armed enemies. There are four configurations to complete.

Unlock Requirements	Acquire new Batsuit

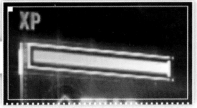

The availability of a Fear Takedown is indicated by the icon just under Batman's health bar.

Fear Takedowns can be performed with the Strike button when sneaking up on enemies who are unaware of Batman's presence. When multiple enemies are clustered nearby, perform a Fear Multi-Takedown by taking the first enemy unaware, then aiming for subsequent enemies and pressing Strike again for each target. Initially, you can subdue up to three enemies at a time with a Fear Multi-Takedown, but you can eventually upgrade the ability to allow for up to five K.O.s at once!

The first trio is simply standing in a semi-circle in the open just in front of the Batpod, allowing Batman to sneak up quite easily.

In this AR Challenge, four trios of armed foes must be dispatched with Fear Multi-Takedowns. The environment and Batman's starting position are the same for each trio, but each trio's position is different, steadily making the stalking a slightly more difficult positioning puzzle.

The second and third trios must be approached by way of grates and crawlspaces nearby; note that it's possible (and here, necessary) to begin the Fear Multi-Takedown from within the cover of a vent or grate crawlspace, or from above a ceiling grate.

Groups that are spread out are still susceptible to Fear Takedowns with some patience.

Detective Mode reveals where nearby grates can be used to safely approach the alert trio.

Fear Takedowns can be initiated from within the cover of crawlspaces.

The third group is inside a structure on the left, allowing you to drop in from above directly into a Fear Takedown.

The time to strike is when the leftmost sentry approaches the others.

The fourth trio of firearm-packing henchmen are more spread out on the upper level, rather than standing in a little cluster, but this still allows for a Fear Multi-Takedown. Dangle from the ladder or ledge just underneath and behind them. When the leftmost guard (relative Batman's starting position) walks close, initiate the Fear Multi-Takedown on him and proceed to the right to take down the remaining two adversaries along the catwalk.

3 PREDATOR FUNDAMENTALS

Strike from the shadows and leave no man standing. Hunt three armed enemies whose positions are randomized each time the training program is run.

Unlock Requirements	Acquire new Batsuit

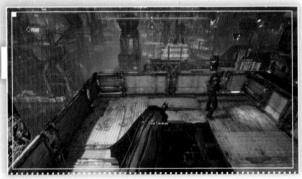

Sneak up on patrols to take them out silently.

Just getting to this point, with the new Batsuit, involved a bit of stealth action. A large portion of the game is spent stalking well-equipped foes, and trying to thin their ranks without alerting them all. In this practice scenario, there are three armed punks patrolling this area. It's up to you to take them all down, and the quieter the better.

While taking down one patrol, pan the camera and use Detective Mode to stay aware of other sentry positions.

If patrols line up correctly, you may be able to clear two or even three at once with a Fear Multi-Takedown.

On the ground, you can crouch to move silently and keep out of their lines of sight, using corner cover if it helps your view or gives you a Corner Takedown chance. Using Detective Mode, you can find some flimsy walls here, which you can use to set Explosive Gel traps for enemies on the other side. There are also floor grates to duck underneath, and air vents to hide in. You can pop out from either for Takedowns when a patrol walks past. Or, prowling from above, you can also practice Glide Kicks and Inverted Takedowns. If someone gets a clean look at you sneaking around, you'll have a split-second to tag them with a Quickfired Gadget before they open fire. If they do, stealth is out, and you'll either want to take them head-on or retreat and lose the attention.

4 GRAPNEL BOOST MK II

Become master of the skies with the Grapnel Boost Mk II. Test your aerial supremacy to the fullest as you grapple, glide, and dive across the Gotham skyline.

Unlock Requirements	Acquire new Batsuit

Tap the Run button repeatedly, then hold it while zipping in toward a long-range Grapple point to engage the Grapnel Boost, which launches Batman into a fast glide. The speed of this boost can be increased through upgrades.

The symbols direct you through a sustainable glide path.

This Challenge helps you learn to really exploit the aerodynamic Batsuit. Once you Grapnel Boost off a nearby smokestack, you'll see Bat signals in midair directing you where to swoop. They're arrayed to demonstrate something important.

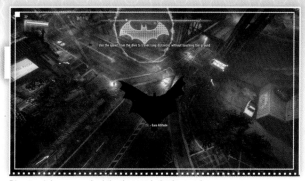

Dive to pick up speed while the symbols descend.

Pull up hard out of the Dive before hitting the ground to gain speed and altitude.

By Diving at high speed and then pitching upward hard, you can regain vertical momentum without touching the ground or any Grapnel Boost point. You can fly in big rollercoaster arcs, diving to regain speed and pitching upward to regain altitude. You can remain in the air indefinitely, and there's even a Trophy (or an Achievement) to unlock involving gliding under bridges across all three islands without touching anything. You won't have to accumulate that much flight time in this challenge, but you need to follow the trail of symbols through the sky and remain airborne for 60 more seconds. You are allowed to Grapnel Boost off of perches and rooftops to pick up more airspeed, but you cannot touch down on anything.

Swoop or Grapnel Boost up to high altitude, then coast to burn up time and enjoy the view.

5 SUMMON, EJECT & GLIDE

Call in the car and shoot for the sky. Learn to work in unison with WayneTech's most powerful weapon.

Unlock Requirements	Acquire new Batsuit

First things first, dive from a glide into the Batmobile.

Pick up speed toward the icon path.

This challenge demonstrates the synergy between the new Batsuit and the Batmobile, which are designed to work in concert. The Batmobile Remote allows you to summon the Batmobile even while gliding above Gotham, as long as you're above a thoroughfare

Eject from the Batmobile and pitch upward to ascend, steering toward the Bat signals in the sky.

The signals direct you back toward a road where you can summon the Batmobile from the air a second time, completing the Challenge.

that the car can navigate. (You can't summon the Batmobile over water or a rooftop, for example.)

Batman will dive and board the car—if you time it right, he'll even dive straight into the Batmobile. From here, you can rumble off immediately, now piloting the car in Pursuit Mode. It's easy to transition right back into a glide from the driver's seat. Accelerate and tap the Run button repeatedly (like during a Grapnel Boost) to eject rapidly upward— hold down the Run/Glide button to transition right into low-altitude flight. Airborne, you'll want to steer toward Bat signals hovering in the sky, directing your flight. The icons direct you in a gentle arc right by a road in front of Panessa Film Studios, where you'll be directed to call the Batmobile again. You can see how fluid it is to swap between driving through Gotham and soaring above it.

6 WEAPON ENERGY DIAGNOSTICS

Unleash the Batmobile's awesome power. Destroy enemy targets while avoiding incoming fire to charge the Secondary Weapon energy and activate the Missile Barrage.

Unlock Requirements	Early Chapter 1 progress.

This is the first AR Challenge you'll encounter, shortly after first deploying the Batmobile early on in the game. After completing this AR Challenge, you can begin to unlock the rest of them.

Secondary Weapon energy is indicated right next to the targeting reticle.

In the same way that building Combos leads to Special Combo Takedowns on foot, in tank combat you'll build combo hits toward Secondary Weapon energy.

This Challenge offers an early opportunity to tangle with Rattler drones while practicing Secondary Weapon use. While piloting the Batmobile in Battle Mode, avoid incoming shells while returning fire to build up Missile Barrage energy. Aim at opposing tank turrets and you'll destroy them in one hit from the Batmobile's main cannon. Use dodge thrusters to jet out of the direct path of any enemy attacks, and blast tanks till Secondary Weapon energy is charged.

Fully-charged Missile Barrage can target several enemies at once, rapidly tilting odds in your favor.

Once Missile Barrage is charged, press 🔲 / ❌ to lock on and fire a missile at a drone target. The next step is charging weapon energy for Missile Barrage level 2, which can target up to four enemies; tap 🔲 / ❌ repeatedly to lock on and fire at multiple targets. Now that you've primed a charged-up Missile Barrage, the final step is to destroy four enemy drones at once with a level 2 Missile Barrage.

COMBAT CHALLENGES

7 COMBO MASTER

Show your enemies no mercy by chaining together as many devastating moves as you can without breaking your flow for a second.

Unlock Requirements	After early Chapter 1 progress, run and transition directly into a dive off a rooftop.

ONE STAR	TWO STAR	THREE STAR	OVERACHIEVEMENT
Achieve a Combo of x10 or more	Achieve a Combo of x25 or more	Achieve a Combo of x50 or more	Overachieve x3

This rooftop brawl against an onslaught of thugs gives you an early chance to hone your Combo skills. Maintain a constant flow of actions by alternating between Striking at foes and Quickfiring Gadgets when it's safe to do so, and Countering or Evading incoming enemy attacks. Take your time, and don't rush actions

To prolong Combos, you must avoid getting hit.

For the sake of the objective, the only criteria here is number of Combo hits. Variety doesn't matter for this particular combat scenario.

or "mash" on Strike or Counter. Your Combo will be broken should you hesitate for too long between actions, whiff a Counter, Strike, or Gadget, or eat an enemy attack.

You'll begin facing off against only four combatants, but they'll increase in number after you start knocking some of them out. Eventually there can be ten or more brawlers in this little simulated space. Take out enemies and keep your Combo going for long enough, and more challenging forces appear—knife-wielding fighters you can't attack head-on, and katana-wielding combat specialists who can flip deftly and perform evasions of their own.

8 TOWER DEFENSE

Use your FreeFlow expertise to takedown a gang of thugs on the roof terrace of Wayne Plaza. Combine your gadgets and combat moves to maximize your rating.

Unlock Requirements	After chapter 3 progress, pick up a floored foe with R2 + ○ / RT + Ⓑ , and then unleash a Critical Beat Down.

ONE STAR	TWO STAR	THREE STAR
Score 4000 points	Score 8000 points	Score 16000 points

The danger up here on the roof of a Wayne tower comes from enemy tacklers, knife-users, and Brutes.

This combat challenge is about maximizing score. Right off the bat, the enemy force is more formidable than in the previous combat challenge, since there are a half-dozen enemies at once, some with bats. After a couple waves of standard enemies, a hulking Brute enemy appears alongside two knife-wielders. You can't take either type of foe head-on, and your normal Counters won't hurt them either. You can bypass their defenses by Redirecting over their heads and attacking from behind, or with a Cape Stun into Beat Down finisher. It's hard to pull off a full Beat Down sequence in a crowd, so you may have to circle the heavier enemies at first, taking out the normal thugs. If you have a Special Combo Takedown built up, you can also spend it taking out one of these advanced enemies in one move. Once you unlock the Blade Dodge Takedown upgrade, the knife-wielders are also easily dispatched, provided you have a little bit of timing skill.

Be ready to drop everything to Counter-Dodge or Evade against an incoming blade swipe.

With the Blade Dodge Takedown upgrade, you can start treating blade swipes as instant K.O.s

When you clear all the thugs up here, including the Brute boss and his blade henchmen, you'll clear the challenge. Your goal is a high score, which you'll get in combat scenarios by avoiding all incoming hits, keeping a Combo going the whole time, and varying your Combo actions. Little things add up, especially as your Combo count increases; Throw Counters are worth double normal Counters, and ditto perfectly timed Critical Strikes over normal Strikes. It's worthwhile, as your multiplier increases mid-Combo, to try to mix in higher-value actions like Aerial Attacks, Beat Downs, and Ground Takedowns, if you can squeeze them off without getting hit.

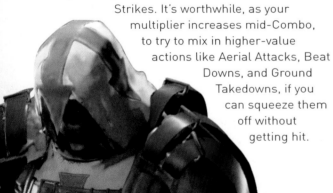

9 AZRAEL'S ATONEMENT

Fight as the Order's angel of vengeance and push your combat skills to the limit. Only perfection is good enough as the challenge will end when taking even a single blow.

Unlock Requirements	Complete side mission "Heir to the Cowl"

ONE STAR	TWO STAR	THREE STAR
Score 7500 points	Score 15000 points	Score 30000 points

You control Azrael of the Order of St. Dumas in this challenge and you have one goal: don't get hit. You won't unlock this

Azrael is a superb close quarters fighter, like Batman himself.

challenge until you complete the Azrael-centric side mission. Dodging or Countering all attacks here is crucial. The battle opens against ten militia fighters at once, but they're initially all standard foes, easily Countered. The only attack they have you can't Counter is their telegraphed tackle, easy to Evade or thwart with a Quickfired Batarang.

Be ready to Cape Stun shielded fighters and Redirect over electrified ones, or avoid them altogether and focus on unarmed targets.

While you should still try and maintain Combos when it's safe, be willing to drop them in favor of Evading/Redirecting to assure safety.

After a couple waves of standard fodder, though, warriors carrying riot shields begin to appear, and then fighters wielding electrified stun rods. Both of these unit types have uncounterable attacks up close and are very dangerous to approach from the front, so exercise extra caution once they're around. Take out stun rod users by Redirecting over them and then striking, or with a Special Combo Takedown. Shield users can be deshelled with a Cape Stun into Aerial Attack sequence, or pulled off balance with the Quickfired Batclaw. If you can avoid getting hit and either build up one huge Combo around 90 hits, or multiple impressive Combos in the 40-50 range, you'll be on your way to earning all three stars.

With two heroes knocking enemy fighters down at once, the Special Combo Multi Ground Takedown becomes even more useful than usual.

10 GOTHAM KNIGHTS

Perfect your dual team combat skills. Reunite the original dynamic duo, Bruce Wayne and Dick Grayson, to defeat the criminals of Gotham City and obtain the highest possible score.

Unlock Requirements	After Chapter 5 progress, deploy three different Quickfire Gadgets in one fight

ONE STAR	TWO STAR	THREE STAR
Score 5000 points	Score 10000 points	Score 20000 points

You can swap seamlessly between Batman and Nightwing.

This tag team fight highlights the combat skills of Batman and one of his closest allies. You can tag between Batman and Nightwing with L1/LB, which can be done mid-Combo. The duo must plow through several waves of attackers, starting with a batch of standard fist fighting thugs and a baseball fan. As you start taking combatants down, shield users show up, and eventually a Brute enters the fray.

Nightwing has his own move set, including a Special Combo Takedown that stuns many fighters much like one of Batman's REC special moves.

Countering the Brute won't hurt him any, and he'll punish you for assaulting him head-on, so you'll have to stun him and then use a full Beat Down attack. This can be very difficult to pull off without getting hit when many of the Brute's henchmen are still circling, so you may need to deplete their ranks before knocking out the boss. Once this fearsome twosome has taken out several waves including the Brute, the challenge will end. There are enough foes to fight here that getting three stars and the WayneTech Upgrade Point is all about good Combo etiquette, so keep a Combo going and avoid needless damage.

PREDATOR CHALLENGES

11 SMASH AND GRAB

Stop the bank heist in Chinatown. Bring down Two-Face's crew before they get away with the loot. Performance is evaluated purely on time taken to defeat all of the thugs.

Unlock Requirements	Progress in side mission "Two-Faced Bandit"

ONE STAR	TWO STAR	THREE STAR
Stop the heist in less than 3:00	Stop the heist in less than 2:00	Stop the heist in less than 1:15

From the heist-related side mission comes this heist-related challenge. Twenty of Two Face's armed goons are trying to sack the bank branch on Bleake Island. Your goal is to knock out enough of them to end the heist. Each time you take one out, another appears. You'll have to dispatch 10 of the thieves before they call it off, and you'll have about five and a half minutes to accomplish this. While you can take your time, the goals are pointed toward speed.

When striking from above, there are plenty of perches above the bank's main floor, along with the roof of the enclosed offices in the center. Takedowns can be used from perches on foes walking underneath, and Glide Kicks can be initiated from anywhere. To come up from below you can move very quickly in ducts underneath the entire length of the bank's floor, even into the vault itself. Running silently under the floor, you can sometimes find loners or small groups briefly separated from view from other thieves. On loners, start a Silent Takedown then just finish it fast with a Knockout Smash ender—the bank alarm is blaring, so sound doesn't matter like it normally does. You're mostly worried about line of sight here. Catch a small group separated, and a Fear Multi-Takedown can quickly eliminate them all. After any Takedowns, quickly return to changing perches above or prowling ducts below, looking for more chances to pick the invaders off. Watch out if you're spotted—enemies will track above with their guns, or drop searing grenades into grates below.

Gun-toting robbers pour in from a garbage truck they've reappropriated.

Gadgets here can give you a big advantage.

The bank's layout allows for many different approaches.

Catch groups separated from each other, dispatch them fast, then return to cover.

The bank is basically rectangular, with the thieves' truck and the bank's vault situated at opposing corners. The vault is their primary target, but the thieves also ransack a couple offices in the middle of the rectangle.

Several features of the bank floor are worth noting. Using the Remote Hacking Device, you can close a gate near the robbers' truck, briefly halting anyone returning from the vault with loot until they get it back open. You can use this to create a bottleneck, ideally setting up a Fear Multi-Takedown x5 (if you've unlocked it). In a side office across the hall from the truck and gate, you'll find a Dye Pack Deterrent panel that can be hacked with the RHD to disperse a choking cloud over any foes nearby. Finally, and most worth noting, there's a shock-panel security floor near the vault itself that can be triggered with the RHD, instantly incapacitating anyone standing on it. This can be three or four knockouts at once, if you time it right. You can set traps of your own as well, using Explosive Gel on the weak walls of the offices. And if you have the Disruptor Gadget and anti-weapon upgrades for it, you can booby-trap some of the guards' guns. Disrupt the gun of a robber that you don't have an easy angle on, so if he spots you taking down an easier mark, he'll take himself out by opening fire.

12 TERMINAL VELOCITY

Analyze the enemy threat, then plan your attacks to stay ahead of these well-equipped armed enemies at Grand Avenue Station. Complete all three mission objectives to earn 3 stars.

Unlock Requirements	After Chapter 5 progress, subdue a Brute or Minigunner with an Environment Takedown.

OBJECTIVE 1	OBJECTIVE 2	OBJECTIVE 3
Use a Remote Hacking Device Takedown point to K.O. a militia thug	Perform a Fear Takedown through a weak wooden wall	Take out the militia Minigunner with an Environment Takedown

Grand Avenue Station is a complex multi-tiered structure. The enclosed Riverside Lounge is situated alongside an outdoor triple-deck. A sentry gun is already set up outside the lounge. It can be blinded with the RHD. Eight sentries patrol the area, including a Minigunner

The varied terrain here allows for many different approaches.

It's possible (and probably wisest) to just avoid the sentry gun's scanning area rather than attempting to sneak up behind it to physically disable it.

and a guard with a portable Detective Mode scanner. There are many vantage points above the structure, which are safe places to observe and traverse the area as long as you don't attract attention.

If you *do* want to attract attention, you can hang a patrolling foe from one of these perches with an Inverted Takedown. This leaves him dangling by his feet and screaming, which naturally attracts the attention of several other guards. This is not automatically negative—string up a distraction with an Inverted Takedown, then immediately Grapple across several other perches to another part of the area. Half the enemy force will leave their normal routes to congregate around their hanging comrade, which gives you an opportunity to pursue targets or set traps elsewhere. Act quickly and you can take out the Minigunner across the stage, or lure the two guards by the Portable Generator here, which can be overloaded into an explosion by the Remote Hacking Device. The Voice Synthesizer, once acquired, makes it much easier to coax patrols into going wherever you want them to.

The Detective Mode monitor usually stays inside the Riverside Lounge, and is a prime candidate for elimination by Fear Takedown through weak wall.

To take out half their force at once, hang one adversary, relocate to avoid being spotted during their initial alert panic, and then Grapple back above and drop down with a Fear Multi-Takedown.

As you remain in Detective Mode during this challenge, a bar slowly fills up in the middle of the screen, indicating the scanner's progress in pinning down Batman's location. You'll also hear the audio comms of the guard with his accomplices as he scans. To thwart the scanning attempts, don't leave Detective Mode on needlessly. It's fine to activate Detective Mode to scan quickly for enemies or environment features, but turn it back off after acquiring intel. This way, this monitor will never detect Batman.

13 REVIVE AND SHINE

Test your stealth skills against a squad of armed militia. With a medic providing back up, the enemy won't stay down for long. Your performance will be rated on number of objectives completed.

Unlock Requirements	Early Chapter 3 progress, perform a Fear Multi-Takedown against three foes

OBJECTIVE 1	OBJECTIVE 2	OBJECTIVE 3
Take no damage during the challenge	Take out the militia Medic last	Perform two separate Fear Multi-Takedowns

This challenge occurs on what is basically a five-level catwalk supporting the monorail. This creates interesting challenges because the six patrolling hostiles are spread out, with good lines of sight between them. Among them is a white-suited Medic, who revives any unconscious ally he finds. If the other patrols discover a subdued partner, they'll call for the Medic. It greatly simplifies completion of the challenge if you carefully stalk and knock out the Medic first, but then you can't get a three star rating.

Open walkways present a challenge for approaching foes. You'll want to come from above or approach dangling from ledges rather than sneaking in a crouched position.

The Medic complicates this scenario all by himself.

The enemies here are spread out among several floors of catwalks. Batman has plenty of movement paths but not much cover.

Gadget combinations like the Voice Synthesizer and Disruptor allow you to booby-trap things like weapon crates, setting traps to take out enemies remotely.

In order to go for three star completion, you'll have to do some planning. The Voice Synthesizer is very helpful here, since it allows you to cluster up pairs of foes wherever you like for Fear Multi-Takedowns. In order to score two Fear Multi-Takedowns against just six enemies, you'll want to open by taking out two or three enemies as far away from the Medic as possible with your initial Fear Multi-Takedown. Now you'll stalk the remaining non-Medics for a Silent Takedown, which you'll need to accomplish in order to enable another Fear Multi-Takedown. Once another Fear Multi-Takedown is locked and loaded, there should only be two or three hostiles left, including the Medic. By now, one of them has probably noticed the growing amount of unconscious friends they have, and the remaining force may be rushing along with the Medic to the nearest victim to revive him. Unleash your second Fear Multi-Takedown against this group, saving the Medic for last.

14 UNDER THE PALE MOONLIGHT

Adapt or perish. Take on the ultimate deployment of armed militia, including one team with optic deflection armor, on the sprawling Panessa Studios rooftop.

Unlock Requirements	During Chapter 7 progress, use the Voice Synthesizer to lure an enemy into a Takedown

OBJECTIVE 1	OBJECTIVE 2	OBJECTIVE 3
Perform a x4 Fear Multi-Takedown	Use the Voice Synthesizer to K.O. a target at a weak wall primed with Explosive Gel	Take out the Boa drone controller last

The studios rooftop is by far the largest and most varied invisible predator challenge environment.

There are high and low tiers to the studios rooftop, and patrols all over the place.

Panessa Film Studios is crawling with advanced militia forces in this challenge, and you have to clear them all out. Mixed into their ranks here are optic deflection troops who can disappear from Detective Mode scans, and a Boa Sentry drone controller. The drone operator works from one of the area's lower hallways, remotely piloting a surveillance drone up top. The rooftop is so big that this drone doesn't have to be a problem as long as you keep track of where it is, but beware that if you lose track of it, it has the altitude to spot you even on vantage point perches above the action. The drone patrols as long as its operator is conscious, so you could just take him out, but you can't get three stars that way. Like with "Revive and Shine," one of your main objectives is to leave the specialty unit for last, but that's actually easier here as long as you're mindful of the drone's position. With Detective Mode on, you can see a line linking the Boa drone with its pilot.

Several areas have flimsy, destructible walls, perfect for fulfilling the Explosive Gel objective.

Every conceivable form of lure and Takedown is possible in this dense, layered area.

The weak walls near the drone controller help fulfill another objective, using the Voice Synthesizer to lure a guard into a prepared Explosive Gel trap. Just direct an enemy unit to investigate near where you've prepped a flimsy wall to explode, then set it off. If you leave the drone controller alone in the underhalls till he's the only one left, you can clear two stars with your last action. Before that, you'll have to earn another star with a five-stage Fear Multi-Takedown. You can't pull this off before fully upgrading your Fear Multi-Takedown, but at least this challenge area has plenty of targets to line up once you do. As in other challenges, when you want guards to clump up together, take one of them down as a honeypot somewhere he will be noticed, then hide nearby. His being found by his accomplices puts them on high alert and sets them to searching the nearby area. Naturally, this is where you can pounce upon them unawares.

15 MIDNIGHT FURY TT

Take on the Bleake Island time trial. Choose your route wisely, looking out for time-bonuses and shortcuts along the way to get the quickest possible time.

Unlock Requirements	After Chapter 3 progress, Eject from the Batmobile and glide over 300 meters

ONE STAR	TWO STAR	THREE STAR
Complete the course in less than 2:15	Complete the course in less than 2:00	Complete the course in less than 1:45

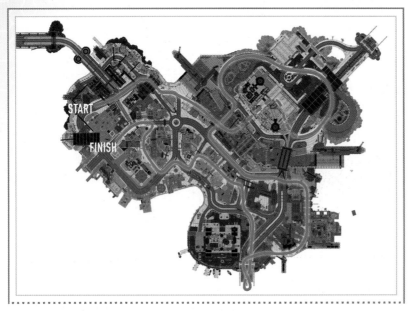

Hourglass pickups, scattered here and there usually just off the main route, knock three seconds off your total. Incorporate them into your route where the detour isn't significant.

Early on, a Bat symbol directs you to smash right through a wooden storage door, forging ahead into a reservoir, where you'll need to make a hard left into an underground tunnel leading under the film studios.

This is the first time trial race you can engage in, burning rubber across (and under) Bleake Island. You'll be guided on the right route by a line indicator on the road and by Bat symbols spinning in the streets ahead. The Bat symbols are like checkpoints you must drive through, as during earlier Gliding challenges. Along the way, you'll see holographic hourglass symbols on the road too, usually off to the side or tucked into a tight corner. These pickups reduce three seconds from your time trial total, so they'll add up and go a long way toward helping you clear the objective with all three stars. The presence of a time pickup in a puzzling spot might also lead you to a shortcut or daring jump.

After barging through the docks, you'll find a jump that leads back to the road right in front of GCPD.

The course will detour you into just barely dipping into Miagani Island before immediately doubling you back across the bridge. Be ready to burn all your Afterburner juice toward Miagani and then power slide right back around.

There are upgrades to increase Afterburner recharge rate, but for the most part clearing the time trials involves avoiding wipeouts, maximizing Afterburner and power slides, improving your racing line, and snagging some hourglass pickups along the way.

16 CITY HEAT TT

Race the clock to complete the Miagani Island track. You'll need to know every street, shortcut and back alley if you want to be the fastest wheels in Gotham.

Unlock requirement	After Chapter 7 progress, use three different Gadgets during one Glide Kick attack.

ONE STAR	TWO STARS	THREE STARS
Complete the course in less than 1:25	Complete the course in less than 1:15	Complete the course in less than 1:05

Miagani is a grid of paved, Afterburner-friendly streets and sharp 90-degree turns.

This course doesn't just stay on city streets, however. Be bold off-roading—you can jump over or smash through most impediments.

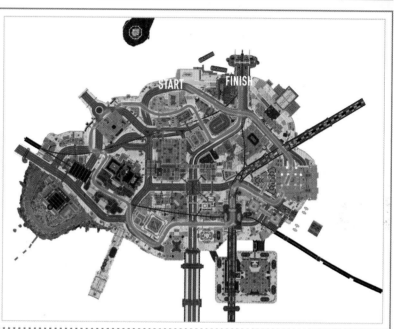

In the home stretch, be ready to plow right into a commercial alley and back onto city streets on the other side.

This challenge is Miagani Island's counterpart to Midnight Fury TT. This street race is a little more straightforward, since most of the action involves burning down straightaways or power sliding through sharp, regular turns. A couple detours take you dramatically into extracurricular areas but otherwise this time trial is about pure street speed. Slide aggressively through the turns to build as much energy as possible for solid Afterburning stretches.

Pass into the parking garage just before the Bank of Gotham near the finish for a time-shaving shortcut and some time pickups.

17 CRUSHONATOR

Race one lap of Riddler's infamous high pressure course. Be careful not to crush yourself along the way. Earn a time bonus by drifting effectively around corners.

Unlock Requirements	Complete fourth Riddler cave during "Riddler's Revenge" side mission

ONE STAR	TWO STAR	THREE STAR
Complete a lap in less than 1:20	Complete a lap in less than 1:10	Complete a lap in less than 1:00

You'll have to disable red or white blocks alternatively to pass through these tracks.

Many different puzzles are spread throughout the elaborate side mission "Riddler's Revenge," featuring Edward Nigma, everyone's favorite puzzler. There are all sorts of stages involving puzzles and combat, but some involve Riddler's time trials too. Once you've experienced them during "Riddler's Revenge," they'll also be available in AR Challenge variants.

Watch out for green panels on the ground and ceiling. These indicate where a green crusher block will smash down. The machine stomping is rhythmic and you can technically drive over the green panels when the crushers are locking back into the ceiling, but it's better to just avoid them altogether.

The way here is marked on the walls with arrows, and blocks line the track and block it in places. You control whether white or red blocks are "active" at any given time. When white blocks are impeding the track, red blocks are withdrawn, and vice versa. You have to use this to your advantage by swapping between having red or white blocks active in line with your progress on the course. A long run of white blocks sometimes precedes a run of red blocks, with a small strip of neutral blocks in between. You'll have to swap red on, travel over the retracted white blocks, then swap them when you're in the small zone in between. There are also places where green blocks smash in place again and again. If you're in a green spot when it comes down, good-bye Batmobile. If you're going for the best time and you get smashed at all, just restart the race. You don't have to pull off any unreal timing passing through dangerous green block fields for a three star rating, you just have to race the whole track cleanly with good Afterburner efficiency, avoiding green crusher areas (and not crushing yourself with white or red blocks).

18 CONDAMNED

Race a single lap of Riddler's most dangerous course, with Mr. E Nigma himself in control of the hazards. Earn a time bonus by drifting effectively around corners.

Unlock Requirements	Complete seventh Riddler cave during "Riddler's Revenge" side mission

ONE STAR	TWO STAR	THREE STAR
Complete a lap in less than 1:30	Complete a lap in less than 1:15	Complete a lap in less than 1:00

This course is a slalom against death. The track itself isn't too complex; it's the obstacles that present the challenge.

The thorniest sections are probably those involving moving slicer traps. Don't overreact approaching them. It's better to pass cleanly and a bit more slowly than it is to fail to pass them at all.

When the track completely banks, just go with it. The downforce of the Batmobile keeps it suctioned against the road. After the first banked section, be ready to Afterburner jump over some horizontal slicing traps.

This short but deadly time trial pits you against a twisting course filled with custom-designed Riddler traps. Spiked spinning obstacles either whirl in place or while traveling side to side on a set path. These tree trunk-like traps can be either vertical or horizontal. Green crusher blocks smash down from the ceiling, as during Crushonator. And the banks of the track itself can become sheer vertical walls; this is a dam, after all. Slicing and crushing obstacles may be present even when you're banked on your side navigating one of these segments. The key here is to keep the pedal to the floor and not to smash into anything. Sounds so easy, doesn't it?

Avoid the crushing and slicing traps while banked vertically, too.

19 MENTAL BLOCKED

Complete a single lap of Riddler's fiendish course on its hardest configuration as quickly as possible. Drift the Batmobile around corners to earn a time bonus.

Unlock Requirements	Complete first Riddler cave during "Riddler's Revenge" side mission

ONE STAR	TWO STAR	THREE STAR	OVERACHIEVEMENT
Complete a lap in less than 1:00	Complete a lap in less than 0:48	Complete a lap in less than 0:42	1 for every additional 4 seconds off

Be ready to bank on corkscrewing tracks here too. You'll sometimes have to bank heavily while also manipulating the red and white blocks.

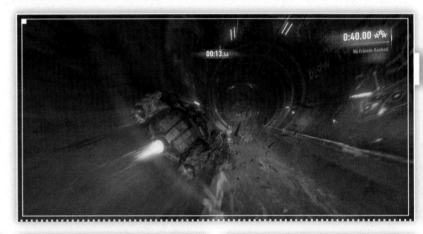

Approaching a red block drop off, you'll have to buckle up and soar over the edge with Afterburner blazing and red blocks active...

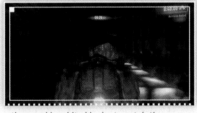

...then enable white blocks to catch the Batmobile...

...then re-enable red blocks to catch yourself yet again.

In a variation of this puzzle, you'll have to jump off red blocks toward a red block barrier, swap to white blocks in midair (retracting the red obstacle ahead), then swap back to red blocks once past the red barrier to deploy a red floor to land upon.

In this Riddler racing challenge, the very first tunnel chamber here will teach you the drill. You'll swap between red or white blocks being active, which opens or closes various sections of the track. Here on Mental Blocked, this can be the floor of the track itself, as well as doors that block the way forward, or barriers over sheer drops. Watch the ground or you may unwittingly pull the proverbial rug out from under your own feet. Swapping between red or white blocks as necessary without taking yourself out is the ticket to success during Mental Blocked. As in other challenges, if you're going for a three star rating, just restart immediately if you ever wipe out or crush the Batmobile. You can sustain things like a clumsy Afterburner exit from a corner slide, but an egregious error torpedoes any high ranking attempt.

20 UNTOUCHABLE

Dodge through a hail of missile fire and survive as long as possible without taking a single hit. Attack is the best form of defense: Earn time bonuses by taking out militia drones.

Unlock Requirements	After Chapter 3 progress, perform 3 Critical Shots in one tank battle

ONE STAR	TWO STAR	THREE STAR
Survive the onslaught for 1:00	Survive the onslaught for 3:00	Survive the onslaught for 6:00

Now the fun starts. Get ready to hold down L2/LT while putting those Battle Mode dodge thrusters to use. This challenge confines you to a small intersection, surrounded by hostile drones. The Batmobile has just a smidgen of armor remaining here—take a single hit and it's over. (This is basically the tank version of Azrael's Atonement.)

But it's not quite as harsh as it sounds. Obviously you wouldn't survive for very long letting tank forces multiply around you without fighting back, but

Each drone kill adds 10 seconds to your survival timer, which goes a long way toward making this a feasible challenge.

start the challenge by immediately taking out several of the Rattler drones with turret shots and you can get a foothold. Blast one or two tanks right at the outset while you start to travel in a circle around what intersection you have to work with. Always pay attention to the Batcomputer's projected vectors of enemy shells and dodge out of the way when you're in enemy sights. The dodge thrusters upgrade that allows for a double thruster dash can be vital here. As you circle and evade with dodge thrusters you should also scan methodically, one-shotting the turrets of each new drone that spawns. It's better to take an extra moment to line up and assure a turret shot than it is to rush the shot and either miss or score a chassis hit; both waste your time and neither kills.

Thin the drone ranks while avoiding hits at all costs. Make sure you don't miss turret shots and you can keep up with their spawning for a fair bit of time, building your Combo as you go.

More drones, and more advanced units, spawn as you hold out. Unleash Secondary Weapons like a fully-charged Missile Barrage as they're available, and go down turrets blazing.

After a few waves of Rattlers, other drones start to appear. Mamba missile pods, Twin Rattlers with two barrels, and Diamondbacks with extra turret plating. The plan stays the same regardless. Get a tank Combo of 10 or more going while dodging incoming fire and you'll be well on your way to three stars here.

Battle the militia's drone tank army beneath the bright lights of Panessa Studios. Take out targets quickly without taking damage to achieve the best score.

Unlock Requirements	After Chapter 1 progress, jump over 50 meters in the Batmobile.

ONE STAR	TWO STARS	THREE STARS
Score 2000 points	Score 4000 points	Score 8000 points

This AR Challenge cannot be unlocked until Lucius Fox activates the Afterburner function on the Batmobile, which fortunately happens very quickly into this dark night. Once Afterburner is available, find one of many sloped surfaces off which to ramp at high speed. Sail at least 50 meters through the air and this Challenge becomes available. Note that there's also a Trophy/an Achievement for ramping 50 meters off eight different spots, and that Gotham City has dozens of sloped spots ripe for Afterburner launching.

There are several waves of Rattlers to destroy before this tank battle is over. Always keep moving, strafing, and circling in Battle Mode, while drawing beads on enemy turrets. Your FPS/action game skills will shine here.

Since you can't Counter as a tank, avoiding hits is even more important than it is on foot. Make liberal use of the dodge thrusters to get out of the path of incoming shells.

This is a pure score attack against a fleet of Rattler drones. These light tanks come equipped with a standard tank turret capable of dumbfiring explosive shells at high velocity. The Batcomputer predicts the paths of enemy shells and displays them while you maneuver in Battle Mode, allowing you to preemptively dodge against Rattler fire. Tanks target and fire in a rhythm—be ready to use dodge thrusters when enemy tank vectors are visible, then draw a bead and blast a turret before the next round of shots starts. Not only does this keep the Batmobile in full armor, but it also allows you to perpetuate a tank Combo, which builds your score multiplier and contributes to Secondary Weapon energy. As in FreeFlow combat, take a hit and your multiplier resets. You'll also lose the tank Combo if you wait about eight seconds between tank hits. The inactivity grace period is much more lenient in tank combat than in hand to hand.

Aside from dodging a drone's fire, you can also beat it to the punch.

Turret shots are worth more points than body shots, and destroy drone tanks in a single hit, so aim for turrets. Zooming in helps with aim, but the turret can swivel faster zoomed out, leaving you with superior maneuverability and wider visibility. If dexterity allows, stay in Battle Mode by holding L2/LT while zooming in and out by clicking Right Stick/R3 as necessary to keep up with the hostile force. Rattlers draw in from all sides, and the battlefield is relatively level, leading to the possibility of making hostiles destroy each other. If you can get the tanks to blast each other with friendly fire, it's worth as much as a turret shot. Mix in Missile Barrage volleys when available on clusters of opportune targets. This Battle Mode combat challenge is all about keeping your multiplier going and not getting hit; if you want that WayneTech Upgrade Point for surpassing 11000 points, just restart the challenge if you get hit.

22 NATURAL SELECTION

Wage war amongst the weeds. With Mambas and Diamondbacks in the field you'll need to be fast and on target if you want to survive. Mix up Secondary Weapon usage to earn bonus points.

Unlock Requirements	After Chapter 3 progress

ONE STAR	TWO STAR	THREE STAR
Score 2500 points	Score 5000 points	Score 10000 points

Enemies can spawn in from every side, and the sloped center gives enemies who congregate there a raised firing position.

This landscaped area by the Botanical Gardens is host to a different mix of hostile drones. Here you'll fight Diamondbacks, Rattler tanks enhanced with turret armor, and Mambas, which deploy a missile pod rather than a dumbfire cannon. The Diamondbacks complicate things because you can't simply take them out in one turret shot, unless you score a Perfect Critical from the front, in their exposed rectangular sighting light. They're also vulnerable if you happen to get shots in on their turrets from the sides or back, where they're not heavily armored. Otherwise, they'll take two turret shots to take down, while you continue to dodge everything trying to destroy the Batmobile. The WayneTech Upgrades to speed up Heavy Turret reload speed can be quite helpful here.

A Mamba lock-on demands your attention. Get the Mamba in your six and then shoot its payload out of the air.

Mambas complicate things by locking on to the Batmobile and launching guided missiles. These vehicles take a few seconds to lock on before firing, and the Batcomputer displays the lock-on in progress by directing you toward the offending Mamba. You can destroy the Mamba to interrupt the firing process. If you don't destroy the Mamba in time, you can shoot the incoming missile out of the air with the Vulcan Gun.

Continue to dodge enemy fire and anti-air incoming missiles, keeping your tank Combo and Secondary Weapon energy flowing.

23 SLUMDOG BILLIONAIRE

Rumble in the ruins against a wide variety of militia drones. The stage is set in the belly of old Gotham as you repel attacks from the ground and sky in a fight for survival.

Unlock Requirements	Most Wanted progress in Campaign for Disarmament

ONE STAR	TWO STAR	THREE STAR
Score 8000 points	Score 16000 points	Score 24000 points

The Combo of Mamba missiles and Dragon UAVs gives you an unusual chance to give the Vulcan Gun a serious workout. Against only light tanks, it's not particularly useful, but here it's crucial.

This is drone tank combat in the bowels of old Gotham against many types of militia drones. This combat space is almost as cramped as during Untouchable, and you'll have airborne Dragon drones to contend with, as well as the usual Rattler family of light tank variants. Dragon drones are little attack helicopters which are agile but very susceptible to the rapid fire Vulcan Gun. Since there are Mambas present during this challenge, keep that in mind when you're shooting down Dragons. While sweeping mini-choppers with the Vulcan Gun, you can also take out any incoming Mamba missiles. The other tanks you are used to by now—turret shots for Rattlers, Perfect shots for Diamondbacks, and dodge thruster out of the way when they're about to fire. Some Diamondbacks come equipped with a triple barrel that fires in a spread pattern, so watch out for that.

The combat here is fast and furious and keeping a perfect tank Combo is critical to get a high score. Go after lengthy tank Combos to close in on the three star target.

The close quarters and plentiful enemies make Missile Barrages unusually useful. You can blindfire a fully charged Missile Barrage in this challenge and fill a big scrapyard with the results.

Dragon air to ground trajectories are projected for you to avoid, just like the ground drones.

BATMOBILE HYBRID CHALLENGES

24 SEEK AND DESTROY

Armored militia vehicles and APCs are on the move on the Gotham streets. It's up to you to run them into the ground. APCs are tougher, but they reward you with double points and time bonuses.

Unlock Requirements	After Chapter 5 progress, score three Vehicle Takedowns without using the Batmobile

ONE STAR	TWO STAR	THREE STAR
Take down 4 armored cars	Take down 8 armored cars	Take down 12 armored cars

The Immobilizer is a reliable and nonlethal way to prevent militia targets from escaping, but it does require two hits to succeed.

This is a free for all chase across Founders' Island, with you in pursuit of a dozen fleeing militia vehicles. This is a different kind of demolition, since these aren't unmanned drones. You just want to disable vehicles, not destroy them. Your primary tool for this in Pursuit Mode is the Immobilizer Gadget. After an initial button press to lock-on to a fleeing enemy vehicle, an additional press launches a homing Immobilizer round once the weapon is charged. If you use only Immobilizer rounds to disable a runaway truck, it'll take two direct hits. If you mix in a little road rage action, smacking into the fleeing vehicle with the Batmobile and tagging it with side swipes, a single Immobilizer hit may be enough to kill their engine.

When you encounter multiple militia trucks at once, lock on one of them with the Immobilizer while you try to run the other one off the road.

No car or truck can withstand a full-throttle impact from the Batmobile.

If you can put enough momentum into a collision, that's the fastest way to disable other cars. If you're chasing one militia vehicle and see another approaching, or crossing at an intersection ahead, feel free to hit the new vehicle head-on, or T-bone them. Their car will be instantly disabled, and the sturdy Batmobile will be fine to resume pursuit against the first target. You'll have two and a half minutes to stop at least a dozen vehicles from fleeing, and each Humvee you take down adds three seconds to your time and each APC adds six seconds. Drive aggressively and be opportunistic about the militia trucks you chase and this should be an easy WayneTech Upgrade Point to earn.

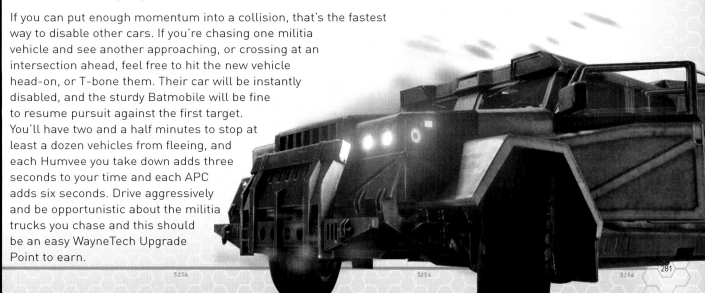

25 KNIGHT TIME STRIKE

Race through the streets to the three conflict zones. Destroy the tanks and move on as quickly as possible. Only the fastest time stays on top.

Unlock Requirements	After Chapter 7 progress, perform 2 Perfect Shots in a row in a drone tank battle

ONE STAR	TWO STAR	THREE STAR
Complete the course in less than 3:30	Complete the course in less than 2:45	Complete the course in less than 2:15

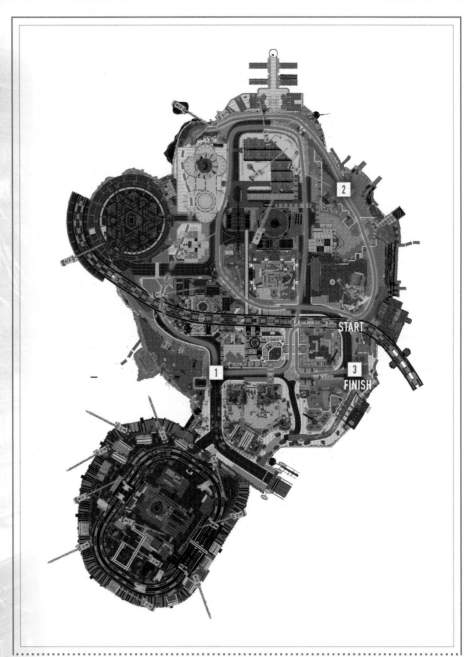

This is Founders' Island's version of a time trial, like Midnight Fury in Bleake Island or City Heat in Miagani. The difference here is that three combat encounters are sprinkled throughout the time trial. You'll race as normal, passing Bat checkpoints and collecting hourglass pickups if possible, but when you arrive at certain places, you'll be jumped by a squad of drone tanks.

The driving portions of this time trial cut across long, uncluttered swaths of Founders' that are begging for Afterburner use.

At the first encounter, you'll be attacked by four Rattler drones. Eliminate them as quickly as possible so you can get back to racing. You don't get time toward your result from these keys, they're merely a bottleneck. You don't get any extra credit for efficient kills beyond just keeping it prompt, but you *will* be penalized for getting hit—successful enemy hits on the Batmobile bleed five seconds off your final result.

Beware the armored Diamondback drone tanks at the final combat zone, which can fire shells in a spread.

At each tank encounter, dispatch the enemy force as quickly as possible without taking hits (if possible).

Race north through a long stretch of old Gotham and you'll end up at encounter two. The situation is about the same, except this time you'll be attacked by five Rattler drones. Again, smash them all quickly and continue racing south and up out of old Gotham.

After a long straight south and an audacious jump down into a construction yard, you'll angle up and out and directly into the third and final combat encounter. Again five Rattlers attack, but this time they're accompanied by two triple-barreled Diamondback drones as well. The quickest solution is to focus on cutting through the five Rattlers quickly without getting hit. This charges up your Secondary Weapon so you can dismiss the Diamondbacks easily with a Missile Barrage, completing the challenge. Upgrades to Afterburner recharge and to Heavy Turret reload speed can both directly contribute to shaving time off your result here. If you speed through the race without wiping out and you don't take more than a hit or two in combat encounters, a WayneTech Upgrade Point should be yours.

26 ROAD RAGE

Race against the clock, chasing down the armored militia transport vehicles, and show them who owns the streets. Earn a time extension for each vehicle taken out.

Unlock Requirements	After Chapter 1 progress, drift continuously in the Batmobile for 3 seconds

ONE STAR	TWO STAR	THREE STAR
Take down 3 armored cars	Take down 6 armored cars	Take down 10 armored cars

This Batmobile AR Challenge is unlocked by drifting continuously in the Batmobile for at least three seconds, which is extremely easy to accomplish—just spin a donut in the street by turning while both accelerating and braking and you'll pull it off. Once unlocked, this Challenge involves a continuous high-speed chase against armored cars running amok on Gotham City's streets. Dispatch the armored cars by slamming into them, side-swiping them, or disabling them with the Immobilizer. Each armored car left inoperative in the road adds 3 seconds to the timer for this challenge, which ticks down continuously until it runs out. Militia vehicles can actually subtract time from *you* if land RPG shots against the Batmobile, so watch out. Henchmen are freewheeling all over the place during this event, so put the pedal to the floor and stay after them aggressively. Dispatching at least six in the allotted time should be no problem.

Militia vehicles can be found in any direction, then stopped with the Immobilizer, or demolition derby style.

Hostiles riding shotgun fire at the Batmobile with handheld rocket tubes, dangerous both because of the damage to the Batmobile and the potential time lost.

27 BIG GAME HUNTER

Only the toughest can triumph. Hunt down six Cobra drones before the enemy can reinforce. Get detected and the challenge will be failed instantly. Watch out, there's something else prowling the streets.

Unlock Requirements	After Chapter 7 progress, unleash any Batmobile Secondary Weapon powered up to level 4.

ONE STAR	TWO STAR	THREE STAR
Destroy 6 Cobra drones in 5:00 or less	Destroy 6 Cobra drones in 3:45 or less	Destroy 6 Cobra drones in 2:30 or less

This dangerous stealth game of cat and mouse pits the Batmobile against the elite tank units of the Arkham Knight's militia, the Cobra drones. These heavy tanks are not to be trifled with—they rumble through the streets searching for targets ahead with blue scanning lights, unleashing devastating strikes once locked on. They are vulnerable (and blind) from behind. In this particular challenge, you cannot afford to even be sighted by a Cobra tank. It's stealth or nothing in this encounter. Needless to say, tread

Cobra drones require discretion. Do not pull out into a road ahead of a Cobra drone, and work carefully to approach them from behind, where their command center can be targeted.

carefully. Watch out for their scanners, of course, and use third-person view to peek around street corners.

It requires a lock-on of several seconds before you can drill a 60mm shell into its core and destroy a Cobra drone, but when you do it goes off with a terrific bang.

If you see blue lights ahead, cautiously back up. You can often just allow Cobras to slowly pass, or use the minimap to find another more vulnerable Cobra nearby.

Once you're behind a Cobra drone that hasn't seen you, you'll need to lock on for several seconds before firing. During this time, continue slowly, cautiously stalking the Cobra. As long as you're securely in the blind spot of the Cobra you're about to destroy, this process shouldn't be interrupted, unless you're spotted by a different Cobra. Keep an eye on the minimap to keep your situational awareness of other potential threats high. After destroying a Cobra drone, vacate the area rapidly; other Cobras will be inbound to investigate what happened, and you don't want to be in their path.

28 DAVID & GOLIATH

Outnumbered and outgunned: stalk six Cobra drones through the streets of Gotham. For each drone destroyed, two more emerge. Any hits to the Batmobile add 30 seconds to the timer.

Unlock Requirements	After Chapter 5 progress, perform 3 Throw Counters in one FreeFlow Combo

ONE STAR	TWO STAR	THREE STAR
Destroy 6 Cobra drones in 5:00 or less	Destroy 6 Cobra drones in 3:45 or less	Destroy 6 Cobra drones in 2:30 or less

This challenge is also against Cobra drones, the militia heavy tanks. Unlike Big Game Hunter, here you can engage with Cobras without the battle instantly ending. It's not explicitly a stealth mission, but since the enemy force is made entirely of heavy tanks, it's still basically a stealth mission. This is especially true since the number of total Cobras increases by two for each Cobra you demolish.

You can lose Cobras that have spotted you by hiding from their red scanners. Go around a corner, park behind a large object, or in an alley.

If you're caught out in the open by multiple Cobras, it's time to get out of there. Swap back to Pursuit Mode, engage the Afterburners, and put anything you can between you and those laser-guided barrels.

When a Cobra sights you, a red laser zeroes in on the Batmobile and you don't have very long to pick a different spot to be. If not, the Cobra's shell deals a hideous amount of damage to the Batmobile's armor. Direct engagement with Cobras is not a sustainable prospect. They can be fooled, however; aside from driving carefully to end up behind them in their patrols, you can use the 60mm Cobra Drone Lure Upgrade to turn your Heavy Turret shell explosions into a distraction for these giants. When you fire after obtaining this upgrade, they are drawn to the location of the shell's detonation instead of the Batmobile's turret.

Once you're heavily incentivized to look for cover by hulking heavy tanks, you'll notice there is a lot of useful debris to hide behind.

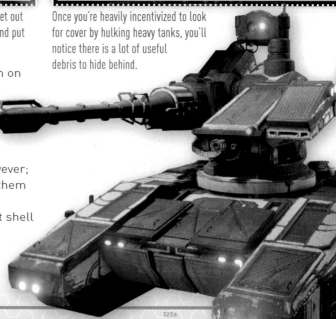

29 DRONE ZONE

Keep your foot down and your finger on the trigger. Combine your driving and battle skills to race between the three combat zones and destroy the drones as fast as you can.

Unlock Requirements	After Chapter 5 progress, call in Batmobile while gliding high above the Gotham Streets

ONE STAR	TWO STAR	THREE STAR
Complete the course in less than 4:30	Complete the course in less than 3:45	Complete the course in less than 3:00

This time trial merges racing and drone warfare like Knight Time Strike, though this challenge is wider-ranging. Starting in Miagani Island, this race detours into some unexpected places, starting with a dockside leap clean over the water onto Founders' Island—no bridges needed here. The first combat encounter also takes place in Founders' Island, against a small contingent of four Rattler drones. Eliminate them as fast as you can, then continue south across the bridge back into Miagani Island.

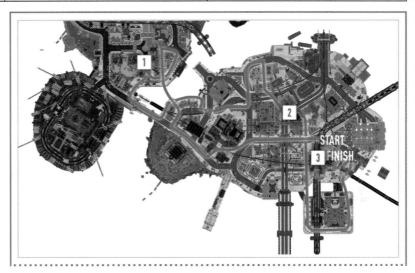

More mandatory leaps are packed into Drone Zone than in other time trials combined.

Be ready for some unexpected twists in the route, including this diversion up an onramp and then off the edge.

The second encounter comes in central Miagani, after cutting back there in a roundabout way, which includes a leap north off the upper deck of the highway before cutting right back south through back alleys. The combat encounter in central Miagani is against a half-dozen Rattler drones, which should be nothing you can't handle by now. Dispatch them cleanly and quickly to move on to the third encounter as fast as possible.

The path to the third encounter involves a thorough and speedy tour of the grounds of WayneTower, involving two huge jumps and a detour through the underground parking area. Finally emerging from WayneTower parking, you'll engage the last cohort of drones in a suffocating space in the shadow of Grand Avenue Station. Apart from the proximity, the other thing to keep in mind here is that one of the Rattlers is an armored Diamondback variant. Destroy the last drones to clear the challenge.

COLLECTIBLE TYPES AND ACQUISITION

While Scarecrow and company are giving Batman plenty to deal with this Halloween Eve, Riddler isn't one to be outdone. In connection to his extensive "Riddler's Revenge" side mission, Edward Nigma has strewn hundreds of challenges all over the environment in the form of trophies you must collect. To clear all of Riddler's challenges, you'll explore every nook and cranny of the islands, putting Batman's Gadgets, Batmobile, and Detective Mode to vigorous use.

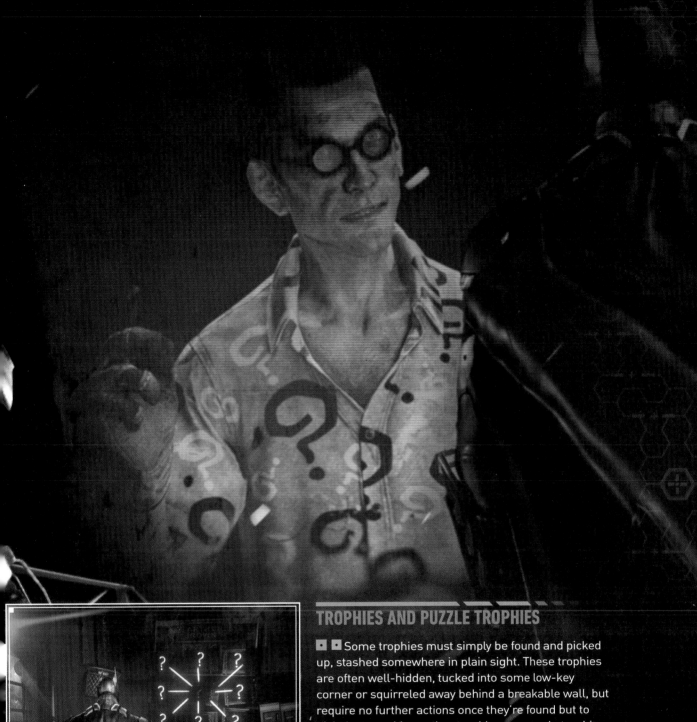

TROPHIES AND PUZZLE TROPHIES

▣ ▣ Some trophies must simply be found and picked up, stashed somewhere in plain sight. These trophies are often well-hidden, tucked into some low-key corner or squirreled away behind a breakable wall, but require no further actions once they're found but to pick them up. Many other trophies are puzzle trophies, and require some small puzzle solution or journey before the trophy is yours. Puzzles vary and often require the use of Gadgets, the Batmobile, or both. Some puzzles have to wait until you acquire Gadgets you lack early on, like the Voice Synthesizer or Remote Hacking Device. For most puzzle trophies, the trophy and its solution are found in the same place, but for a few you must begin your investigation in one place before racing to or searching for a different destination. Each area has its own collection of Riddler trophies, with overlap on just a handful that begin on one island and end on another.

TROPHY REWARDS

Every trophy you collect counts toward Riddler grid completion. Collecting a trophy may also unlock a 3-D model for viewing in the Showcase, or a piece of Concept Art. For more on Riddler grids and unlocks, see the Achievements, Trophies, and Unlocks chapter.

RIDDLE REWARDS

Solving a riddle also unlocks a Gotham City Story entry. These bonus, capsule stories provide even more backstory on the characters of *Arkham Knight* than their Bio entries (which are unlocked through story and side mission progress).

RIDDLES

In addition to trophies, there are riddles to solve. A riddle is a rhyming couplet that alludes to some figure in Batman's orbit. To solve the riddle, scan the correct feature in the environment. The solution might be a poster, or an outfit, or a particular building, or even some faraway structure on the horizon.

Hold up on the D-Pad to scan potential riddle solutions.

DESTRUCTIBLES

Each area also has its own set of destructible objects brought in by the forces threatening Gotham. These must be found and broken. On the islands, Militia Shields representing the Arkham Knight's occupying forces can be destroyed with the Batmobile's main turret. In interior spaces, other kinds of destructibles can be smashed with Gadgets like the trusty Batarang.

DESTRUCTIBLE REWARDS

Each area has 15 destructibles. For every five you wreck, you unlock one more slot on that area's Riddler grids.

UNCOVERING RIDDLER CHALLENGE LOCATIONS

While you can collect most trophies and solve most riddles as soon as you can freely explore a given area, you won't know where any of the puzzles and riddle solutions are. There are two solutions to that. One is to track down and interrogate Riddler Informants, and the other is, of course, the guide you're reading. When perched above the streets of Gotham City not actively engaged in a mission, you can scan the looting crowds below with Detective Mode in search of Riddler Informants. Detective Mode displays them with a glowing green hue. Swoop in and subdue all the thugs except for the Informant. Be sure to leave them for last so the interrogate option appears. An interrogation adds the location of some Riddler challenges near that area to the map. The locations you can shakedown from green-glowing informants are general, and may just be in the vicinity of the challenge, or from a good vantage to find it.

When engaging a gang surrounding an informant, it's okay to briefly smack or counter the informant if it's your best move, to avoid a hit or keep a Free Flow Combo going. Just make sure you don't subdue the informant. (A mere counter or stray regular hit won't subdue a target if he still has friends around.)

Walking through Gotham City Police Department Lockup with Detective Mode on, you may be surprised: there's a Riddler informant right in the heart of GCPD! This one you can interrogate for locations simply by approaching him, no accomplice-clearing necessary.

Lots of the fun of the *Arkham* games comes from discovery and surprise, so it's recommended that you don't plow too deeply into challenge locations and unlocks here until you've explored much of the game on your own. Then, you can use these pages together with the Achievements, Trophies, and Unlocks chapter as a reference to clean up what you've missed, filling up your Riddler grids and completing "Riddler's Revenge."

SOLVING PUZZLES

Trophies that are out in the open can simply be scooped up, and solving riddles is a matter of knowing what to look at. Trophies hidden behind destructible walls can be accessed by eliminating the wall. Depending on the position of the flimsy segment, you can use the Batmobile turret to blast walls, you can utilize Explosive Gel, or you can forcibly glide right through them.

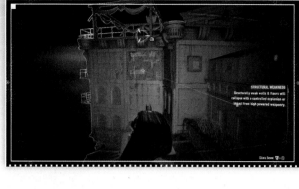

Looking around with Detective Mode reveals the solution for many puzzles. If there's a green platform, you may need to stand (or park) on it while looking for a target; multiple green platforms are a signal that you need to trick a robot into triggering them in synch with you. Question mark triggers often need to be struck with the Batarang or Remote Controlled Batarang as the ultimate objective of a puzzle.

For some two-location puzzles, the Batmobile's Forensic Scanner pulse can reveal traces of Riddler's work.

Follow the trail to its destination to reveal a secret area.

Riot bombers are poor saps wired by Riddler to explode, but you can disarm them and save their lives with an electrified Remote Batarang.

First, pilot the Remote Batarang at street level to reveal which looter was booby-trapped by Riddler.

Then, pilot a Remote Batarang through an exposed electrical current...

...before piloting the sparking Batarang into the combustible thug, disarming the explosive.

Some other puzzles also require steering a Remote Batarang through some exposed electrical element before striking a target.

More complex puzzles require you to juggle several Gadgets, sometimes including the Batmobile.

Batman can't walk across an electrified floor, but a Riddler robot can.

Using the Voice Synthesizer, the robot is ordered to retrieve a Riddler trophy.

The sentry gun that would otherwise chew the robot to bits with gunfire is temporarily blinded with the Remote Hacking Device.

The Batmobile's Power Winch is used to carefully electrify and open a door underneath the Film Studios.

Inside, another Winch stop can be latched upon. From here, a Batmobile EMP briefly disables the force field just overhead...

...which grants a short window to eject and immediately deploy a Line Launcher perk before the force field returns. From up here, it's a cinch to nail three Riddler switches with the Batarang, disabling the shield for good and unlocking the Riddler trophy.

BLEAKE ISLAND

Includes Gotham City Police Department Lockup. Panessa Film Studios collectibles are in their own section later in this chapter.

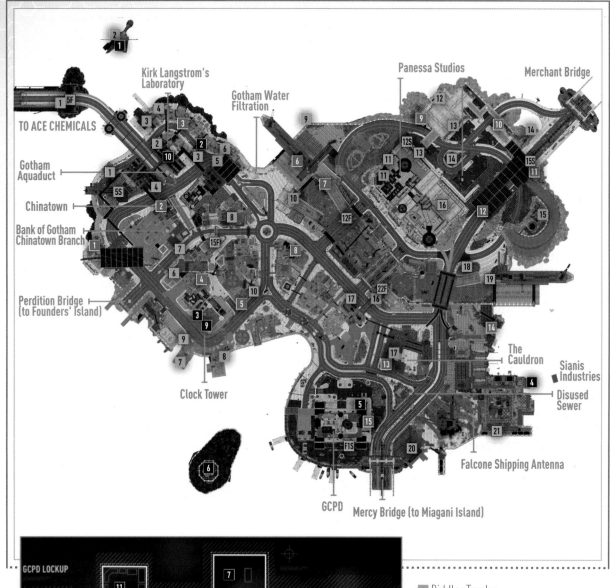

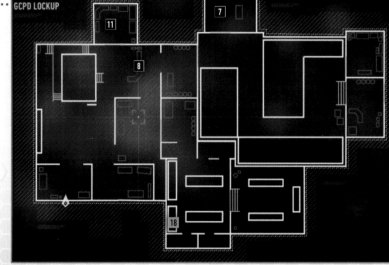

- ◉ Riddler Trophy
- ◎ Riddler Trophy (Requires Puzzle)
- ▣ Destructible
- ⬛ Riddle

BLEAKE ISLAND MILITIA SHIELD DESTRUCTIBLES

Bleake Destructible 1

Bleake Destructible 2

Bleake Destructible 3

Bleake Destructible 4

Bleake Destructible 5

Bleake Destructible 6

Bleake Destructible 7

Bleake Destructible 8

Bleake Destructible 9

Bleake Destructible 10

Bleake Destructible 11

Bleake Destructible 12

Bleake Destructible 13

Bleake Destructible 14

Bleake Destructible 15

BLEAKE ISLAND RIDDLES

Bleake Riddle 1

"Bones stripped bare beneath a warning light, pay heed, seafarers, not to feel his bite."

Bleake Riddle 2

"An open house for bed and dinner, is this sanctuary run by saint or sinner?"

Bleake Riddle 3

"I bet you weren't invited to this lavish do, I wonder how many went dressed up as you?"

Bleake Riddle 4

"Overgrown, abandoned, the inmates set free, madness could never be held in me." (The answer lies in the distance.)

Bleake Riddle 5

"Hope shines brightly in a city this dark, find the source of that signal and you'll soon hit your mark."

Bleake Riddle 6

"She stands at our center that we may not weaken, a symbol of hope, a towering beacon."

Bleake Riddle 7

"Always looking for names to besmirch, where does this newsman conduct his research?"

Bleake Riddle 8

"A souvenir from a previous life, why hold with a hand when a hook will suffice?"

Bleake Riddle 9

"Joining your mission can come with a cost, this empty reminder shows just what she lost." (Not accessible before acquiring the Remote Hacking Device.)

Bleake Riddle 10

"A bat uses these to see at night, the doc's didn't work and his cure caused a fright."

Bleake Riddle 11

"Business is best when Bats need killing, a mercenary's life should receive top billing." (The right object in the room to solve the riddle doesn't appear until the final chapter of the story.)

BLEAKE ISLAND RIDDLER TROPHIES

These trophies must simply be picked up, though they may be well-hidden.

Bleake Trophy 1

Bleake Trophy 2

Bleake Trophy 3

Bleake Trophy 4

Behind a weak, destructible wall.

Bleake Trophy 5
Found in Gotham Water Tunnels while searching for Penguin's fourth weapon cache.

Bleake Trophy 6

Behind a weak, destructible wall.

Bleake Trophy 7

Bleake Trophy 8

Snag the underhanging trophy with the Batclaw.

Bleake Trophy 9

Bleake Trophy 10

Bleake Trophy 11

Access the trophy's room through the floor grates.

Bleake Trophy 12

Behind a weak, destructible wall.

Bleake Trophy 13

Behind a weak, destructible wall.

Bleake Trophy 14

Bleake Trophy 15

Bleake Trophy 16

Bleake Trophy 17

Behind a destructible ceiling tile.

Bleake Trophy 18

The trophy case in GCPD is breakable.

BLEAKE ISLAND RIDDLER PUZZLE TROPHIES

These trophies require that a small puzzle or challenge be solved before they can be acquired.

Bleake Puzzle Trophy 1

Crushonator puzzle.

Bleake Puzzle Trophy 2

Requires Voice Synthesizer, acquired in chapter 6.

Bleake Puzzle Trophy 3

Riot bomber puzzle, available after completing Bleake Puzzle Trophy 7.

Bleake Puzzle Trophy 4

Requires the Batmobile's Power Winch.

Bleake Puzzle Trophy 5S

Start. Requires Batmobile's Forensic Scanner pulse, which creates a path of clues toward your objective.

5F

Finish.

Bleake Puzzle Trophy 6

Requires Voice Synthesizer and a sample of Riddler's voice. Get it by taking down any Riddler robot after acquiring the Voice Synth Gadget.

Bleake Puzzle Trophy 7

First available riot bomber puzzle.

Bleake Puzzle Trophy 8

Battle waves of Riddler robots for the trophy.

Bleake Puzzle Trophy 9

Requires the Remote Electrical Charge, which can charge generators.

Bleake Puzzle Trophy 10

Another riot bomber puzzle.

Bleake Puzzle Trophy 11

Park upon the glowing green platform nearby and the wall becomes a Batmobile shooting gallery.

Bleake Puzzle Trophy 12S 12F

Start. Requires Batmobile's Forensic Scanner pulse.

Bleake Puzzle Trophy 13

Puzzle underneath Panessa that requires the Power Winch, EMP, Line Launcher Perch, and Batarang.

Bleake Puzzle Trophy 14

Power Winch puzzle in front of Panessa Film Studios.

Bleake Puzzle Trophy 15S

A race from the start here to the finish.

15F

Finish.

Bleake Puzzle Trophy 16

A Voice Synthesizer puzzle that requires coordination with a Riddler robot.

Bleake Puzzle Trophy 17

Remote Batmobile Power Winch puzzle.

Bleake Puzzle Trophy 18

Requires Power Winch and Explosive Gel.

Bleake Puzzle Trophy 19

Pinball puzzle.

Bleake Puzzle Trophy 20

The Power Winch activates a wall of targets.

Bleake Puzzle Trophy 21

Puzzle requires giving the train a helpful tug with the Power Winch.

Bleake Puzzle Trophy 22S

A race from the start on Miagani Island to the finish.

22F

The finish.

MIAGANI ISLAND

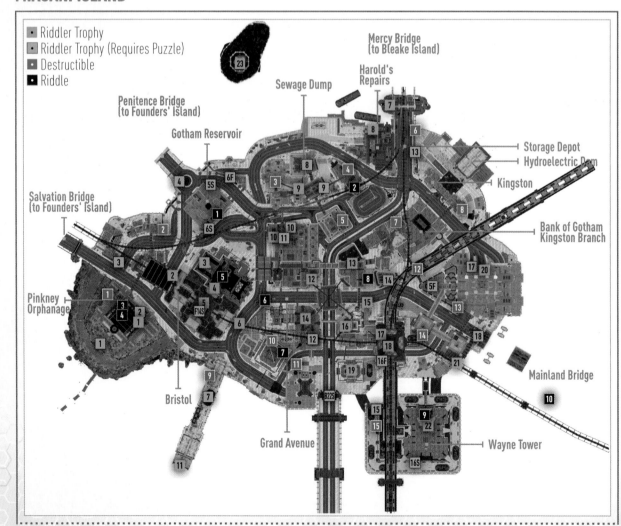

- Riddler Trophy
- Riddler Trophy (Requires Puzzle)
- Destructible
- Riddle

MIAGANI ISLAND MILITIA SHIELD DESTRUCTIBLES

Miagani Destructible 1

Miagani Destructible 2

Miagani Destructible 3

Miagani Destructible 4

Miagani Destructible 5

Miagani Destructible 6

Miagani Destructible 7

Miagani Destructible 8

Miagani Destructible 9

Miagani Destructible 10

Miagani Destructible 11

Miagani Destructible 12

Miagani Destructible 13

Miagani Destructible 14

Miagani Destructible 15

Miagani Riddle 1

"Friends of the Waynes though not as wealthy, their memorial ward keeps Gotham healthy."

Miagani Riddle 2

"The League of Assassins stuck blades through hearts, now they impale each other's art."

Miagani Riddle 3

"You forced this contraption over my brain, I'll reward you with punishment, debasement and pain." (Not accessible before acquiring the Remote Hacking Device.)

Miagani Riddle 4

"It doesn't take much to tame a Cat, make them wear this and then call the bat."

Miagani Riddle 5

"A natural cure for Scarecrow's doom, your savior's gone but still in bloom." (Correct object of focus doesn't appear until late in the story.)

Miagani Riddle 6

"Are you suffering from a mental split? Take out the trash before you defend it!"

Miagani Riddle 7

"Disarming, charming, quite the inquisitor. She'll pull back the vale, whoever her visitor."

Miagani Riddle 8

"A former warden who had a Strange turn, his appointment as mayor was a cause for concern."

Miagani Riddle 9

"The Prince of Gotham sits high in his tower, yet this picture recalls a happier hour."

Miagani Riddle 10

"The highest building in Arkham City. A Strange man worked here, who took no pity."

MIAGANI ISLAND RIDDLER TROPHIES

These trophies must simply be picked up, though they may be well-hidden.

Miagani Trophy 1

Miagani Trophy 2

Miagani Trophy 3

Miagani Trophy 4

Miagani Trophy 5

Miagani Trophy 6

Miagani Trophy 7

Miagani Trophy 8

Behind a weak, destructible wall.

Miagani Trophy 9

Behind a weak, destructible wall.

Miagani Trophy 10

Behind a weak, destructible wall.

Miagani Trophy 11

Miagani Trophy 12

Inside the donuthole.

Miagani Trophy 13

The diner from the game's introduction should look familiar.

Miagani Trophy 14

Behind a weak, destructible wall.

Miagani Trophy 15

On a ledge overlooking the tunnel occupied by the militia in Chapter 3.

Miagani Trophy 16

Miagani Trophy 17

Behind a weak, destructible wall.

Miagani Trophy 18

Miagani Trophy 19

Glide in through breakable windows.

Miagani Trophy 20

Miagani Trophy 21

Behind a weak, destructible wall.

Miagani Trophy 22

In a room found partway up Wayne Tower.

Miagani Trophy 23

Behind a weak, destructible wall.

MIAGANI ISLAND RIDDLER PUZZLE TROPHIES

These trophies require that a small puzzle or challenge be solved before they can be acquired.

Miagani Puzzle Trophy 1

Riddle pillar by Orphanage.

Miagani Puzzle Trophy 2

Missile Barrage shooting gallery.

Miagani Puzzle Trophy 3

Riot bomber puzzle.

Miagani Puzzle Trophy 4

Riddler robot puzzle.

Miagani Puzzle Trophy 5S

Race from the start here to the finish.

5F

Finish.

Miagani Puzzle Trophy 6S

Requires Batmobile's Forensic Scanner pulse. Begin searching here.

6F

Conclude Forensic scouring here.

Miagani Puzzle Trophy 7

Riddler robot puzzle.

Miagani Puzzle Trophy 8

Miagani Puzzle Trophy 9

Riot bomber puzzle.

Miagani Puzzle Trophy 10

Riddler robot brawl.

Miagani Puzzle Trophy 11

Power Winch puzzle.

Miagani Puzzle Trophy 12

Power Winch reveals sentry gun trap room.

Miagani Puzzle Trophy 13

Puzzle behind a weak, destructible wall.

Miagani Puzzle Trophy 14

Power Winch puzzle.

Miagani Puzzle Trophy 15

Riot bomber puzzle.

Miagani Puzzle Trophy 16S

Use Batmobile's Forensic Scanner pulse to follow a trail that starts here.

16F

Finish here.

Miagani Puzzle Trophy 17

Power Winch puzzle.

Miagani Puzzle Trophy 18

Power Winch puzzle.

FOUNDERS' ISLAND

Includes Gotham Water Tunnels. Collectibles for the Airships and the Hideout are in their own sections later in this chapter.

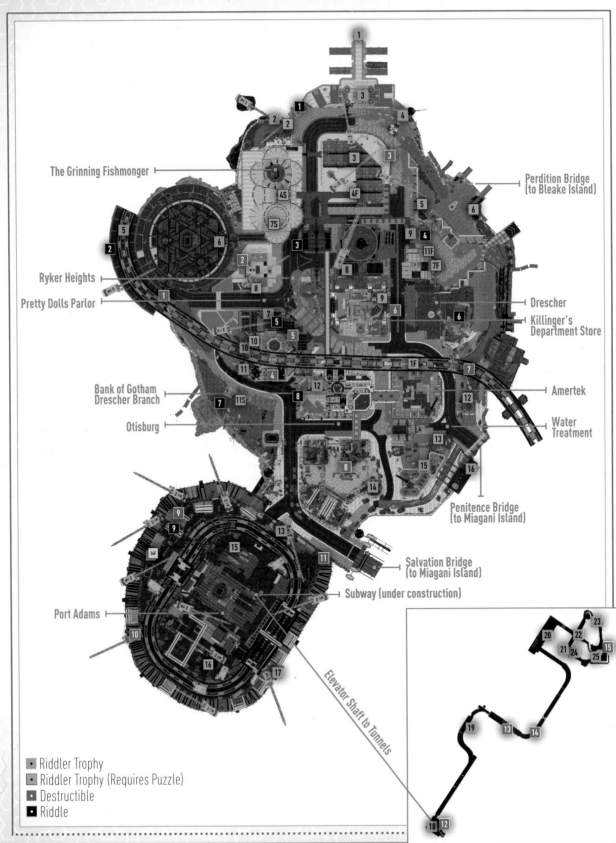

The Grinning Fishmonger

Perdition Bridge (to Bleake Island)

Ryker Heights

Pretty Dolls Parlor

Drescher

Killinger's Department Store

Bank of Gotham Drescher Branch

Amertek

Otisburg

Water Treatment

Penitence Bridge (to Miagani Island)

Salvation Bridge (to Miagani Island)

Subway (under construction)

Port Adams

Elevator Shaft to Tunnels

- ▪ Riddler Trophy
- ▣ Riddler Trophy (Requires Puzzle)
- ▫ Destructible
- ■ Riddle

FOUNDERS' ISLAND DESTRUCTIBLES

Founders' Destructible 1

Founders' Destructible 2

Founders' Destructible 3

Founders' Destructible 4

Founders' Destructible 5

Founders' Destructible 6

Founders' Destructible 7

Founders' Destructible 8

Founders' Destructible 9

Founders' Destructible 10

Founders' Destructible 11

Founders' Destructible 12

Founders' Destructible 13

Founders' Destructible 14

Founders' Destructible 15

FOUNDERS' ISLAND RIDDLES

Founders' Riddle 1

"A psycho killer's grim design, what has an angle but just one line?"

Founders' Riddle 2

"A million dollar home for a spoilt child, his parents are dead but his parties are wild."

Founders' Riddle 3

"He saved the date! All Hallow's Eve! But this calendar killer took his leave."

Founders' Riddle 4

"He lives and dies in seven days, this beast you've tamed but his song still plays."

Founders' Riddle 5

"Roll up! Roll up! For the circus of strange, this porcine professor is clearly deranged."

Founders' Riddle 6

"An ancient order, lust for power consumed, their patron saint is here entombed."

Founders' Riddle 7

"This tumbledown ruin's not looking its best, what do you expect from the Penguin's old nest?"

Founders' Riddle 8

"This cold corporation changed his life forever, curing his wife now a chronic endeavor."

Founders' Riddle 9

"Far away the deflated brute roams, leaving behind what he couldn't ship home."

Founders' Riddle 10

Scan the Batmobile to unlock the Batmobile Cameo.

FOUNDERS' ISLAND RIDDLER TROPHIES

These trophies must simply be picked up, though they may be well-hidden.

Founders' Trophy 1

Founders' Trophy 2

Behind a weak, destructible wall.

Founders' Trophy 3

Behind a weak, destructible wall.

Founders' Trophy 4

Founders' Trophy 5

Founders' Trophy 6

Founders' Trophy 7

Founders' Trophy 8

Founders' Trophy 9

Gain entry during "The Perfect Crime" side mission.

Founders' Trophy 10

Founders' Trophy 11

Behind a weak, destructible wall.

Founders' Trophy 12

Behind a weak, destructible wall.

Founders' Trophy 13

Founders' Trophy 14

Founders' Trophy 15

Behind a weak, destructible wall.

Founders' Trophy 16

Founders' Trophy 17

Founders' Trophy 18

Founders' Trophy 19

Founders' Trophy 20

Founders' Trophy 21

Founders' Trophy 22

Founders' Trophy 23

Founders' Trophy 24

Founders' Trophy 25

FOUNDERS' ISLAND RIDDLER PUZZLE TROPHIES

These trophies require that a small puzzle or challenge be solved before they can be acquired.

Founders' Puzzle Trophy F1S

Race from the start on Bleake Island to the finish on Founders'.

1F

Finish.

Founders' Puzzle Trophy 2

Power Winch and Line Launcher puzzle.

Founders' Puzzle Trophy 3

Founders' Puzzle Trophy 4S

Race from the start high up here to the finish under the streets.

4F

Finish.

Founders' Puzzle Trophy 5

Power Winch puzzle.

Founders' Puzzle Trophy 6

Founders' Puzzle Trophy 7S

Begin Batman Forensic Scanner pulse trail.

7F

Finish.

Founders' Puzzle Trophy 8

Riddler robot Voice Synthesizer puzzle.

Founders' Puzzle Trophy 9

Riddler robot switch puzzle.

Founders' Puzzle TTrophy 10

Batmobile Power Winch reveals trap room.

Founders' PuzzleTrophy 11S

Begin Batmobile Forensic Scanner pulse trail.

11F

Finish.

Founders' Puzzle Trophy 12

Riddler robot Voice Synth puzzle that requires blinding a sentry gun with the Remote Hacking Device.

Founders' Puzzle Trophy 13

Power Winch ball puzzle.

Founders' Puzzle Trophy 14S

Race from the start here in Miagani Island to the finish in Founders'.

14F

Finish.

Founders' Puzzle Trophy 15

Riddler robot puzzle crate.

Founders' Puzzle Trophy 16

Puzzle requiring the Remote Batmobile, Power Winch, and Remote Batarang.

AIRSHIPS

Enter Airships from northwest Founders' Island.

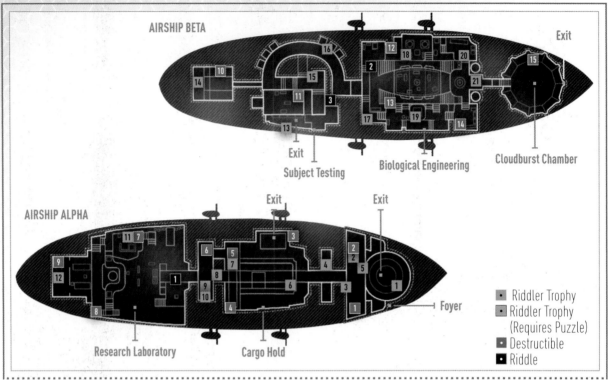

- ■ Riddler Trophy
- ◉ Riddler Trophy (Requires Puzzle)
- ▪ Destructible
- ● Riddle

AIRSHIPS INSECT CRATE DESTRUCTIBLES

Airships Destructible 1

Airships Destructible 2

Airships Destructible 3

Airships Destructible 4

Airships Destructible 5

Airships Destructible 6

Airships Destructible 7

Airships Destructible 8

Airships Destructible 9

Airships Destructible 10

Airships Destructible 11

Airships Destructible 12

Airships Destructible 13

Airships Destructible 14

Airships Destructible 15

AIRSHIPS RIDDLES

Airships Riddle 1

"No Dark Knight, Stagg's pet is no figment, it's just lacking the usual pigment."

Airships Riddle 2

"A bragging reporter's worse than a narc, but perhaps the assassin has found his mark?"

Airships Riddle 3

"Need something moved quickly, in a freezer? This company's owned by a cockney geezer!"

AIRSHIPS RIDDLER TROPHIES

Airships Trophy 1

Use Remote Hacking Device to tilt Airship.

Airships Trophy 2
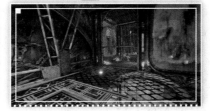

Airships Trophy 3

Use unlocking and locking magnetic blocks and tilting the Airship to reveal hidden vent.

Airships Trophy 4

Target puzzle at bottom of passage.

Airships Trophy 5

Exposing trophy behind vent requires Remote Electrical Charge.

Airships Trophy 6

Magnetic block puzzle requires Airship tilting to reveal path to trophy under the floor.

Airships Trophy 7

Airships Trophy 8

Tap L2 rapidly multiple times.

Airships Trophy 9

Puzzle accessed through ceiling port requires Line Launcher.

Airships Trophy 10

Trophy guarded by sentry gun.

Airships Trophy 11

Remote Hacking Device unlocks monkey puzzle.

Airships Trophy 12

Remote Hacking Device unlocks monkey puzzle.

Airships Trophy 13

Batarang targets on the first Airship.

Airships Trophy 14

Airships Trophy 15

Trophy guarded by sentry guns.

Airships Trophy 16

Airships Trophy 17

Remote Hacking Device unlocks monkey puzzle.

Airships Trophy 18

Airships Trophy 19

Remote Electric Charge puzzle found in vents.

Airships Trophy 20

Airships Trophy 21

Remote Hacking Device unlocks monkey puzzle.

PANESSA FILM STUDIOS

Enter Panessa Film Studios from northeast Bleake Island.

- ■ Riddler Trophy
- ■ Riddler Trophy (Requires Puzzle)
- □ Destructible
- ■ Riddle

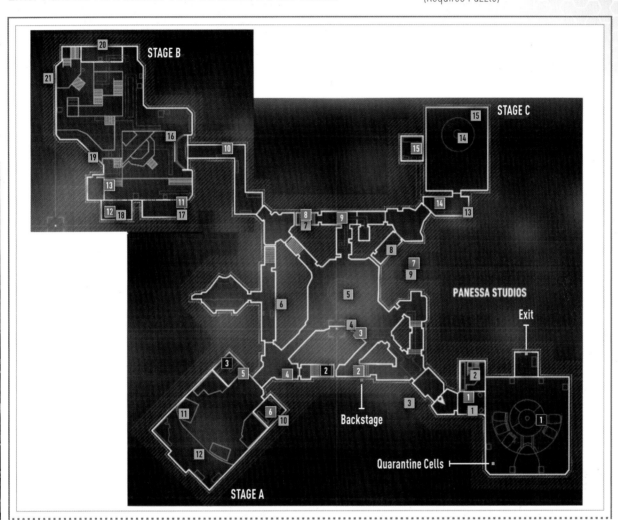

STUDIOS JACK IN THE BOX DESTRUCTIBLES

Studios Destructible 1

Studios Destructible 2

Studios Destructible 3

Studios Destructible 4

Studios Destructible 5

Studios Destructible 6

Studios Destructible 7

Studios Destructible 8

Studios Destructible 9

Studios Destructible 10

Studios Destructible 11

Studios Destructible 12

Studios Destructible 13

Studios Destructible 14

Studios Destructible 15

STUDIOS RIDDLES

Studios Riddle 1

"You? A father figure? Don't make me laugh. You overwork and break your staff."

Studios Riddle 2

"She and her love are no longer together, she'll keep the flames burning forever and ever."

Studios Riddle 3

"A visual artist with burning ambition: prove he made movies before his ignition."

STUDIOS RIDDLER TROPHIES

Studios Trophy 1

Tic-Tac-Toe Batarang puzzle.

Studios Trophy 2

Electrifying Remote Batarang puzzle.

Studios Trophy 3

Riddler robot puzzle.

Studios Trophy 4

Robot core puzzle.

Studios Trophy 5

Statue Batarang puzzle.

Studios Trophy 6

Puzzle requires Line Launcher over electric floor.

Studios Trophy 7

Gun crate explosion reveals puzzle.

Studios Trophy 8

Studios Trophy 9

Electrified Remote Batarang puzzle behind weak, destructible wall.

Studios Trophy 10

Studios Trophy 11

Giant robot puzzle.

Studios Trophy 12

Trophy protected by sentry guns.

Studios Trophy 13

No-look Batarang puzzle.

Studios Trophy 14

"Riddler Says" puzzle.

Studios Trophy 15

Slot machine puzzle.

Studios Trophy 16

Trophy retrievable after stopping fan.

Studios Trophy 17

Rolling ball puzzle.

Studios Trophy 18

Puzzle requires Remote Batarang through vents.

Studios Trophy 19

Studios Trophy 20

Studios Trophy 21

Behind a weak, destructible wall.

Line Launcher puzzle found above ceiling port.

HIDEOUT

Enter the Hideout from the old city in central Founders' Island.

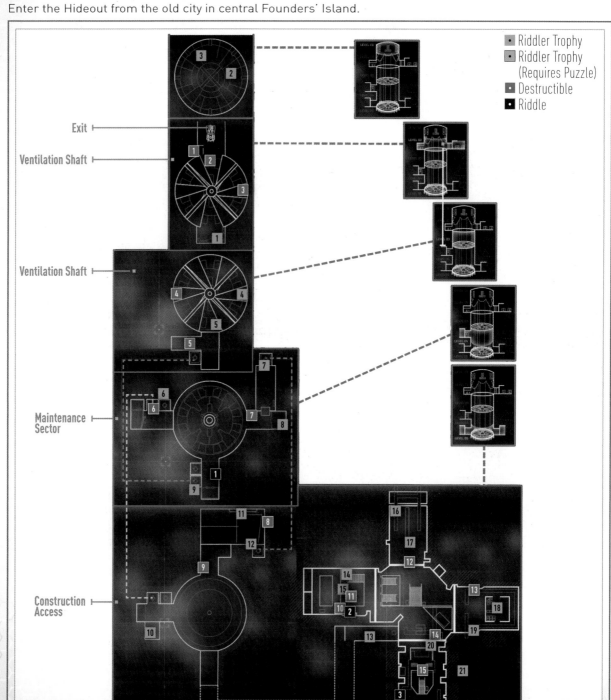

HIDEOUT SPIDER DRONE DESTRUCTIBLES

Hideout Destructible 1

Hideout Destructible 2

Hideout Destructible 3

Hideout Destructible 4

Hideout Destructible 5

Hideout Destructible 6

Hideout Destructible 7

Hideout Destructible 8

Hideout Destructible 9

Hideout Destructible 10

Hideout Destructible 11

Hid eout Destructible 12

Hideout Destructible 13

Hideout Destructible 14

Hideout Destructible 15

HIDEOUT RIDDLES

Hideout Riddle 1

"With a fluffy white coat and ears standing tall, what burrowed the hole in which Alice did fall?"

Hideout Riddle 2

"Vengeance burns darkly inside the betrayed, as they stare at reminders of debts unpaid."

Hideout Riddle 3

"A psychotic doctor who caught the fear bug, the fruits of his research: a powerful drug."

HIDEOUT RIDDLER TROPHIES

Hideout Trophy 1

Some weak walls can be blasted with the Batmobile's main turret as you descend down the generator shaft.

Hideout Trophy 2

Use the Remote Electrical Charge to power pipes.

Hideout Trophy 3

Hideout Trophy 4

Ball transfer puzzle.

Hideout Trophy 5

Descending ball shooting gallery.

Hideout Trophy 6

Use Remote Hacking Device through glass floor.

Hideout Trophy 7

Behind weak, destructible wall.

Hideout Trophy 8

Remote Electrical Charge rotation puzzle accessed through vents.

Hideout Trophy 9

Hideout Trophy 10

Remote Batarang against sentry gun.

Hideout Trophy 11

Hideout Trophy 12

Hideout Trophy 13

Hideout Trophy 14

Use Remote Electrical Charge for box rotation puzzle.

Hideout Trophy 15

Hideout Trophy 16

Symbol matching wall.

Hideout Trophy 17

Hideout Trophy 18

Hideout Trophy 19

Remote Hacking Device reveals Remote Electrical Charge puzzle.

Hideout Trophy 20

Snag trophy with Batclaw.

Hideout Trophy 21

Remote Hacking Device reveals gun sentry and robot puzzle.

ACHIEVEMENTS, TROPHIES, AND UNLOCKS

There wouldn't be much need for a reclusive billionaire to moonlight as the world's greatest detective if there wasn't plenty to do out there. On top of the extreme problems being caused citywide by Scarecrow, Arkham Knight, and their cohort, many other important players in Bruce Wayne's life have crashed the proceedings. There are over a dozen side missions that accompany the main story. Challenge rooms return in the form of AR Challenges, which offer situational skirmishes spanning every gameplay type. And Riddler has again blanketed Gotham City in various puzzles. For almost anything you complete, whether main story progress, side missions, or collecting Riddler trophies, you're probably earning something here.

ACHIEVEMENTS AND TROPHIES

MAIN STORY

Many Achievements and Trophies are earned for playing through the central story of *Arkham Knight*. Each chapter is covered in-depth in this guide's walkthrough section, so look there if you run into trouble taking back Gotham City. For the Knightfall Achievement, you need at least eight side missions completed at the end of the game. I AM the Batman! is the capstone Achievement of *Arkham Knight* and requires that you complete the game once, then play through and complete it again in New Game Plus mode, in Knightmare difficulty.

ICON	NAME	XBOX ONE GAMERSCORE	PLAYSTATION 4 TROPHY	UNLOCK CONDITION
	Journey into Knight	10	Bronze	Chapter 1 progress
	Trail of Fear	10	Bronze	Chapter 1 progress
	The Frequency of Fear	20	Bronze	Chapter 1 progress
	Fear of Faith	10	Bronze	Chapter 2 progress
	As the Crow Flies	20	Bronze	Chapter 2 progress
	No Man's Land	10	Bronze	Chapter 3 progress
	Living Hell	10	Bronze	Chapter 3 progress
	Cold World	20	Bronze	Chapter 3 progress
	A Battle Within	10	Bronze	Chapter 4 progress
	Dark Wings Fly Away in Fear	20	Bronze	Chapter 4 progress
	With a Vengeance!	10	Bronze	Chapter 5 progress
	Strange Deadfellows	10	Bronze	Chapter 5 progress
	Creature of the Night	25	Bronze	Chapter 5 progress
	Brotherhood of the Fist	10	Bronze	Chapter 6 progress
	A Heart Broken in Two	25	Bronze	Chapter 6 progress
	City of Fear	20	Bronze	Chapter 7 progress
	Who Rules the Night	30	Bronze	Chapter 7 progress
	Judgment Day	30	Bronze	Chapter 8 progress
	Fear of Success	20	Bronze	Chapter 9 progress
	Be Not Afraid	30	Bronze	Chapter 9 progress
	Master of Fear	50	Bronze	Completing the Main Path
	Knightfall	50	Gold	Endgame Completion at 100%
	The Long Halloween	50	Silver	Complete the Main Path in New Game +
	I AM the Batman!	—	Platinum	Unlocking all other Trophies

MOST WANTED – SIDE MISSIONS

Many Achievements and Trophies are earned by completing side missions. Longer side missions usually award several Achievements across their course. A few side mission Achivements only appear on Xbox One, and have no PlayStation 4 Trophy counterpart.

ICON	NAME	XBOX ONE GAMERSCORE	PLAYSTATION 4 TROPHY	UNLOCK CONDITION
	Death of Innocents	15	Bronze	Complete "The Line of Duty" side mission
	The Monster Machine	20	Bronze	Complete "The Perfect Crime" side mission
	Scar of the Bat	15	Bronze	Complete "Creature of the Night" side mission
	The Road Home	15	Bronze	Complete "Armored and Dangerous" side mission
	Days of Fire	15	Bronze	Complete "Gotham on Fire" side mission
	Angel in the Dark	20	Bronze	Complete "Heir to the Cowl" side mission
	Gates of Gotham	10	Bronze	Complete "Occupy Gotham" side mission
	Streets of Gotham	10	Bronze	Complete "Own the Roads" side mission
	Gotham Underground	10	Bronze	Complete "Campaign for Disarmament" side mission
	Dark Allegiances	20	Bronze	Complete three previous side missions and confront their orchestrator
	Beautiful Boy	10	Xbox One only	Destroy Penguin's second weapon cache
	Blind Love	10	Xbox One Only	Destroy Penguin's third weapon cache
	Practice Run	10	Xbox One Only	Destroy Penguin's fourth weapon cache
	Touch of Death	20	Bronze	Complete "Gun Runner" side mission
	Two Faces of Fear!	10	Xbox One only	Stop the Miagani Island bank heist during "Two-Faced Bandit" side mission
	Two Sides of the Same Coin!	10	Xbox One only	Stop the Founders' Island bank heist during "Two-Faced Bandit" side mission
	Jekyll & Hyde	20	Bronze	Complete "Two-Faced Bandit" side mission
	The Cult	10	Bronze	Complete "Lamb to the Slaughter" side mission
	Double Jeopardy	10	Bronze	Complete "Friend in Need" side mission

"RIDDLER'S REVENGE" RELATED

The largest side mission in *Arkham Knight* involves saving a curious cat from a demented trickster genius. Riddler is holding Catwoman captive and there are many challenges for Batman to overcome to save her and stop Riddler. These Achievements also serve as collectible Achievements, since you have to find scores of Riddler trophies in the course of this side mission. This side mission, along with all others, is covered in the Most Wanted chapter.

ICON	NAME	XBOX ONE GAMERSCORE	PLAYSTATION 4 TROPHY	UNLOCK CONDITION
	The Road to Hell	10	Bronze	Complete the first Riddler trial.
	Pieces of the Puzzle	10	Bronze	Complete the second Riddler trial.
	Riddler on the Rampage	10	Bronze	Complete the fourth Riddler trial.
	The Burning Question	10	Bronze	Complete the fifth Riddler trial.
	Death by Design	10	Bronze	Complete the seventh Riddler trial.
	Lethal Pursuits	10	Bronze	Complete the ninth Riddler trial.
	The Cat and the Bat	10	Bronze	Complete the third Riddler trial.
	The Primal Riddle	10	Bronze	Complete the sixth Riddler trial.
	The Riddle Factory	10	Bronze	Complete the eighth Riddler trial.
	Nine Lives	10	Bronze	Complete the last Riddler trial.
	Riddle Me That	30	Bronze	Complete "Riddler's Revenge" side mission

AR CHALLENGE RELATED

AR Challenges are unlocked over the course of *Arkham Knight* through completing various specific actions. These futuristic, augmented reality challenge rooms allow consequence-free practice for any type of situation. Once an AR Challenge is unlocked, you can access it either from the main menu or from the challenge's location somewhere in Gotham City. You can earn up to three stars for performance in each challenge, and each 23 new stars you earn unlocks another challenge-related Achievement.

ICON	NAME	XBOX ONE GAMERSCORE	PLAYSTATION 4 TROPHY	UNLOCK CONDITION
	Sins of Youth	10	Bronze	Collect 23 Stars in AR Challenges
	Fortunate Son	15	Bronze	Collect 46 Stars in AR Challenges
	Absolution	20	Bronze	Collect 69 Stars in AR Challenges

BATMOBILE STUNTS

The Batmobile, perhaps the most significant addition to *Arkham Knight*, has several Achievements tied to various behind-the-wheel tasks. You will most likely unlock most of these through normal gameplay.

ICON	NAME	XBOX ONE GAMERSCORE	PLAYSTATION 4 TROPHY	UNLOCK CONDITION
	Dirty Tricks	5	Bronze	Achieve 3 minutes of drifting time in the Batmobile. Can be accomplished simply by spinning in a donut for 3 minutes.
	A Leap of Faith	5	Bronze	Complete 8 different jumps over 100 meters each. Need to unlock Batmobile Afterburner first.
	Savage Metal	5	Bronze	Use the Batmobile to take out 10 milita vehicles without using the Immobilizer. Simply crashing into them works.
	Point of Impact	5	Bronze	Score 5 perfect shots in a row without taking damage. Use single shots from the Vulcan Cannon and aim for the rectangular light on the front of drones.
	Seduction of the Gun	5	Bronze	Score 50 critical shots on light tanks by aiming for their cannons or their rectangular lights.
	Choice of Weapons	5	Bronze	Use all 5 Batmobile weapons in one tank battle: the Vulcan Gun, the Heavy Cannon, the EMP, the Missile Barrage, and the Drone Hack. Can't be accomplished until all Batmobile weapons are acquired.

MISCELLANEOUS BATMAN STUNTS

Aside from the incredibly noteworthy addition of the Batmobile to Batman's peacekeeping arsenal, his suit and Gadgets have also received some performance tweaks. The enhanced glide potential of the Batsuit, with more speed and lift gained pulling up from dives, allows for flight across all three islands without needing rooftop or Grapnel support. And the speed boost gained from diving off a high building (or ejecting from the Batmobile) grants enough momentum to sustain a low-altitude glide. As for stringing together more than 15 moves, this might sound like a lot, but it adds up quickly. Each basic action counts (Strike, Counter, Cape Stun, Evade, Redirect over foe, etc.), as well as each Quickfired Gadget (Batarang, Batclaw, Explosive Gel, and others later in the game). Various Takedowns each count as distinct actions too, like Ground Takedowns and Environment Takedowns. Then there are all the combat moves available through WayneTech upgrades that allow you to upgrade the Dark Knight as you see fit. Batman isn't lacking for variety, so the key issue is to keep the Free Flow Combo going.

ICON	NAME	XBOX ONE GAMERSCORE	PLAYSTATION 4 TROPHY	UNLOCK CONDITION
	Cycle of Violence	5	Bronze	Use 100 Quickfire Gadgets in Free Flow Combat.
	Brutality 101	5	Bronze	String together over 15 moves in the same Free Flow Combo.
	Blunt Trauma	5	Bronze	Perform every type of Predator Takedown. (Standard, from behind; popping out of a vent tunnel; swinging down from a ledge above; jumping down from a ledge above; smashing through a ceiling/glass; Inverted Takedown from a perch; popping up from a grate; popping down through a grate above; Ledge Takedown; Corner Takedown; Takedown through a weak wall; Grapnel Boost Takedown; Line Launcher Takedown; Environment Takedown.)
	Death and Glory	5	Bronze	Take out 20 thugs with Fear Takedowns.
	Run Through the Jungle	5	Bronze	Glide underneath the three main bridges between islands in one airborne period without touching the ground or using a Grapple boost.
	The Real Deal	5	Bronze	Takedown 20 moving cars without using the Batmobile.
	Gotham After Midnight	5	Bronze	Glide for 400 meters while less than 20 meters from the ground.

AR CHALLENGES

All AR Challenges have a story progression prerequisite. You must have more than a certain amount of progress to unlock a given AR Challenge. Most AR Challenges also have a secondary task you must perform before the Challenge can be attempted.

AR CHALLENGE PREREQUISITES

AR CHALLENGE TYPE	AR CHALLENGE	FIRST AVAILABLE	UNLOCK CONDITION
Tutorial	Throw Counter	Chapter 1 progress	—
Tutorial	Fear Multi-Takedown	Chapter 1 progress	—
Tutorial	Predator Fundamentals	Chapter 1 progress	—
Tutorial	Grapnel Boost MKII	Chapter 1 progress	—
Tutorial	Summon, Eject and Glide	Chapter 1 progress	—
Tutorial	Weapon Energy Diagnostics	Chapter 1 progress	—
Combat	Combo Master	Chapter 1 progress	Run directly into a dive off a rooftop.
Batmobile Combat	One Man Army	Chapter 1 progress	Use Afterburners to jump over 50 meters in the Batmobile.
Hybrid	Road Rage	Chapter 1 progress	Drift continously for over three seconds.
Combat	Tower Defense	Chapter 3 progress	Pick up floored enemy into Beat Down.
Predator	Revive and Shine	Chapter 3 progress	Take out three enemies with a Fear Multi-Takedown.
Batmobile Race	Mightnight Fury TT	Chapter 3 progress	Eject from Batmobile into a glide that lasts over 300 meters.
Batmobile Combat	Untouchable	Chapter 3 progress	Perform three critical shots in one tank battle.
Batmobile Combat	Natural Selection	Chapter 3 progress	—
Combat	Batman and Nightwing: Gotham Knights	Chapter 5 progress	Use three different Quickfire Gadgets in one Free Flow Combo.
Predator	Terminal Velocity	Chapter 5 progress	Take out a brute-level enemy with an Environment Takedown.
Batmobile Combat	Slumdog Billionaire	Chapter 5 progress	—
Hybrid	Seek and Destroy	Chapter 5 progress	Takedown the cars of joyriding thugs on foot or from a glide.
Hybrid	David and Goliath	Chapter 5 progress	Perform 3 Throw Counters in one Free Flow Combo.
Hybrid	Drone Zone	Chapter 5 progress	Call the Batmobile and plummet into the driver's seat from a glide.
Predator	Under the Pale Moonlight	Chapter 7 progress	Use the Voice Synthesizer to order an enemy into a trap.
Batmobile Race	City Heat TT	Chapter 7 progress	Use three different Gadgets in one glide attack.
Hybrid	Knight Time Strike	Chapter 7 progress	Perform 2 perfect shots in a row in a drone tank battle.
Hybrid	Big Game Hunter	Chapter 7 progress	Charge up and fire any secondary Batmobile weapon at level 4.
Combat	Azrael: Azrael's Atonement	Complete "Heir to the Cowl" side mission	—
Batmobile Race	Crushonator	Progress in "Riddler's Revenge" side mission	—
Batmobile Race	Condamned	Progress in "Riddler's Revenge" side mission	—
Batmobile Race	Mental Blocked	Progress in "Riddler's Revenge" side mission	—
Predator	Smash and Grab	Progress in "Two-Faced Bandit" side mission	—

CHARACTER BIOS

A rich cast of characters surrounds Batman. You can learn more about the characters of the *Arkham* series by collecting their Bios. Most of these are earned either through main story progress or by investigating side missions. Only one is uncovered by solving a particular Riddle. Any audio tapes you earn by completing Riddler Grids can be played back from within Bios.

CHARACTER BIO PREREQUISITES

Aaron Cash	Chapter 1 progress	Johnny Charisma	Chapter 6 progress
Albert King	Chapter 6 progress	The Joker	Chapter 2 progress
Alfred	Chapter 2 progress	Kirk And Francine Langstrom	"Creature of the Night" side mission progress
Arkham Knight	Chapter 2 progress	Lucius Fox	Chapter 3 progress
Azrael	"Heir to the Cowl" side mission progress	Man–Bat	Complete "Creature of the Night" side mission
Batman	Always available	Martha Wayne and Thomas Wayne	Chapter 9 progress
Bruce Wayne	Always available	Nightwing	Chapter 3 progress
Catwoman	Chapter 3 progress	Oracle	Chapter 1 progress
Christina Bell	Chapter 6 progress	Penguin	Chapter 3 progress
Deacon Blackfire	Chapter 9 progress	Poison Ivy	Chapter 1 progress
Deathstroke	Chapter 9 progress	Professor Pyg	Complete "The Perfect Crime" side mission
Fire Chief	"The Line of Duty" side mission progress	Red Hood	Chapter 9 progress
Firefly	"Gotham on Fire" side mission progress	Riddler	Chapter 3 progress
Gordon	Chapter 1 progress	Robin	Chapter 5 progress
Harley Quinn	Chapter 6 progress	Scarecrow	Chapter 2 progress
Henry Adams	Chapter 6 progress	Simon Stagg	Chapter 4 progress
Hush	Complete "Friend in Need" side mission	Batgirl	Bleake Island Riddle 9
Jack Ryder	Chapter 1 progress	Two–Face	"Two–Faced Bandit" side mission progress
Jason Todd	Chapter 6 progress	Vicki Vale	Chapter 9 progress

SHOWCASE – CHARACTER MODELS

Arkham Knight is one of the first games designed with the newest generation of consoles in mind, and it shows. The art design and character models are worth appreciating, and you can do just that using the Showcase. Most Showcase models are unlocked for viewing by collecting certain Riddler Puzzle Trophies.

CHARACTER SHOWCASE PREREQUISITE

Aaron Cash	Bleake Island Puzzle Trophy 18	Hush	Complete "Friend in Need" side mission
Ace Workers	Miagani Island Puzzle Trophy 12	Jack Ryder	Complete "Lamb to the Slaughter" side mission
Albert King	Studios Trophy 10	Jason Todd	Studio Trophy 15
Alfred Pennyworth	Miagani Island Puzzle Trophy 1	Jim Gordon	Bleake Island Puzzle Trophy 4
Arkham Knight	Founders' Island Puzzle Trophy 14	Johnny Charisma	Studio Trophy 14
Arkham Knight Militia	Hideout Trophy 11	The Joker	Hideout Trophy 1
Arkham Knight Militia Checkpoint Commander	Complete "Own the Roads" side mission	Kirk Langstrom	Complete "Creature of the Night" side mission
Arkham Knight Militia Combat Specialists	Founders' Island Puzzle Trophy 10	Lucius Fox	Airships Trophy 7
		Man-Bat	Complete "Creature of the Night" side mission
Arkham Knight Militia Heavy Armored Weapons Expert	Hideout Trophy 14	Nightwing	Founders' Island Puzzle Trophy 6
Arkham Knight Militia Mini-gunners	Founders' Island Puzzle Trophy 13	Oracle	Bleake Island Puzzle Trophy 13
Arkham Knight Militia Personal Guard	Hideout Trophy 10	Paramedics	Miagani Island Puzzle Trophy 11
Azrael	Complete "Heir to the Cowl" side mission	Penguin	Complete "Gun Runner" side mission
Batman (New Suit)	Early story progress	Penguin Brutes	Airships Trophy 2
Batman (Old Suit)	Early story progress	Penguin Thugs	Airships Trophy 11
Batman Unmasked	Founders' Island Puzzle Trophy 11	Poison Ivy	Founders' Island Puzzle Trophy 3
Blackfire Cult Members	Complete "Lamb to the Slaughter" side mission	Police Officers	Miagani Island Puzzle Trophy 2
Catwoman	Founders' Island Puzzle Trophy 8	Primates	Airships Trophy 17
Christina Bell	Studio Trophy 19	Professor Pyg	Complete "The Perfect Crime" side mission
Civilians	Hideout Trophy 7	Red Hood	Late story completion
Deacon Blackfire	Complete "Lamb to the Slaughter" side mission	Reporters	Late story completion
Deathstroke	Complete "Campaign For Disarmament" side mission	Riddler	Miagani Island Puzzle Trophy 7
Deceased Scientists	Airships Trophy 15	Riddler 2	Complete "Riddler's Revenge" side mission
Demon	Bleake Island Puzzle Trophy 21	Riddler Robots	Bleake Island Puzzle Trophy 8
Dollotrons	During "The Perfect Crime" side mission	Rioters	Bleake Island Puzzle Trophy 20
Family	Late story progress	Robin	Studio Trophy 2
Firefighters	Complete "The Line of Duty" side mission	Scarecrow	Hideout Trophy 4
Firefly	Complete "Gotham on Fire" side mission	Sick Joker	Airships Trophy 6
Harley Quinn	Studios Trophy 7	Simon Stagg	Airships Trophy 20
Harley Quinn Brutes	Studios Trophy 18	Two-Face	Complete "Two-Faced Bandit" side mission
Harley Quinn Mini-gun Brutes	Studios Trophy 20	Two-Face Thugs	Miagani Island Puzzle Trophy 17
Harley Quinn Thugs	Hideout Trophy 20	Vicki Vale	Late story completion
Henry Adams	Studio Trophy 13	Waitress	Miagani Island Puzzle Trophy 14
		Young Joker	Studio Trophy 5

SHOWCASE – VEHICLE MODELS

The vehicles of *Arkham Knight* also merit a close look, which the Vehicle Showcase allows. As with Character Showcase models, most of these are discovered by collecting Riddler Puzzle Trophies.

VEHICLE SHOWCASE PREREQUISITE

Batwing	Airships Trophy 21	Dragon Drone	Hideout Trophy 6
Bat Pod	Bleake Island Puzzle Trophy 1	Boa Sentry Drone	Airships Trophy 4
Batmobile	Early story progress	Serpent Drone	Miagani Island Puzzle Trophy 18
Batmobile 2	Hideout Trophy 5	Relay Drone	Bleake Island Puzzle Trophy 2
Militia APC	Complete "Armored and Dangerous" side mission	Python Drone	Studios Trophy 21
Armored Vehicle	Bleake Island Puzzle Trophy 19	Militia Radar	Studios Trophy 6
Excavator	Hideout Trophy 21	Police Car	Miagani Island Puzzle Trophy 6
Arkham Knight's Gunship	Complete "Occupy Gotham" side mission	SWAT Van	Airships Trophy 9
Rattler Drone	Bleake Island Puzzle Trophy 11	Police Helicopter	Founders' Island Puzzle Trophy 1
Diamondback Drone	Miagani Island Puzzle Trophy 5	Taxi	Studios Trophy 4
Mamba Drone	Bleake Island Puzzle Trophy 22	North Refrigeration Truck	Airships Trophy 14
Twin Rattler Drone	Studios Trophy 11	Hell's Gate Refuse Truck	Progress in "Two-Faced Bandit" side mission
Cobra Drone	Founders' Island Puzzle Trophy 2	School Bus	Founders' Island Puzzle Trophy 5
Cloudburst Tank	Hideout Trophy 2		

CONCEPT ART

Before the high-quality Showcase-worthy models were built, the world of *Arkham Knight* started as sketches and concept art. Many pieces of concept art can be unlocked by picking up Riddler Puzzle Trophies. A few are also tied to certain side missions.

CONCEPT ART PREREQUISITE

Ace Chemicals	Bleake Island Puzzle Trophy 17
Ace Chemicals	Miagani Island Trophy 10
Ace Chemicals	Miagani Island Puzzle Trophy 10
Ace Chemicals	Bleake Island Puzzle Trophy 15
Ace Chemicals	Miagani Island Puzzle Trophy 16
Ace Chemicals	Miagani Island Puzzle Trophy 8
Ace Chemicals	Airships Trophy 18
Bank	Progress in "Two-Faced Bandit" side mission
Bank	Progress in "Two-Faced Bandit" side mission
Miagani Island	Founders' Island Puzzle Trophy 4
Miagani Island	Airships Trophy 3
Miagani Island	Miagani Island Trophy 14
Miagani Island	Hideout Trophy 3
Miagani Island	Miagani Island Trophy 8
Miagani Island	Bleake Island Puzzle Trophy 6
Miagani Island	Founders' Island Trophy 15
Miagani Island	Airships Trophy 16
Miagani Island	Miagani Island Puzzle Trophy 4
Miagani Island	Airships Trophy 5
Miagani Island	Bleake Island Puzzle Trophy 5
Miagani Island	Studios Trophy 9
Founders' Island	Founders' Island Puzzle Trophy 7
Founders' Island	Founders' Island Puzzle Trophy 16
Founders' Island	Miagani Island Puzzle Trophy 13
Founders' Island	Founders' Island Puzzle Trophy 12
Bleake Island	Bleake Island Puzzle Trophy 9
Bleake Island	Bleake Island Trophy 13
Bleake Island	Founders' Island Trophy 2
Clocktower	Airships Trophy 10
Clocktower	Bleake Island Puzzle Trophy 12

Batman	Full story completion
GCPD	Bleake Island Trophy 16
Hideout	Hideout Trophy 8
Hideout	Hideout Trophy 12
Hideout	Hideout Trophy 19
Hideout	Hideout Trophy 18
Hideout	Hideout Trophy 13
Hideout	Hideout Trophy 9
Hideout	Hideout Trophy 16
Poison Ivy	Hideout Trophy 15
Poison Ivy	Founders' Island Puzzle Trophy 9
Film Studios	Studios Trophy 12
Film Studios	Founders' Island Puzzle Trophy 15
Film Studios	Studios Trophy 17
Film Studios	Studios Trophy 1
Film Studios	Studios Trophy 8
Penguin	Bleake Island Puzzle Trophy 14
Professor Pyg	Founders' Island Trophy 7
Riddler	Studios Trophy 3
Riddler	Airships Trophy 8
Riddler	Complete sixth Riddler trial during "Riddler's Revenge" side mission
Airships	Airships Trophy 12
Airships	Airships Trophy 19
Airships	Airships Trophy 1
Airships	Airships Trophy 13
Wayne Office	Studios Trophy 16
Wayne Manor	Late story completion
Joker 1	Full story completion
Joker 2	Full story completion
Joker 3	Full story completion

GOTHAM CITY STORIES

Riddler left trophies lying around all over the city, but he has also set up Riddles to solve. These are couplets that point to a particular thing, place, or view. You can submit a possible Riddle solution by looking at something and scanning the environment by holding up on the D-Pad. Each Riddle unlocks a Gotham City Story.

GOTHAM CITY STORY PREREQUISITES

Aaron Cash	Bleake Island Riddle 8
Alfred	Founders' Island Riddle 2
Arkham City	Miagani Island Riddle 10
Azrael	Founders' Island Riddle 6
Bane	Founders' Island Riddle 9
Batgirl	Bleake Island Riddle 9
Calendar Man	Founders' Island Riddle 3
Catwoman	Miagani Island Riddle 4
Deacon Blackfire	Bleake Island Riddle 2
Deadshot	Airships Riddle 2
Deathstroke	Bleake Island Riddle 11
Firefly	Studios Riddle 3
Gordon	Bleake Island Riddle 5
Harley Quinn	Studios Riddle 2
Hush	Miagani Island Riddle 1
Jack Ryder	Bleake Island Riddle 7
Jason Todd	Hideout Riddle 2
The Joker	Bleake Island Riddle 4
Killer Croc	Bleake Island Riddle 1
Lady of Gotham	Bleake Island Riddle 6

Lucius Fox	Scan the Batmobile
Mad Hatter	Hideout Riddle 1
Man-Bat	Bleake Island Riddle 10
Martha and Thomas Wayne	Miagani Island Riddle 9
Mr. Freeze	Founders' Island Riddle 8
Nightwing	Airships Riddle 3
Oracle	Bleake Island Riddle 3
Penguin	Founders' Island Riddle 7
Poison Ivy	Miagani Island Riddle 5
Professor Pyg	Founders' Island Riddle 5
Quincy Sharp	Miagani Island Riddle 8
Ra's	Miagani Island Riddle 2
Riddler	Miagani Island Riddle 3
Scarecrow	Hideout Riddle 3
Simon Stagg	Airships Riddle 1
Solomon Grundy	Founders' Island Riddle 4
Tim Drake	Studios Riddle 1
Two-Face	Miagani Island Riddle 6
Vicki Vale	Miagani Island Riddle 7
Zsasz	Founders' Island Riddle 1

RIDDLER GRIDS AND AUDIO TAPES

Riddler has hidden away some big surprises and privileged conversations behind his network of collectibles. Every Riddler trophy you collect, puzzle you complete, and riddle you solve unlocks one spot on one of these Grids. Destructibles (Militia Shields, Insect Crates, Jack in the Boxes, and Spider Drones) also go toward clearing every space on the Grids. Completing a Grid unlocks an exclusive audio tape, playable once unlocked from certain Bio pages.

Grids for the three main islands have 18 fields each, and are completed with 17 Riddler challenges solved and five Destructibles smashed. Grids for smaller interiors have nine spaces, requiring eight completed Riddler challenges and five Destructibles demolished. If you're on your way to completing a Grid and unlocking an audio tape, cross-reference with the Riddler Collectibles chapter to track down anything you need.

☐ Trophy	▦ Trophy (Bombs)	☐ Riddle	▪ Destructible

BLEAKE ISLAND GRIDS

Unlock Riddler tapes by completing Bleake Island Grids.

BLEAKE ISLAND TAPE 1

Bleake Riddle 9	Bleake Trophy 1	Bleake Trophy 12	Bleake Trophy 8	Bleake Puzzle Trophy 16	Bleake Puzzle Trophy 18
Bleake Puzzle Trophy 7 (bomber)	5 Bleake Destructibles broken	Bleake Puzzle Trophy 1	Bleake Riddle 8	Bleake Puzzle Trophy 14	Bleake Trophy 18
Bleake Puzzle Trophy 22	Bleake Riddle 1	Bleake Riddle 11	Bleake Puzzle Trophy 13	Bleake Trophy 6	Bleake Trophy 14

BLEAKE ISLAND TAPE 2

Bleake Puzzle Trophy 6	Bleake Trophy 5	Bleake Puzzle Trophy 5	Bleake Puzzle Trophy 3 (bomber)	Bleake Riddle 2	Bleake Trophy 16
Bleake Puzzle Trophy 4	Bleake Riddle 7	Bleake Riddle 4	Bleake Trophy 10	Bleake Puzzle Trophy 21	Bleake Puzzle Trophy 11
Bleake Riddle 5	Bleake Trophy 13	Bleake Trophy 3	Bleake Puzzle Trophy 19	Bleake Trophy 7	10 Bleake Destructibles broken

BLEAKE ISLAND TAPE 3

Bleake Puzzle Trophy 17	Bleake Trophy 2	Bleake Trophy 4	15 Bleake Destructibles broken	Bleake Trophy 9	Bleake Riddle 10
Bleake Trophy 17	Bleake Puzzle Trophy 9	Bleake Puzzle Trophy 12	Bleake Puzzle Trophy 8	Bleake Puzzle Trophy 20	Bleake Trophy 11
Bleake Puzzle Trophy 10 (bomber)	Bleake Riddle 3	Bleake Puzzle Trophy 2	Bleake Trophy 15	Bleake Riddle 6	Bleake Puzzle Trophy 15

MIAGANI ISLAND GRIDS

Unlock Penguin tapes by completing Miagani Island Grids.

MIAGANI ISLAND TAPE 1

Miagani Riddle 4	Miagani Puzzle Trophy 9 (bomber)	Miagani Puzzle Trophy 10	Miagani Trophy 7	Miagani Trophy 18	10 Miagani Destructibles broken
Miagani Trophy 19	Miagani Riddle 1	Miagani Puzzle Trophy 13	Miagani Puzzle Trophy 1	Miagani Riddle 10	Miagani Trophy 6
Miagani Trophy 3	Miagani Puzzle Trophy 4	Miagani Trophy 9	Miagani Trophy 5	Miagani Puzzle Trophy 2	Miagani Trophy 10

MIAGANI ISLAND TAPE 2

Miagani Puzzle Trophy 5	Miagani Trophy 14	Miagani Trophy 20	Miagani Trophy 16	Miagani Puzzle Trophy 17	Miagani Trophy 22
Miagani Puzzle Trophy 8	15 Miagani Destructibles broken	Miagani Riddle 9	Miagani Puzzle Trophy 15 (bomber)	Miagani Trophy 4	Miagani Riddle 8
Miagani Puzzle Trophy 18	Miagani Riddle 5	Miagani Trophy 21	Miagani Trophy 23	Miagani Puzzle Trophy 11	Miagani Trophy 13

MIAGANI ISLAND TAPE 3

Miagani Puzzle Trophy 6	Miagani Puzzle Trophy 3 (bomber)	Miagani Trophy 11	Miagani Puzzle Trophy 16	Miagani Trophy 17	Miagani Riddle 7
Miagani Riddle 2	Miagani Puzzle Trophy 7	Miagani Puzzle Trophy 14	Miagani Riddle 6	Miagani Trophy 1	Miagani Trophy 15
Miagani Puzzle Trophy 12	Miagani Trophy 8	5 Miagani Destructibles broken	Miagani Trophy 12	Miagani Riddle 3	Miagani Trophy 2

FOUNDERS' ISLAND GRIDS

Unlock Scarecrow tapes by completing Founders' Island Grids.

FOUNDERS' ISLAND TAPE 1

Founders' Riddle 9	Founders' Trophy 4	Founders' Puzzle Trophy 7	Founders' Trophy 7	Founders' Trophy 22	Founders' Puzzle Trophy 5
Founders' Puzzle Trophy 9	Founders' Riddle 6	Founders' Trophy 17	Founders' Puzzle Trophy 14	15 Founders' Destructibles broken	Founders' Riddle 3
Founders' Riddle 2	Founders' Trophy 12	Founders' Puzzle Trophy 13	Founders' Trophy 14	Founders' Puzzle Trophy 12	Founders' Trophy 11

FOUNDERS' ISLAND TAPE 2

Founders' Puzzle Trophy 11	Founders' Trophy 20	Founders' Trophy 13	Founders' Trophy 8	Founders' Puzzle Trophy 15	Founders' Riddle 7
Founders' Trophy 18	Founders' Trophy 16	Founders' Riddle 10	Founders' Trophy 19	Founders' Trophy 6	Founders' Puzzle Trophy 4
Founders' Puzzle Trophy 6	Founders' Riddle 8	Founders' Puzzle Trophy 3	Founders' Trophy 9	5 Founders' Destructibles broken	Founders' Trophy 3

FOUNDERS' ISLAND TAPE 3

10 Founders' Destructibles broken	Founders' Trophy 1	Founders' Trophy 24	Founders' Riddle 4	Founders' Puzzle Trophy 10	Founders' Trophy 25
Founders' Trophy 15	Founders' Riddle 5	Founders' Puzzle Trophy 8	Founders' Puzzle Trophy 1	Founders' Puzzle Trophy 2	Founders' Trophy 23
Founders' Puzzle Trophy 16	Founders' Trophy 5	Founders' Trophy 21	Founders' Trophy 10	Founders' Riddle 1	Founders' Trophy 2

AIRSHIPS GRIDS

Unlock Simon Stagg tapes by completing Airships Grids.

AIRSHIPS TAPE 1

Airships Trophy 11	5 Airships Destructibles broken	Airships Trophy 16
Airships Trophy 17	Airships Trophy 6	Airships Trophy 13
Airships Trophy 3	Airships Trophy 9	Airships Riddle 3

AIRSHIPS TAPE 2

Airships Trophy 10	10 Airships Destructibles broken	Airships Trophy 14
Airships Trophy 2	Airships Riddle 2	Airships Trophy 5
Airships Trophy 20	Airships Trophy 8	Airships Trophy 19

AIRSHIPS TAPE 3

Airships Trophy 7	Airships Trophy 4	Airships Trophy 15
15 Airships Destructibles broken	Airships Trophy 1	Airships Riddle 1
Airships Trophy 12	Airships Trophy 18	Airships Trophy 21

STUDIOS GRIDS

Unlock Harley Quinn tapes by completing Studios Grids.

STUDIOS TAPE 1

Studios Trophy 20	Studios Trophy 17	Studios Riddle 3
15 Studios Destructibles broken	Studios Trophy 16	Studios Trophy 21
Studios Trophy 15	Studios Trophy 14	Studios Trophy 2

STUDIOS TAPE 2

Studios Trophy 9	5 Studios Destructibles broken	Studios Trophy 6
Studios Trophy 12	Studios Trophy 1	Studios Trophy 13
Studios Trophy 4	Studios Trophy 18	Studios Riddle 1

STUDIOS TAPE 3

Studios Trophy 7	10 Studios Destructibles broken	Studios Trophy 5
Studios Trophy 10	Studios Riddle 2	Studios Trophy 3
Studios Trophy 8	Studios Trophy 19	Studios Trophy 11

HIDEOUT GRIDS

Unlock Arkham Knight tapes by completing Hideout Grids.

HIDEOUT TAPE 1

Hideout Trophy 1	Hideout Trophy 21	Hideout Trophy 14
Hideout Riddle 2	Hideout Trophy 13	10 Hideout Destructibles broken
Hideout Trophy 10	Hideout Trophy 5	Hideout Trophy 9

HIDEOUT TAPE 2

Hideout Trophy 19	Hideout Trophy 15	Hideout Trophy 18
Hideout Trophy 16	Hideout Riddle 1	Hideout Trophy 4
15 Hideout Destructibles broken	Hideout Trophy 8	Hideout Trophy 3

HIDEOUT TAPE 3

Hideout Trophy 6	Hideout Trophy 17	5 Hideout Destructibles broken
Hideout Trophy 2	Hideout Trophy 12	Hideout Trophy 7
Hideout Trophy 20	Hideout Riddle 3	Hideout Trophy 11

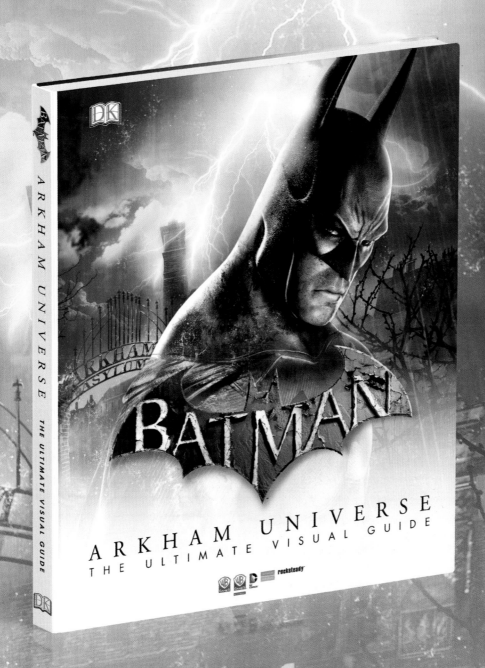

ARKHAM KNIGHT

SIGNATURE SERIES STRATEGY GUIDE

Written by Michael Owen and Joe Epstein

Copyright © 2015 DC Comics.

BATMAN: ARKHAM KNIGHT software © 2015 Warner Bros. Entertainment Inc. Developed by Rocksteady Studios. BATMAN and all characters, their distinctive likenesses, and related elements are trademarks of DC Comics © 2015. All Rights Reserved. WB GAMES LOGO, WB SHIELD:™ & © Warner Bros. Entertainment Inc. (s15)

BradyGAMES, a division of Penguin Group (USA). BradyGAMES® is a registered trademark of Penguin. All rights reserved, including the right of reproduction in whole or in part in any form.

DK/BradyGames, a division of Penguin Group (USA).
6081 East 82nd Street, 4th Floor
Indianapolis, IN 46250

The ratings icon is a registered trademark of the Entertainment Software Association. All other trademarks and trade names are properties of their respective owners.

BASED ON A GAME RATED BY THE ESRB

Please be advised that the ESRB ratings icons, "EC", "E", "E10+", "T", "M", "AO", and "RP" are trademarks owned by the Entertainment Software Association, and may only be used with their permission and authority. For information regarding whether a product has been rated by the ESRB, please visit www.esrb.org. For permission to use the ratings icons, please contact the ESA at esrblicenseinfo@theesa.com.

ISBN: 978-0-7440-1616-1

Printing Code: The rightmost double-digit number is the year of the book's printing; the rightmost single-digit number is the number of the book's printing. For example, 15-1 shows that the first printing of the book occurred in 2015.

18 17 16 15   4 3 2 1

Printed in the USA.

Batman created by Bob Kane.

BRADYGAMES STAFF

VP & Publisher ▶ **Mike Degler**

Editorial Manager ▶ **Tim Fitzpatrick**

Design and Layout Manager ▶ **Tracy Wehmeyer**

Licensing ▶ **Aaron Lockhart**
▶ **Christian Sumner**

Marketing ▶ **Katie Hemlock**
▶ **Paul Giacomotto**

Digital Publishing ▶ **Julie Asbury**
▶ **Tim Cox**
▶ **Shaida Boroumand**

Operations Manager ▶ **Stacey Beheler**

CREDITS

Senior Development Editor ▶ **Jennifer Sims**

Senior Graphic Designer ▶ **Carol Stamile**

Senior Production Designer ▶ **Areva**

FREE EGUIDE!

Go to www.primagames.com/code and enter this unique code to access your FREE eGuide!

BRMA-CNNG-7P8Q-Y2YT

BRADYGAMES

www.primagames.com

DC COMICS™

www.dccomics.com

rocksteady™

www.rocksteadyltd.com

WB GAMES

www.warnerbros.com

Copyright © 2015 DC Comics.